To look around at our crumbling world culture is to readily realize we are, in fact, in a war of spiritual proportions. Talk to just about anyone about what is transpiring and they typically relay how they cannot believe how quickly the governmental, legal, moral, familial, and spiritual fabric is simply unraveling at breakneck speed. In light of this reality, how should the Church respond to push back the forces of evil? How should Christians, as soldiers of Christ, prepare themselves to achieve victory?

Terry Tyrrell's *Forward into Battle* is an excellent field manual designed to teach believers how to answer these two pivotal questions. As a former officer in the armed forces, Terry weds his military expertise on the earthly plane with his depth of biblical knowledge regarding spiritual battle tactics in a way that effectively equips one to engage darkness with the power of God's light. This is, no doubt, a timely work for the challenging day in which believers live.

Reverend Marty Baker
Senior Pastor, Burke Community Church
Burke, Virginia

We are in a war that is both spiritual and cultural. To succeed in this war, we need a blending of conviction, motivation, and practical know-how. Terry provides all three in *Forward into Battle*. He speaks perceptively from experience, dedicating the book to Gary Combs—one of my heroes during my tenure on the faculty at the U.S. Air Force Academy—and others. This is not light, bedtime reading; it is a vital call to arms that requires a response. Having known Terry since his time as a cadet, I can testify to his commitment in actually doing what he writes about. *Forward into Battle* is not just for the military, but for everyone who is called to the battle for the souls of men and women.

Major General Jerry E. White (U.S. Air Force, Retired), PhD
International President Emeritus, The Navigators and author
of *Honesty, Morality and Conscience* and *To Be A Friend*
Colorado Springs, Colorado

In *Forward into Battle*, Terry Tyrrell comprehensively describes the pervasiveness of spiritual warfare. He demonstrates this truth in personal stories, historical anecdotes, and biblical illustrations woven through the framework of every aspect of the metaphor of military service—from entry to retirement and beyond. Terry thoroughly covers every facet of the Christian life. He shows how an aggressive enemy continues to fight against and attempts to defeat and destroy the believer throughout a lifetime (a military career) and provides prescriptions on how to live, fight, and win as a warrior through the power of the Holy Spirit. At the end of each chapter, Terry provides practical helps for self-evaluation: how to grow as a follower of Jesus Christ and how to disciple others. A must read—an excellent Bible study for anyone, especially military men and women!

Colonel Bobby Little (U.S. Army, Retired)
Executive Director, Christian Embassy—A Cru Ministry
Washington, D.C.

If you don't believe spiritual warfare exists, Satan has already won one of the most significant battles he will ever have with you. Our evil adversary is constantly on the attack, seeking to prevent you from becoming the man or woman God wants you to be. In *Forward into Battle*, Terry Tyrrell sets out military analogies to life as a follower of Jesus to help you understand the reality of spiritual conflict and how you can engage in it victoriously.

As you read the book, you will discover how to become a warrior in God's army and how to relate to our divine Commander. You'll gain a better appreciation for the devil's tactics, our spiritual weaponry, and our mission. You'll learn about godly leadership and the rewards that await you when your earthly service comes to an end. I have no doubt that you will be better prepared to confront and defeat Satan's attacks as you seek to live faithfully and fruitfully for Christ.

Brigadier General David B. Warner (U.S. Air Force, Retired)
Executive Director, Officers' Christian Fellowship
Englewood, Colorado

Whether you are opposed to war or not, you're in one. It's a spiritual war fought without bullets and bombs with consequences that are far more deadly than physical war. They have to do with eternal life and death. Drawing from both military experiences and the Word of God, Terry Tyrrell has identified and passed on practical principles that will help us win this war, individually and corporately—not by retreating, but by going forward! This work will be inspirational and instructive whether you have a military background or not.

Chris Adsit
National Director, Branches of Valor
and author of *Personal Disciplemaking*
Eugene, Oregon

A long career in both terrestrial and heavenly warfare is drawn together in *Forward into Battle*, which will be of especial benefit to the many with uniformed experience. Terry has woven his deep Biblical understanding with his wealth of military insights; readers will benefit from his width of scriptural exposure and examples from his long, uniformed career, drawn together into some greatly valuable "so what should I now do?" applications. Read and mark slowly; learn and inwardly digest for life.

Captain Richard Meryon (Royal Navy, Retired)
Former Executive Director, Christian Vision for Men U.K.
and later Director of the Garden Tomb in Jerusalem
Bath, England

As a military officer, I value actionable intelligence, the tools and training to execute my mission, and a leader with integrity and authority. Terry highlights all these and more in *Forward into Battle* as he describes why, how, and Who we serve as soldiers in God's army. While a member of Terry and Elizabeth's Bible study during my assignment to RAF Mildenhall, I benefited from their mentorship as an officer and a Christian. I can hear Terry's voice through *Forward into Battle* as he connects through personal stories, teaches through the Word, and challenges through analysis. His guidance will surely help believers, both new and seasoned, to become more devoted followers of Christ, better prepared to battle against the forces of darkness.

Major Sarah Hedrick, U.S. Air Force
Tyndall Air Force Base, Florida

When the Army introduced the short-lived tag line "An Army of One" with the first commercial showing a single soldier running through the desert, I remember thinking THAT WOULD NEVER HAPPEN! Our strength is in our cohesive teams and in our joint armed forces. My long-time friend, Terry Tyrrell, takes us to the heart of what it means to be a warrior and leader in the Army of God—to take up our weapons as a team to fight and defeat the forces of evil. *Forward into Battle* is a treasure trove of truths and marching orders from our Warriors' Manual—the Bible.

Lieutenant General R.L. VanAntwerp (U.S. Army, Retired)
Former Commanding General, U.S. Army Corps of Engineers
and former President, Officers Christian Fellowship
West End, North Carolina

I have known Terry Tyrrell since we were in high school together. After graduation Terry went off to the Air Force Academy while I continued in "normal" civilian life. He has spent the rest of his life in the armed forces, or in serving in ministry to the armed forces. In *Forward into Battle*, Terry brings his military experience to bear on the meaning of spiritual warfare. He uses the analogy of military service to illuminate the whole Christian life, from beginning to end. Terry's deep sincerity and commitment, which I have never seen waver, come through. For those serving in the military, I am sure this will be particularly helpful. But it is surely relevant to all believers.

Tim Stafford
General Editor, *God's Justice: the Holy Bible*
and author of many books and magazine articles
Santa Rosa, California

Spiritual warfare is a reality. As Christians, we live in a hostile world of anxiety-filled explosives intended to weaken, then destroy our relationship with God. We can either view ourselves as outnumbered and beleaguered followers of Jesus Christ grasping for signs of end-times, or we can see ourselves as God sees us—a tenacious remnant, called by name, clothed in the full armor of God—to carry forth His banner of redemption into battle.

Terry Tyrrell does an excellent job of drawing parallels between a career warrior in the armed forces and a faithful warrior in God's army. Whether you're a new recruit or a seasoned soldier, in a war zone on the other side of the world or on the other side of town, feeling battle-ready or battle-weary, you'll be inspired and challenged by the vivid analogies and the thought-provoking questions in each chapter of *Forward Into Battle*.

Colette Rau
U.S. Navy Wife
Annapolis, Maryland

The Lord Jesus taught us using parables; they are powerful, unforgettable stories of truth that teach us how to live. *Forward into Battle* is a book of parables that capture the intensity and excitement of warriors in the military as they call us to "fight the good fight" against Satan's army. This is a must-read for chaplains and lay ministers in our armed forces—as well as for every spiritual warrior who serves as a follower of Christ.

Chaplain, Major General, Charles C. Baldwin
(U.S. Air Force, Retired)
Former U.S. Air Force Chief of Chaplains
Charleston, South Carolina

Forward into Battle

SERVING AS WARRIORS IN GOD'S ARMY

Terry Tyrrell

Forward into Battle: Serving As Warriors in God's Army
Copyright © 2017 by Terry Tyrrell

Library of Congress Cataloging-in-Publication Data

Tyrrell, John T.
Forward into Battle: Serving As Warriors in God's Army/Terry Tyrrell
ISBN: 154290305X
ISBN 13: 9781542903059
Library of Congress Control Number: 2017901681
CreateSpace Independent Publishing Platform
North Charleston, South Carolina

All Scripture references are from the NEW AMERICAN STANDARD BIBLE®, Copyright © 1960, 1962, 1963, 1968, 1971, 1972, 1973, 1975, 1977, 1995 by The Lockman Foundation. Used by permission.

All rights reserved. No part of this publication may be reproduced, stored in a retrieval system, or transmitted in any form or by any means—electronic, mechanical, photocopy, recording, or any other—except for brief quotations in printed reviews, without the prior permission of the author.

Cover design: Drew Swartz

Printed in the United States of America

Dedication

To Gary Combs, who encouraged me to become a soldier in God's army, prayed with me as I received Christ as my Savior, and was my first model of what Jesus expected of me as a warrior under His command; to Brigadier General (Retired) Orwyn Sampson and Ron Soderquist, who served as outstanding examples of leadership as I carried out my duties on the spiritual battlefield; and to the many other Christian warriors I've been privileged to serve alongside for nearly five decades.

Foreword

IN THE CHURCHES I attended while growing up in California in the 1950s and 1960s, we often sang the stirring hymn "Onward, Christian Soldiers." I still remember some of Sabine Baring-Gould's lyrics:

> Onward, Christian soldiers, marching as to war,
> With the cross of Jesus going on before!
> Christ, the royal Master, leads against the foe;
> Forward into battle, see his banner go!
>
> Like a mighty army moves the church of God;
> Brothers, we are treading where the saints have trod;
> We are not divided; all one body we,
> One in hope and doctrine, one in charity.[1]

Back in those days, I supposed this language was purely symbolic. What the songwriter undoubtedly had in mind were the principles of hard work, unity, and upholding tradition. After all, Jesus spoke of peace, love, and acceptance. Surely He wouldn't condone violence. Many years later, I realized Baring-Gould's encouragement was literal, not figurative. Since the days of Adam and Eve, Earth has been the theater of operations for a great spiritual battle that will continue until Christ returns to destroy the evil that runs uncontrolled upon the planet.

On December 1, 1969, Congressman Alexander Pirnie pulled the first birth date from a container at the Selective Service headquarters in Washington, D.C. All young men born September 14 in the years between 1944 and 1950 were assigned draft number one. Those born on my birthday—June 22—were given number 247. Eventually, all men with numbers up to 195 who weren't deferred were directed to report for possible induction into the military.

In God's draft of spiritual warriors, the rebirth-days of all Jesus' followers—the dates we receive Christ as Savior—are put into capsules and drawn one by one. Regardless of the date we become Christians, we're all assigned draft number one, and the Lord inducts everyone—men, women, and children—with number one into His army. There are no exceptions. No one receives a deferment. No one can opt out as a conscientious objector. We all serve God for the rest of our earthly lives as the forces of good do battle with the forces of evil.

Some Christians, focusing on the love Christ displayed during His earthly ministry, detest war and might feel offended by these military analogies. They refuse to serve in their nations' armed forces and suggest others should also decline. Some protest against the military and the government officials who send troops into combat. When I mentioned to a friend I was writing on this topic, he warned me it wouldn't go over well. "Christians are basically pacifists," he suggested. "They won't want to read about armies and war."

While I respect the views of Christians who oppose wars between nations, we all must recognize that spiritual warfare exists and will continue until the Lord puts an end to it. No matter how committed we are to following the loving model of Jesus, we're all members of a heavenly force locked in battle with Satan and his wicked troops.

If you walk into any Christian bookstore and ask to be directed to the section on spiritual warfare, you'll find several excellent books explaining how to defend yourself when Satan attacks. Others outline how to recover when the devil has inflicted major damage in your life. While wise guidance on these topics is valuable, defensive and recovery operations aren't the only challenges we face.

We also must take the battle to the enemy. God doesn't expect His warriors to hide away in spiritual bunkers that will preserve us from the potentially devastating attacks of our adversary. He sends us into the midst of the fighting, directing us to strike our foe with an offensive barrage that will drive back his advances and, ultimately, defeat him totally.

Most authors approach spiritual warfare from the perspective of individual followers of Christ. But as wars on Earth are fought by adversarial armies, spiritual wars are fought by opposing forces. Since the serpent deceived Adam and Eve in the Garden of Eden, God's warriors have battled the forces of Satan. For the members of God's army to carry out our orders with precision, we must fight as a cohesive unit.

How can we be prepared to fight the good fight and to prevail over our cunning adversary? As with life's other challenges, we can turn to scripture for instruction and encouragement. God's word provides some excellent guidance for our service as warriors in His army.

In *Forward into Battle*, we'll discover what scripture has to say about the radical transformation we undergo when we change allegiance to serve in His forces. We'll build a solid foundation for our service by exploring the basics of becoming a follower and working on a team. And we'll prepare for spiritual combat by ensuring we understand our mission and are fully up to speed on intelligence concerning our enemy.

With this background, our focus will shift to how we're to conduct battlefield operations, employing the weapons God provides to accomplish the orders He lays out. The Lord will call some of us to be leaders in this battle, and we'll learn from Jesus and others who have gone before us how to get the most from our troops. We'll also consider our final transition as we retire from active duty and receive recognition for our years of service.

Understanding the similarities between membership in a nation's armed forces and in the army of God will enable us to serve honorably and effectively in spiritual combat. I trust the message I have to share, forged over more than three decades of military duty, will be valuable to all who serve in the Lord's army as side by side we move forward into battle.

Terry Tyrrell
Bury St. Edmunds, England

How to Get the Most from *Forward into Battle*

FORWARD INTO BATTLE provides a "big picture" of the Christian life by comparing it to service in the military. After all, everyone who becomes a member of God's family immediately takes on a role in His army, fighting the forces of evil commanded by our archenemy Satan. Rather than explaining how to walk day by day as a follower of Jesus, the book lays out a strategic overview on life before becoming a Christian, receiving Christ as Savior, carrying out the mission and duties God gives us, and being rewarded when our time on Earth ends.

Each of the six sections of *Forward into Battle* begins with a short introduction to plot the course for its two chapters. Twelve **readings** combine lessons from scripture and illustrations from life to explain what we should know and how we can put this knowledge into practice. A number of footnotes in each chapter refer you to passages from God's word, and longer sections of scripture are mentioned parenthetically. Those who wish to explore more deeply will find these references helpful. Approach the chapters prayerfully, asking God to reveal His truth and how it applies to your life.

Following major military operations, those involved in the planning and execution assess what went right and what went wrong. Using this analysis, leaders can better prepare for future combat. At the end of each chapter of this book, a set of ***lessons learned*** summarizes the reading's highlights.

To help you to put into action the principles outlined in the book, each chapter concludes with two exercises. You can use the ***unit analysis*** in a weekly group discussion. Read the introduction and answer the questions prior to your meeting. This will prepare you to discuss points you've picked up in the reading. Because there isn't sufficient space to answer the questions in the book, you might want to go to www.forwardintobattle.com on the Internet to download and print a copy of the unit analysis as you complete each chapter.

If you use the unit analysis in a group study, you may want to call on the same facilitator each session, or you may choose to rotate this responsibility. Whichever approach you select, be sure to allow each person in the group to share what God has revealed while going through the reading and answering the questions. Some members may tend to dominate while others remain silent. One of the most important duties of the person in charge is to ensure a balance of input from all.

In your group discussion, you may find you don't have enough time to deal with every question in the unit analysis. If this happens, you have two options. First, the leader may want to focus on what he or she feels are the most helpful questions, discussing some on the list and skipping others. A second approach would be to spread the unit analysis over two sessions for each chapter. One hint for using your time wisely: Don't look up verses that are paraphrased in a question.

Not everyone will be able to gather with others to discuss the unit analysis. If this is true for you, you may want to ask a more mature follower of Jesus to disciple you through the entire book, or you may choose to call on this person to help with specific sections you find challenging. In either case, first take time on your own to consider the questions thoughtfully and prayerfully. Then seek advice from your trusted friend. Discuss the main points of the reading and the questions in the unit analysis, and ask for help in better understanding any areas you're finding difficult.

The second exercise provides the opportunity to prepare a ***personal battle plan***. All too often as we study God's word, the goal is to obtain greater knowledge of what His inspired authors have written. While this is very important in our spiritual growth, it's crucial that we apply in our lives what we learn in our study. Once again, you'll find copies of the battle plan material you can complete at www.forwardintobattle.com.

As you prepare your plans, be specific and honest. After you complete each plan, take two steps to ensure you carry out your proposed actions. First, commit them to prayer regularly, asking God to give you the strength and wisdom to accomplish what you set out to do. Second, ask another Christian to pray for you and hold you accountable. This may be someone in your discussion group, the person discipling you, or another person you trust.

Get together with your friend following each group meeting. Discuss how you've resolved to move forward, and ask this person to pray for you regularly. Begin the next one-on-one meeting with an honest evaluation of how you've succeeded and where you've fallen short. Add discussion of the current week's plan, and you and your friend will have a prayer agenda for the next seven days.

In addition to reading, discussing, and planning using *Forward into Battle*, it may be helpful for you to spend time in your daily devotions focusing on the material at www.forwardintobattle.com. These 120 devotions are composed of excerpts from the book and a question or two to stimulate your thinking and prayer.

As you trust in the Lord and tap into the help of His Spirit and other followers of Christ, I'm confident God will richly bless your efforts to give Him first place in your life, to conform to the image of His Son, and to carry out your duties faithfully.

 Members of the armed forces, their families and friends, and other interested people can find additional helpful spiritual resources and information at www.CruMilitary.org, the website of Cru Military, a ministry of Cru (formerly Campus Crusade for Christ).

Contents

Foreword	xi
How to Get the Most from *Forward into Battle*	xv
Signing Up for Service: A Radical Transformation	1
Chapter 1 Growing Up in Hostile Territory	5
Chapter 2 Changing Allegiance	24
Training in the Basics: Foundation for Service	47
Chapter 3 Becoming a Follower	51
Chapter 4 Working on A Team	75
Anticipating Combat: Preparation for Conflict	96
Chapter 5 Understanding the Mission	100
Chapter 6 Gathering Intelligence	132
Engaging the Enemy: Operations on the Battlefield	154
Chapter 7 Drawing Our Weapons	158
Chapter 8 Fighting and Winning	183
Leading a Unit: Assumption of Command	211
Chapter 9 Learning from Those Who Have Gone Before Us	215
Chapter 10 Getting the Most from the Troops	242

Completing the Mission: A Final Transition   268
Chapter 11   Retiring From Active Duty   272
Chapter 12   Receiving Recognition for Service   294

Epilogue   321
Acknowledgements   324
References   326

Signing Up for Service: A Radical Transformation

I ENTERED THE world a mere five years after World War II ended. As I was growing up, it wasn't unusual to hear stories of how my father and uncle had served bravely in the armed forces in the 1940s. I learned at a tender age of man's inhumanity to man as my elders recounted the brutal efforts by the Germans and the Japanese to extend their influence in Europe and the Pacific. I heard tales of cruel treatment of civilian and military prisoners in concentration camps. I also learned of my father's and uncle's dramatic scrapes with death.

My father, Bob, enlisted in the Navy. Following basic training and technical school, he was assigned to the USS Half Moon as it patrolled the South Pacific. He climbed steadily in rank and soon became a fire controller first class. His duties: leading a team of anti-aircraft gunners as they protected the ship from Japanese fighter planes. He and his fellow gunners were successful in their task. Despite several close calls, the Half Moon suffered only minor damage.

Uncle Ray signed up for pilot training and headed from California's hot and dry Central Valley to Craig Army Airfield in hot and muggy Alabama. He became a fighter pilot and was posted to the Royal Air Force base at East Wretham in England, joining a unit of the U.S. Army Air Forces 8th Air Force.

Ray flew escort missions, protecting huge American bombers as they dropped their ordnance on enemy targets on the continent. On his 63rd combat mission, Ray's aircraft was hit by German fire. He spent the last year of the war as a guest of the Third Reich in prisoner-of-war camps in Poland and Germany. General Patton and his 14th Armored Division forces liberated Ray and his fellow prisoners as the war ended.

Though their service was much different, these brave warriors both left behind comfort and security to travel to faraway lands to fight for peace, freedom, and democracy. A sense of patriotism prompted them to give up their previous lifestyle and to step courageously into the unknown. As they prepared to enter combat, they realized the sacrifices that would be demanded of them. Both were willing to give up their lives, if necessary, to protect their nation and its allies. This was quite a radical transformation for a couple of young men whose previous existence revolved around doing what they wanted to do, when they wanted to do it.

A little more than a quarter century later, I experienced a similar transformation. A couple of days after my eighteenth birthday, I sat in the small airport in Fresno, California, ready for my first airplane ride. As I waited to board a United Airlines flight to Los Angeles for the first leg of a journey to Colorado Springs, I was engulfed in a sea of emotions. I thought about my decision to enter the Air Force Academy and all I'd be giving up. I was leaving behind my family and my girlfriend. I'd turned down scholarships to a couple of prestigious universities. I'd no longer have the freedom to choose what I'd wear, what I'd eat, when I'd go out, or when I'd return home.

Only one person from my high school had taken this path prior to me. He made it through basic training and then decided to give up his government-funded education. I had little idea what I was getting myself into. I knew the program would push me to my limits intellectually, physically, and emotionally, but I didn't know how this would happen. I knew even less about what life in the Air Force would be like. Despite this anxiety, I felt a strong desire to do something for my country, to repay the nation for the freedoms I'd taken for granted over the previous 18 years.

In a spiritual sense, we go through a transformation every bit as radical as entering the military when we become Christians. The world we're born into is much different from the world the Lord created for His children. From God's perspective, ***we live in hostile territory***. As we survey the landscape, we see evil all around us. Satan employs a variety of sinister tactics to entice us to seek instant gratification in doing things God doesn't want us to do. Because these temptations can lead to great pleasure, the devil is very often successful in separating us from God, not only during our days on Earth, but for eternity.

Jesus warned His disciples about the evil world, explaining the hostility His followers face is identical to what He experienced. "'If the world hates you, you know it has hated Me before it hated you. If you were of the world, the world would love its own; but because you are not of the world, but I chose you out of the world, therefore the world hates you.'"[1] Christ repeated these thoughts when He prayed, "'The world has hated them [His followers], because they are not of the world, even as I am not of the world. I do not ask Thee to take them out of the world, but to keep them from the evil one.'"[2]

Fortunately, God provides a way—and only ***one*** way—for us to escape the solid grip the world's evil has on our lives. He gives us the opportunity to desert Satan's forces and to enlist in His army. In the Father's infinite love, He sent His Son into the world to save us from an eternity apart from Him. As we receive Christ as Savior—as we sign up to serve as warriors under Jesus' command—***we change allegiance***, escaping Satan's rule over us and becoming citizens of the kingdom of heaven.

How does this transformation from citizens of the world to members of God's family and warriors in His army take place? Christ told His followers of the unique path open to all who desire to make this transition. "'I am the way, and the truth, and the life; no one comes to the Father, but through Me.'"[3] Jesus explained eternal life was life apart from slavery to evil. "'And this is eternal life,'" He said, "'that they may know Thee, the only true God, and Jesus Christ Whom Thou has sent.'"[4]

These brief references reveal the worldly corruption into which every human is born and the new, everlasting relationship we can have with the Creator and Sustainer of the universe. Throughout Jesus' three-year ministry, He taught we must forsake the influence of Satan and begin to know God and serve as His warriors. Let's take a look at what's involved in this process.

CHAPTER 1

Growing Up in Hostile Territory

God is the only being who is good, and the standards are set by Him. Because God hates sin, He has to punish those guilty of sin. Maybe that's not an appealing standard. But to put it bluntly, when you get your own universe, you can make your own standards.

Francis Chan[1]

FROM MY VANTAGE point, California's Central Valley in the mid-1960s didn't seem to be a combat zone. As in all large cities and most good-sized towns, Fresno included an area my parents told me to avoid at night. If there were to be any evil deeds committed under the cover of darkness, more than likely they'd take place in this neighborhood. Tales of knife attacks, shootings, and robberies were enough to keep my friends and me well away from this territory.

I only ventured "across the tracks" in the safety of a school bus transporting my teammates and me to a baseball or basketball game. Rumors of a brick being hurled through a window of another team's vehicle had us all worried and gave new meaning to the phrase "home-field advantage." I've never seen so many teenage athletes suddenly become refined gentlemen, graciously insisting others precede them down the bus steps and through the crowd of students from the host school welcoming us to their campus.

While my teammates and I avoided serious injury at the hands of opposing spectators through my high-school sports career, we couldn't escape the nightly reports of the conflict in Southeast Asia. Everyone knew someone who had enlisted in the military, and we often wondered how our friends were getting on in Vietnam, Cambodia, Laos, or Thailand.

As anchormen Chet Huntley and David Brinkley reported news of the war on television each evening, we hoped and prayed the soldiers we knew would survive their tours of duty. Although combat footage was broadcast regularly, it wasn't until years later as we watched movies about the conflict that we fully appreciated the harsh physical, mental, and emotional toll the war had taken on the brave, young Americans who served so far away.

When we think about hostility, it's quite easy to visualize criminal attacks on innocent folks who stray into the wrong side of town. Scenes of military combat also come quickly to mind. Physical violence, though, is only one dimension of the hostility that exists in our world. All of us are surrounded every day by a spiritual battle that is every bit as deadly as the brutality of murder or the ravages of war. We all reside in hostile territory.

Rebellion in Heaven

Before God created the world, He filled the heavens with angels who were superior in power and knowledge to the humans who'd come later.[2] The perfect relationship between the Creator and the created was threatened as God gave these spiritual beings the ability to choose whether or not to obey Him.

Peace in the spiritual realm ended when Lucifer—a wise, beautiful, and previously blameless angel—thought he could elevate himself above God and rebelled. The Lord punished Lucifer's arrogance by banishing him from heaven along with one third of His angels who'd joined the rebellion.³ From that day, the forces of God have been at war with the forces of His former angel, who's now called Satan. And every human resident of Earth has been caught up in this violent spiritual combat.

Satan's initial battle—which he won easily—separated Adam and Eve from their heavenly Father. The Lord had placed them in the Garden of Eden, a beautiful setting He desired all people to experience throughout their earthly lives. (See Genesis 2.)

The devil deceived Adam and Eve into disobeying God's command not to eat the fruit from the tree of the knowledge of good and evil. Although the Lord cursed Satan, the devil must have cackled in delight as God drove Adam and Eve from their beautiful garden. (See Genesis 3.) Their disobedience had a dramatic effect on all of us. We've inherited the rebellious nature of our first ancestors and are born with an allegiance not to God but to Satan. Because the whole world is subject to the devil's power, we all enter life as members of his forces. As Apostle Paul tells Timothy, Satan holds us captive to do his will.⁴

Darkness on Earth

The world since the failure of Adam and Eve is nothing like the paradise God had created for mankind to enjoy. One of the characteristics of this hostile territory is darkness. In both the Old and New Testaments, we see references contrasting physical and spiritual darkness and light.

In the chaos that existed as God formed the Earth, darkness covered the planet. The Lord then spoke light into being, defining day and night.⁵ Because the world was dark before God created what He called good, the absence of light took on figurative meanings. Darkness was used to describe Sheol—the underground residence of the dead. Job calls it "'the land of darkness and deep shadow; the land of utter gloom as darkness itself.'" He also refers to darkness to describe how man's separation from God produces murder, theft, and adultery.⁶

This theme carries into the New Testament. According to Apostle John, those living in darkness don't recognize the light Christ brought to the world.[7] Jesus explained that evil people hate the light and love the darkness because it hides their wicked deeds. He urged the multitudes to walk by His light while He was among them so they wouldn't be overtaken by darkness, adding that those who walk without the light have no idea where they're going.[8]

Apostle Paul tells us Satan blinds the minds of those who don't believe in Jesus so they fail to recognize the light of the gospel and the glory of Christ.[9] This darkness prevents people from seeing God, from knowing He's always present. We're unaware of all He has done and is doing for us.

Since the Lord placed humans on the planet, He's demonstrated His character, power, and nature in everything He's created. We haven't been grateful for all God has done for us; we've had no place in our hearts for Him. In our human wisdom, we worshiped and served not the Creator but the things He created. In disgust, God allowed us to satisfy our physical cravings by engaging in impure activities.[10]

All who try to live morally pure lives are subject to attacks by Satan and by wicked people around them. Apostle Peter explains that those who follow their sensual desires will speak evil about God's way of truth, trying to deceive others with lies. As an example, Peter mentions Lot, who'd been tormented daily by the lawless deeds of unprincipled men in Sodom prior to the town's destruction.[11]

We All Fall Short

In this darkness, wickedness runs rampant. Jesus warned that man's corrupt heart produces immoral thoughts, murder, sexual relations outside marriage, theft, and untruthfulness.[12] Apostle John summarized the evil deeds of mankind as lust of the flesh, lust of the eyes, and the boastful pride of life.[13]

Paul sent warnings about the evil deeds done in darkness to young churches across the Mediterranean. Many of his letters included lengthy lists of what followers of Christ must avoid. Among the most common offenses were jealousy, greed, envy, gossip, arrogance, pride, anger, quarrels, drunkenness, and sexual immorality.[14] And Paul wasn't just talking about actions that characterized those outside the church. The apostle expected to discover many of these practices when he visited church members in the region. Obviously, the new believers were having trouble living righteous lives.

You get the picture. When we enter the world, we're totally self-centered. These wayward traits combine to form our human nature. Although we may try to conform to the legal and moral codes of society and the manners we're taught as youngsters, every one of us has an inner core that is corrupt. Even those whose actions and intentions seem mostly good aren't free of moral shortcomings.

We'd like to think people are basically good but a few turn to evil, but this isn't the message of God's word. In his letter to the Roman Christians, Paul quotes a conclusion King David had come to almost a thousand years earlier: "'There is none righteous, not even one.'"[15] The apostle concludes we all sin and fall short of God's glory.[16] Everyone who has lived, is alive now, or will one day be born into the world begins life in hostility toward God, fighting as His enemy.[17]

Take Me, for Example
How does this view of the hostile territory in which we live square with reality? To answer this question, let's return to California's Central Valley in the mid-20th century. While those growing up on "the right side of the tracks" were quick to judge those living in the evil environment across the railway lines, all of us were equally guilty of wrongdoing in the eyes of the Lord.

"They" turned to assault, stealing cars, and breaking into shops and homes. "We" engaged in wayward acts that were neither as well publicized nor condemned. In the more up-market section of town, I heard locker-room tales of the sexual exploits of some of my teammates. The use and abuse of drugs and alcohol, while not as widespread as in years just ahead, was beginning to be a problem in our high school.

Before I became a Christian, I was so afraid of upsetting God that I mustered all my strength to resist temptation. I was a good student and a fair athlete, so between studying, practices, and games, I didn't have a lot of spare time for unwholesome activities. With 20-20 hindsight and more than six decades of life behind me, I can see the shortcomings in my life that disqualified me from the ranks of the perfect. Although I was not as bad as I could have been, I was not as good as I should have been. I lived in a world filled with constant peer pressure that chipped away at my meager human resolve. Eventually, I gave in to the desire for instant satisfaction doing things I knew were wrong.

It wasn't a sudden, dramatic fall from grace but a gradual descent from what was right to what was pleasurable and comfortable. Our affluent neighborhood was populated by families much better off than we were. The most popular students arrived for classes decked out in designer fashions, challenging anyone who wanted to be cool to follow suit. Unable to afford such luxury, I was delighted to discover a name-brand flannel shirt hanging in the back of my father's closet.

A devious plan immediately blossomed in my eager-to-be-accepted mind. I coerced my mother to secretly cut the label out of my dad's shirt, purchase a much-less-expensive brand at the local discount store, and sew the label into my new shirt. I walked down the hallowed halls of my school with the shirt over my arm, label clearly visible for all to see. (No one actually wore these shirts; they were merely vain displays of status.)

My foolproof plan would've worked perfectly except for one tragic flaw. Everyone else carried shirts with patterns identical to one another but different from my counterfeit version. No matter how hard I tried to explain that the company had come up with a new design, I was met with a condescending look that shouted, "You're not one of the cool guys!" I was certain the principal would reveal my attempt to be accepted during his morning announcements over the public address system. Fortunately, he never became aware of the plot!

This desire for acceptance manifested itself in other ways. The "in crowd" in the late 1960s was composed largely of varsity athletes. During my high-school sports career, however, I was a perpetual junior-varsity player. I was never able to wear the distinctive dark blue and white jacket with the large, light-blue B (for Bullard) that was awarded to varsity team members. No matter how hard I tried to associate with this elite circle of athletes, I couldn't gain entry. Finally, in my senior year, I earned a varsity letter in baseball. It was awarded to me a week or two prior to my June graduation, much too late in the California heat to wear the long-coveted jacket.

Pride wasn't my only shortcoming. Somewhere along the line, I lost the motivation or ability—or both—to hide emotional responses to difficult situations. Anger often bubbled to the surface. I shouted at my parents, younger brother, and friends when things didn't go my way. Questions or comments that seemed to make demands on me or challenge my views produced angry responses, over time driving a wedge between me and family and friends.

Frustration led to sarcasm, which, combined with my desire for acceptance, resulted in my only trip to the high-school dean's office. The 30 students in my American government course were poised for an end-of-term exam when the teacher requested we put away all books and papers, pointing to a stack of notes I'd turned upside down at the top corner of my desk. In an attempt at humor at the teacher's expense, I turned to the class and explained, "I can read through these papers to get all the answers." The dean's office was only two minutes from my classroom, but that was one of the longest walks of my life.

Pride. An overwhelming desire for acceptance. Anger. Sarcasm. Disrespect. These may not be the worst shortcomings in a teenage boy, but at the time, I was trying as hard as I could to earn God's favor. I mistakenly thought I had to be without fault to gain His approval and to secure a spot in heaven, and still I was unable to live a life pleasing to Him.

I'm Not Alone
Failure to measure up to God's standard is evident in all of us. If you doubt humans are born into the world with the tendency to be something other than what God desires, try this easy experiment. Place two toddlers on the floor and remove everything but one toy. Put it between the tots and watch the fireworks begin.

In virtually every case, greed becomes very apparent very quickly. Only in the rarest situation does the child who first gains control of the toy extend it lovingly to the other. Usually the possessor of the treasure puts a stranglehold on it with one hand while fighting off the adversary with the other hand, all the while shouting meaningless noises that translate "This belongs to me. Don't even think about taking it away!" This is our nature, inherited from Adam and Eve, who, like us, wanted it their way and not God's way.

Our shortcomings don't disappear as we get older, as I learned through the unknowing instruction of a dear lady I once visited in San Francisco. Her beautiful home and garden were immaculate. In fact, when I arrived, she gave me a tour of the house and explained how I was to care for each room. Among the requirements was that I dry the tub and bathroom sink—with a clean, pressed towel—after every use.

The 70-year-old was always the picture of fashion when she left the house: a smart suit, white gloves, and hat. She'd been a pillar in her church for decades. I detected absolutely no character flaws in this gentle woman—until she got behind the wheel of her 15-year-old car, which looked as if it had just rolled off the showroom floor.

During my visit, we drove to the Fleishhacker Zoo, continued out to observe Seal Rock through telescopes along the shoreline, and cruised through Golden Gate Park. When we came across a member of an ethnic group other than hers as he waited on the curb to cross the street, my kind hostess became agitated, eventually announcing people of his nationality shouldn't have been allowed into the United States in the first place! The verbal abuse lasted no more than a minute, but it was obvious she'd expressed some deeply held opinions that elevated her and people like her to lofty positions at the expense of others who—by color or national origin—were different from her.

Like a teen motivated by pride, a toddler unwilling to share, or an elderly lady with a condescending view of others, we all fall short of what God wants us to be. Our flaws may be large or small, but we all have them. And because one of the Lord's moral attributes is justice, we're all subject to His judgment.

Our Actions Bring Reactions

From our earliest days, we're exposed to a simple yet profound truth: Our words and deeds produce consequences. Some responses to our behavior are good. A hug and a kiss for a child's small act of kindness when Mom isn't feeling well. A slap on the back for making the winning basket or knocking in the winning run. A reward of cookies and milk when all the leaves are raked into piles. On other occasions, we wish we could have avoided the results of our shortcomings. Banishment to the bedroom for destroying sister's new book. A few lashes with Dad's belt after he learns we disobeyed when Mom requested toys be put away.

Of course, these rewards and punishments are meant to prepare us for life as teens and adults when parental supervision decreases and then vanishes altogether. Those who understand the concept can look forward to living constructively within the standards of society. Those who fail to learn this lesson—or who aren't exposed to it—often struggle through subsequent decades. In the same way, a lifetime spent in spiritual darkness produces much more severe consequences. As Prophet Isaiah warned, "Woe to those ... whose deeds are done in a dark place."[18]

What can evildoers expect? Apart from a pardon from God, the identical end awaits all members of the human race, from those whose deeds have been noble by the world's standards to those who, in defiance of God, have devoted their lives to evil pursuits. One fate awaits the wise and the foolish.[19] The fate of all is death.

Apostle Paul explains that sin—any violation of God's requirements—entered the world through Adam, and sin led to death for mankind because all sinned.[20] James, the brother of Jesus, agrees. He explains we're all tempted when we're carried away and enticed by our own lust, which then gives birth to sin, which brings forth death.[21]

Surely, you counter, one who engages in an evil deed doesn't, in the midst of it, fall to the ground in pain as life ebbs from his or her body. You're absolutely correct. But because we're all born with a nature that leads us to commit wicked acts, it's only a matter of time before we violate God's standards. Were toddlers to be struck dead physically at their first offense, the world would be a lonely place. No one would live long enough to perpetuate the species, and mankind would cease to exist! Therefore, when we fail to live as God commands, our vital bodily functions don't cease instantly.

Sin Produces Separation

The Bible tells us God created man in His Own image.[22] The Father is spirit and does not have a body,[23] so the family resemblance we bear cannot be physical. In addition to our bodies, each of us possesses a soul and a spirit. The soul is what makes us who we are. It's the combination of our minds, emotions, and wills. It includes our senses, desires, affections, and appetites. The spirit is the part of us that enables us to connect with God.

When Apostle Paul tells us the wages of sin is death, he means that if we don't measure up to God's standards, we'll be separated from Him eternally. When our earthly bodies eventually wear out and return to dust,[24] the immaterial aspects of humans—our souls and spirits—will exist forever in one of two places. Those who choose to follow Christ can look forward to eternity in the presence of God. Everyone who rejects Christ and does evil can expect to be separated from God and experience tribulation and distress that will never end.[25]

Author C.S. Lewis explains two types of people exist in our world. One group is composed of those who seek to follow the Lord's commands, those who say to God, "Thy will be done." The other is made up of those who turn their backs on the Lord, those to whom God says, "Thy will be done." The relationship with God we choose in life carries into eternity.[26]

I hear murmurings of doubt. In the words of the old television westerns, some are urging, "Whoa, 'pardner;' slow down just a minute. I've walked this planet for a few years now, and the people I've come across aren't evil, at least not most of them. How can you lump everyone together and suggest we're born unworthy to exist in God's presence?"

I'm not making this judgment; it comes directly from the word of God. We know from scripture God is perfect. On several occasions, He reminded the Israelites He is holy.[27] As King David tells us, God hates wickedness.[28] He won't permit anything that isn't pure to enter His presence. The Lord demonstrated He wouldn't tolerate evil when He expelled

Lucifer and his band of dissenting angels from heaven. In the same way, He won't allow humans, who are also unrighteous, to enter His unspoiled kingdom.

From our limited, human perspective, we don't look upon ourselves as bad. By comparison to historical and modern-day evildoers, we can't be considered wicked. It should be the terrorists, mass murderers, and other nasty people who deserve to exist apart from God eternally. The problem is that we look at ourselves and others from the outside. We see kind acts and hear encouraging words and conclude they come from basically good people.

God, on the other hand, examines what to us is invisible. While we pay attention to outward appearance, the Lord looks at our hearts.[29] When He does, what He detects in 100 percent of the people who have existed, exist now, or will exist in the future—apart from Jesus—is a nature incompatible with His own. The Lord described this universal flaw after He'd delivered Noah and his clan from the great flood. He proclaimed that from our youth, the intent of our hearts is evil.[30]

So what do we conclude after this upsetting review of mankind from God's perspective? His word tells us we begin our days on Earth living inconsistently with what He desires. Among the consequences of this disobedience is a planet totally different from the beautiful world He presented as a gift to Adam and Eve. As we survey the depths to which we and our ancestors have fallen, we must admit we live in hostile territory. We are born citizens of this evil world, and our inherited guilt brings with it a sentence of eternal separation from the Lord.

In God's love, though, He extends to us all a single way to overcome this hostility. The holy, righteous Lord will allow us to come into His presence—now and for eternity—if we change our allegiance, join His army, and pledge to fight the ongoing spiritual battle on His side rather than as soldiers of Satan's evil forces. We can make this turnaround only through receiving God's Son, Jesus Christ, as our Savior.

Lessons Learned

- God created a beautiful planet upon which His children could enjoy a personal relationship with Him while He met all their needs.
- Adam and Eve disobeyed the Lord, and this brought His punishment on them and all subsequent generations.
- God's sentence is that we begin life as followers of His evil and powerful adversary, Satan.
- We've inherited our ancestors' nature of rebellion, and this accounts for the evil we see around us, from minor infringements to major acts of wickedness.
- No one has the ability to live a life free of wrongdoing, and even one unrighteous deed is enough to separate us from God for eternity.
- In God's unlimited love, He provides a way for us to forsake our allegiance to Satan and take up a position in His forces, fighting against our former leader and his evil troops.

Unit Analysis

*To download Unit Analysis and Personal Battle Plan material,
please go to www.forwardintobattle.com.*

Take a look around and you'll notice the world is not such a pretty place. Sure, God has blessed us with a planet filled with natural beauty. And man has designed and constructed some marvelous buildings. But look deeper than just the physical environment. If you were able to see into the hearts of men and women, you'd discover anything but beauty. You'd find greed, envy, and jealousy. You'd come across anger, frustration, and hate. We're not as bad as we could be, but we all fall short of perfection. We all think or say or do the wrong thing once in a while—if not often. Whether our shortcomings are huge or relatively insignificant, whether they come frequently or seldom, they form a barrier between us and God, Who is holy and righteous.

1. Over the past week, how have people around you—in your family, at work, at school, at church, or in recreational pursuits—demonstrated some of the traits that separate mankind from God? (Don't mention anyone's name, or someone may use you as an example!)
2. Despite his elevated status in the heavenly realms, Lucifer opted to rebel against the Lord. What does Isaiah 14:12-13 tell us about the reason Lucifer went astray? Now take a look at Genesis 3:1-7. In verse 5, how was the serpent's temptation of Eve similar to his own failure? Do you think Satan uses the same strategy today he employed in the Garden of Eden? Discuss how he may have tempted you in a way similar to his attack on Eve.
3. We tend to look at ourselves and many of those around us and conclude we're not bad people. After all, we've never done anything ***really*** evil. According to Romans 3:23, how would Apostle Paul respond to our claims of innocence? Read Romans 5:12. What is the source of the rebellious attitude we all possess when we enter the world?
4. In several of his letters, Paul lists behaviors that illustrate our human nature. What does Galatians 5:19-21 tell us about our natural inclinations? In Matthew 15:18-19, where does Jesus suggest the desires to take part in these evil activities come from?
5. Our words and deeds—good and bad—produce reactions from those around us. You've probably heard someone remark, "I really shouldn't have said (or done) that, and now I'll just have to live with the consequences." In a spiritual sense, what does Paul tell us in Romans 6:23 is the consequence of our rebellion toward God? How does James 1:13-15 support Paul's assertion? Describe the difference between physical death and spiritual death.

6. Among God's character traits are holiness and righteousness. Because the Lord is perfect, He's totally holy and thoroughly righteous. And because God never changes, He's always been holy, is now holy, and will always be holy. Take a look at Leviticus 11:44-45 and Psalm 5:4-6. Given God hates evil, could He ever allow an always imperfect, occasionally evil person into His presence? If we all fall short of God's standard, who could ever be worthy to approach the Lord?
7. Because of Adam's rebellion, we come into this world outside God's family. To whom is our allegiance initially directed? Who's giving us orders, and what's he calling us to do? Though we may resist the rebelliousness Satan tries to coax us into, how—when we fail to defeat his temptations—does he use us to achieve his evil purposes? What's the impact of our evil thoughts, words, and deeds on those around us?
8. Do you sense the need for people to break out of the hold Satan has over us? Where do you stand today? Are you serving in God's army, or are you among the sinister forces under Satan's command?

Prayer Points

- Praise God that His word helps us to understand the hostile environment on Earth
- Thank the Lord that He offers to rescue us from the world's darkness even though we could never be good, strong, or wise enough to come into His presence
- Ask God to help you understand how you fit into the great spiritual battle between His soldiers and the forces of evil
- Commit to responding to the Lord's invitation to forsake allegiance to Satan and to become a warrior in His army

Personal Battle Plan

1. Every day, we're targets for Satan's temptations. Our wicked enemy derives great delight when we fall short of what God wants us to be, when we do what God desires we avoid. Think back over the past week or so. **List the three or four areas in which the devil has attacked you most frequently**.
2. Now conduct a battle-damage assessment, considering some of the areas in which Jesus, John, and Paul tell us men and women commonly fail to defeat Satan's temptations. Beginning with a **review of your thought life** over the past several years, evaluate how frequently you've been a casualty of war in the following areas:

	Never A Problem	Sometimes Fall Short	Often Give In

a. Jealousy (resentful of a rival or of a person enjoying success or advantage)
b. Envy, covetousness (unhealthy craving for what someone else possesses)
c. Greed (excessive desire for more than one needs or deserves)
d. Arrogance (overbearing, unwarranted pride or feelings of self-importance)
e. Evil, impure, filthy thoughts
f. Malice (desire to harm another person)
g. Dislike of others

	Never A Problem	Sometimes Fall Short	Often Give In

    h. Indifference toward or hatred of God
    i. Idolatry (worship of people or things unworthy of reverence)
    j. Other wrong thoughts (be specific)

3. Turn next to **an evaluation of your words**. Using the same scale, determine those areas in which you've spoken in an inappropriate manner.

	Never A Problem	Sometimes Fall Short	Often Give In

    a. Angry outbursts
    b. Disputes, dissension, strife (quarreling)
    c. Enmity (expressing hostility)
    d. Insolence (speaking with bold disrespect)
    e. Deceit (representing as true what is known to be false)
    f. Slander (making false statements that damage a person's reputation)
    g. Gossip (repeating idle talk and rumors)
    h. Coarse (vulgar, obscene, crude) jesting, silly talk
    i. Boasting (talking proudly about oneself)
    j. Other bad words (be specific)

4. As a final review, **assess your actions** to determine in which areas you may have failed to live up to God's standards.

	Never A Problem	Sometimes Fall Short	Often Give In
a. Drunkenness, carousing			
b. Sexual promiscuity, adultery, sensuality			
c. Disobedience			
d. Untrustworthiness			
e. Theft			
f. Murder			
g. Other immoral, wicked actions (be specific)			

5 Using your responses above, **list the three areas in which you struggle most** in trying to be the person God wants you to be. Commit to pray daily that the Lord will give you the strength to defeat Satan's attacks in these areas. Thank God for His promise in I Corinthians 10:13: "No temptation has overtaken you but such as is common to man; and God is faithful, Who will not allow you to be tempted beyond what you are able, but with the temptation will provide the way of escape also, that you may be able to endure it."

6. Throughout the Bible, we learn God is holy and righteous. We also see all mankind has a habit of giving in to temptation, some more often and more dramatically than others. **Reflect on God's purity**, and ask Him to help you understand why He won't allow imperfect man to enter His perfect presence.

7. Because Adam and Eve failed to follow God's instructions, each person on Earth is born with allegiance to the devil. **Honestly assess whom you follow today: God or Satan.** Have you ever made a

conscious decision or taken any action to desert from the forces of evil? If you have, write down what you've done to overcome Satan's hold on you. If not, make a note of why you're content to continue in the direction you're headed or why you believe a change of allegiance may be necessary.

8. **Prepare for the next session** by contemplating the tremendous agony Jesus endured as He died on the cross more than 2,000 years ago.

CHAPTER 2

Changing Allegiance

The purpose of God for man is to make him holy. Not happiness first, and holiness if possible, but holiness first and bliss as a consequence. The real you is the self which Christ could make you. You were not built to abide in sin. God made you for Himself, and deep-set in your heart there are longings after holiness.

W. E. Sangster[1]

THROUGHOUT MY TEENAGE years, I led a very ordinary life. My father was an insurance salesman, my mother a homemaker. My parents, my younger brother, and I lived in a very nice house across the street from my high school. I was neither popular nor unpopular, a member of the unnoticed majority that passes quietly through the educational system.

This doesn't mean I merely existed through these years, content to be involved in nothing. I earned respectable grades and participated in a variety of extracurricular activities. I began playing baseball in Little League and kept at it through my senior year in high school. Although never a star, I played a few innings in most games, enjoying my role as a utility infielder and cheerleader/comedian during my time riding the bench. My basketball career had come to an end the previous year when, after starting the first dozen games for the junior varsity team, the coach discovered a player who could score about 15 points per game more than I could.

I had several clusters of friends—baseball and basketball teammates, students who shared several classes with me, and members of my church youth group—but I didn't have a "best friend." On the dating scene, I had an on-again, off-again relationship with a wonderful girl who was an excellent student, was interested in sports, and was an aspiring guitar player and folk singer. I didn't have a care in the world!

Well, that's not entirely true. Did I mention this was the 1960s? At that time, the U.S. was involved in a military conflict in Southeast Asia. As a teenage male, I became most interested in the news that the U.S.—for the first time since 1942—was considering holding a draft of young men of service age. Graphic television reports of the gruesome reality of war had convinced me that serving as a soldier in the jungles of Vietnam wasn't the life for me.

At the same time, my father and my uncle suggested I consider competing for an appointment to the relatively new U.S. Air Force Academy (USAFA) in Colorado. As my high-school days dwindled and the possibility of a draft became more likely, my anxiety about hand-to-hand combat coupled with a desire to serve my nation in some way led me to apply to the Academy.

After reviewing my results on a Civil Service exam and interviewing me in his office, Congressman B.F. Sisk nominated me as an alternate from his district. USAFA officials at the institution enrolled not only the primary nominees for the class of 1972 but also several of the alternates. I was among them.

On June 23, 1968—just two and a half weeks after graduating from high school—I kissed my mother and my girlfriend good-bye, shook hands with my father and brother, and boarded a United Airlines aircraft for my first-ever flight. Actually, it was three flights as I winged my way first from Fresno to Los Angeles, then on to Denver, and finally south to Colorado Springs.

I set out for the Academy dressed in a double-breasted, gold sports coat; brown slacks; and a brown-and-gold-striped tie. I also sported a pair of brown, wingtip shoes. My parents had purchased this outfit for me shortly prior to my departure, even though I wouldn't be allowed to wear civilian clothes for most of the initial 12 months of my cadet career.

Upon arrival in Los Angeles, I joined the equivalent of a squadron of 18-year-old men who, I deduced, also were headed for USAFA. What gave them away was that unlike me, all were wearing shiny, black, military shoes, which we'd been instructed to bring with us. I was certain the fashion faux pas of my fellow passengers would elevate me significantly in the eyes of the upper-class cadets who'd greet us upon our arrival at the Academy.

Throughout the flights, I pondered the great changes about to take place in my life. I had no curfew over my final couple of years in high school, and I recognized my time would not be my own at the Academy. My civilian wardrobe would soon be packed away in a storage room, to be removed only during two short holidays we'd be granted our first year. I'd trade my room at home—decorated to my tastes and cleaned when and if I wished—for a three-man dormitory room that would require constant tidying. I was about to begin a year filled with academic, military, and athletic challenges that would start before dawn and keep me running until late into the night.

My several hours speculating on the future ended abruptly when a stewardess announced we'd be landing in Colorado Springs momentarily. A bus with Air Force Academy emblazoned across the side transported us to the school, and 44 faces pressed against the windows as we pulled up to the area that included dorms, dining hall, and academic buildings. Upper-class cadets greeted us cordially and led us to various stations where we began our transition. First stop: the barbershop. More than 1,000 heads were shaved that day, and the shorn locks must have set an Academy record for volume and weight! (Did I mention this was the 1960s?)

Incoming cadets made further stops to be measured for uniforms, receive shots (using an electric, pistol-like device that caused even some of the more sturdy young men to quiver), and sign for post-office boxes. After a full day of processing and a couple of meals in the cavernous dining hall, we were led to a large theater where we were introduced to the Commandant of Cadets, the first military general most of us had ever seen. A highly decorated fighter pilot who'd been a hero in Vietnam, he gave us a short pep talk. I then followed his lead in repeating these life-changing words:

> I, John Terry Tyrrell, having been appointed an Air Force Cadet in the United States Air Force, do solemnly swear that I will support and defend the Constitution of the United States against all enemies, foreign and domestic, that I will bear true faith and allegiance to the same; that I take this obligation freely, without any mental reservation or purpose of evasion, and that I will well and faithfully discharge the duties of the office on which I am about to enter. So help me God.

Upon completing this oath, I was no longer one of the protected; I was on the road to becoming one of the protectors. As men younger than I were fighting and dying on battlefields in Southeast Asia, I'd vowed to take up the battle against any current or future enemy that challenged our nation and our way of life. I was prepared to give my life should this be necessary. In a matter of a few seconds, I became set apart from the other 464 18-year-olds who'd been handed diplomas by our high-school principal a couple of weeks earlier.

While not much more than appearance had changed in my few hours at USAFA, I'd embarked on a transition that eventually would yield a person not even my closest friends back in Fresno would know or fully understand. I wouldn't be marching off to war any time soon, but I'd begin to develop the skills, knowledge, and values to serve as a military officer. In the physical realm, moving from life as a civilian to membership in the U.S. military is the most radical transformation I've experienced.

Stepping into the Light

The transformation from loyalty to Satan to allegiance to God is every bit as radical a change as giving up civilian life to enter the armed forces. It's also very similar. In the spiritual warfare that's existed since the days of Adam and Eve, humans begin their lives among the forces of Satan. Motivated by a desire to please ourselves, we engage in selfish activities that delight God's adversary and cause the Lord great sadness. In our natural existence, we do our own thing, satisfying our needs and urges as we wish.

A new soldier must lay aside a former lifestyle and follow the direction of the commander, and a recruit in God's army must follow the Lord's command. While new military members must prepare themselves for an eventual call to conflict, God's warriors begin to adopt the character and strategies they'll employ as they battle the satanic forces from which they've defected. Military troops are different from their peers outside the forces, and God's followers are set apart through their efforts to break away from Satan's influence over mankind.

What exactly is involved in transferring allegiance from Satan to God? As we've seen, those living apart from the Lord exist in darkness. Those who join God's army move from darkness to light. This transformation is similar to what happened when Jesus healed a blind man. After the man had lived in darkness all his life, Jesus opened his eyes to physical light. For the first time, he could see the world around him. In the same way, Christ overcomes the darkness Satan produces so we can discern the spiritual light of God. We're able to see the Lord's truth that the devil has hidden from us through the years. (See John 9.) John's gospel contains several passages that explain this change.

John tells us Christ was light sent into the dark world. Unfortunately, those who existed in darkness had no idea God had sent His Son to illuminate their paths. The light of Jesus pierced the darkness for a few who recognized He wasn't just another mortal. Their appreciation of Christ's divine nature caused them to break allegiance with the devil and vow to follow Jesus. The apostle explains Jesus gave these people the right to become children of God.[2]

On several occasions, Jesus discussed the differences between life in His light and life in darkness. The religious leaders of His day often tried to trick Christ into breaking God's commands. Jesus used one of these tests to announce how He'd come to the aid of those who'd forsake their role in Satan's forces. "'I am the light of the world,'" He said. "'He who follows Me shall not walk in darkness, but shall have the light of life.'"[3]

Jesus referred to Himself as the source of light in a dark world. He urged those in His audience to "'walk while you have the light, that darkness may not overtake you; he who walks in the darkness does not know where he goes. While you have the light, believe in the light, in order that you may become sons of light.'"[4]

Christ preached and performed many miraculous signs, yet those deceived by Satan's schemes refused to step out of the darkness of evil into the light He offered. Saddened by their refusal to grasp the truth, Jesus cried out, "'I have come as light into the world, that everyone who believes in Me may not remain in darkness.'"[5] His frequent contrasting of light and darkness was intended to help listeners understand change was necessary if they were to become the people God intended. They'd have to move from their natural state to a supernatural existence, pledging allegiance to God through trusting in His Son as their one true Leader.

Nicodemus learned of this transition in a secret meeting with Jesus. The wealthy Jewish leader came to Christ one night to avoid the disapproval of fellow members of the nation's highest ruling body. Nicodemus simply complimented Jesus as a gifted teacher and acknowledged His skill must have come from God.

Making the Transition

Christ didn't thank Nicodemus or affirm the truth of his statement. Instead, Jesus offered advice as relevant today as it was 2,000 years ago:

"'Truly, truly, I say to you, unless one is born again, he cannot see the kingdom of God.'"[6] He explained this rebirth isn't physical; it's spiritual. We're not children of God when we're born into this dark world. To belong to the kingdom of God—to become His sons and daughters—we must go through a spiritual transformation illuminated by the light of Jesus.

None of Christ's early followers understood this better than Paul. After Jesus' resurrection, He appeared to the future apostle as he traveled to Damascus. Christ told Paul He was sending him to the Gentiles "'to open their eyes so that they may turn from darkness to light and from the dominion of Satan to God.'"[7] For the rest of his life, Paul proclaimed that people must make the transition from darkness to light. We have a choice: We can switch to God's path for our lives, or we can remain on Satan's path.

Paul reminded the Ephesians that before pledging their allegiance to Christ, they lived in darkness. He encouraged his readers to walk as children of light, begging them not to participate in the wicked deeds of darkness. To the church in Colosse, Paul wrote that Jesus had delivered them from the domain of darkness, where they'd been alienated, hostile, and engaged in evil practices.[8]

A God of Love

Why does God want us to break ranks from among Satan's followers and pledge allegiance to Him? The answer comes into focus as we understand God's love isn't simply something He has or something He does. It's His nature: God is love.[9] In His unlimited love, the Creator of the universe wishes to establish an intimate relationship with all humans, a relationship that will endure through eternity. Unfortunately, no one has totally pleased God. Each of us has disobeyed the Father, some more than others.[10]

Because sinful man could never stand in the presence of holy God, the fate for all mankind was eternal separation from the Father. In His overwhelming love for us, though, God devised a plan. He sent His Son to Earth to take on the penalty we deserve. Jesus paid for our disobedience through His death on the cross so that everyone who trusts in Him as Savior may live forever with the Father, Son, and Holy Spirit.[11] This is the only way we can break allegiance to Satan, the only way we can make the transition from darkness to light.

God reveals His love to us in grace—blessing us when we don't deserve it—and mercy—withholding punishment we've earned by our evil thoughts, words, and deeds. King David praised God that He is gracious and merciful, slow to anger, and great in lovingkindness.[12]

The grace of God is much like the gifts children receive at Christmas. Although they have a habit of disobeying the rules, fighting with brothers and sisters, and making nuisances of themselves, Mom and Dad still love them so much they want to give them that special present when the family gathers around the Christmas tree. Though the children may not have earned their gifts, the excitement in their faces makes the undeserved blessing a joy for their parents.

God's grace is revealed through some of His earliest dealings with the Jews. Although they constantly failed to trust and obey Him, He showed favor to them. In the midst of their complaining during the exodus from Egypt to the Promised Land, the Lord provided food for His people. He also enabled them to defeat their foes along the way and then gave them a good and spacious land flowing with milk and honey as their new home. Since these early days, God has treated those He's adopted as sons and daughters with grace.

Jesus constantly poured out grace. On one occasion, a crowd of 4,000 men and many more women and children had been listening to Him teach for three days. Jesus felt compassion for them and multiplied seven loaves of bread and a few small fish into a meal that satisfied all and also generated seven baskets full of leftovers.[13] Jesus was moved when He encountered a widow in the town of Nain who was about to bury her only son. Christ consoled the grieving mother and raised her son from the dead.[14] Now that's grace!

God treats us with mercy when He withholds the punishment we deserve because of our rebellion against Him. Let's go back to our example of Christmas. Let's say Mom and Dad give six-year-old Ashley a beautiful doll, but her eight-year-old brother Justin rips the head off the doll within an hour of opening the gifts. Under normal circumstances, the children's parents would sentence Justin to an afternoon in his room. In the spirit of the holiday and filled with love, though, Mom and Dad choose not to punish Justin. After making sure he understands the error of his ways, they allow Justin to enjoy the remainder of the day's activities and the special Christmas goodies Mom has baked over the past week. This is mercy.

We see God's mercy through His forgiveness. King David tells us God is forgiving and good, abounding in love to all who call to Him.[15] David knew this from experience; earlier he'd called on God to have mercy according to His unfailing love. (See Psalm 51.) Based on the king's repentance, God forgave David's adulterous relationship with Bathsheba.

Jesus also expressed mercy through forgiveness. One evening, a sinful woman crashed a dinner party at the home of a high official so she could honor Christ. She began crying and wet His feet with her tears. Then she wiped them with her hair, kissed them, and poured perfume on them. As the high-powered guests looked on in amazement, Jesus forgave the woman's many sins, telling her, "'Your faith has saved you; go in peace.'"[16]

Though it's impossible to describe fully God's love for us, we know it's:

- ***Unconditional*** – He loves the good and the bad and sent His Son to save all.[17]
- ***Undeserved*** – By our nature, we're sinful. He's holy. He chooses to love us anyway.[18]
- ***Unlimited*** – In His great love, He adopted us and has given us an eternal inheritance.[19]
- ***Unsurpassed*** – No one else could love us as much as God does; He demonstrated this by sending His dear Son to die for us.[20]

- ***Unending*** – His love for us is everlasting.[21]
- ***Unbreakable*** – Nothing can separate us from God's love.[22]
- ***Unable to be comprehended*** – His love surpasses knowledge.[23]

In the final analysis, God's love, grace, mercy, and forgiveness come together at the cross. As Apostle Paul wrote, "Because of His great love with which He loved us, even when we were dead in our transgressions, [God] made us alive together with Christ (by grace you have been saved)."[24] And Peter, Jesus' disciple and close friend, rejoiced that because of God's great mercy, He has allowed us to become part of His family through Jesus' resurrection from the dead.[25]

Another of Jesus' inner circle, John, puts it this way: "By this the love of God was manifested in us, that God sent His only begotten Son into the world so that we might live through Him. In this is love, not that we loved God, but that He loved us and sent His Son to be the propitiation [atoning sacrifice] for our sins. ... The Father has sent the Son to be the Savior of the world."[26]

Jesus Died for All

Few of us truly understand the concept of sacrifice. Perhaps a couple of stories will help. During World War II, the 4th and 5th Battalions of England's Suffolk Regiment were sent to Singapore in an attempt to keep the British colony out of Japanese hands. The two units were mostly new recruits with no battle experience. They were quickly defeated, and those who survived became prisoners of war. Many were forced to build the Burma Railway, enduring the brutality of Japanese guards, starvation, and disease. In the two battalions, 557 men died as prisoners of war, more than four times the number killed in action.[27]

In *Miracle on the River Kwai*, Ernest Gordon tells a true story about a group of prisoners working on the railway. At the end of the day, their tools were collected, and a Japanese guard shouted that a shovel was missing.

He demanded to know who'd taken it. The guard worked himself into a fury and ordered whoever was guilty to step forward. No one moved. "All die! All die!" he shrieked. The guard cocked his rifle and aimed it at the prisoners. At that moment, one man stepped forward, and the guard clubbed him to death with the rifle while the prisoner stood silently. When the work party returned to the camp, the tools were counted again, and all the shovels were accounted for. The man had stepped forward as a substitute to save the others.[28]

A year or two later, the U.S. Army's 105th Infantry Division was fighting the Japanese on Saipan, a small island in the western Pacific Ocean. On July 7, 1944, Lieutenant Colonel William O'Brien's battalion was attacked by an overwhelming enemy force of between 3,000 and 5,000. In bloody, hand-to-hand combat, the Japanese eventually overran American positions. After being seriously wounded, and with casualties mounting and ammunition running low, Lieutenant Colonel O'Brien refused to be evacuated. Armed with a pistol and a .50-caliber machinegun mounted atop a jeep, he kept the enemy at bay as his troops retreated to safety. His body was later found surrounded by the Japanese soldiers he'd killed.[29]

Nearby, Private Thomas Baker was wounded early in the attack. He fired on the Japanese until he was out of ammunition, and then he carried on the fight unarmed. A comrade carried him 50 yards to the rear of the fighting, but he refused to be moved any farther because he didn't want to risk the lives of other American troops. Private Baker was propped up against a tree and was given a pistol and eight bullets. As the other members of his battalion withdrew, they looked back and saw Private Baker taking fire so they could escape. His body—flanked by eight dead Japanese troops—was recovered later. For their gallant sacrifice, Lieutenant Colonel O'Brien and Private Baker (who afterwards was promoted to sergeant) were awarded the Medal of Honor.[30]

These three men gave up their lives so others could live. Nearly 2,000 years earlier, Jesus died as a substitute for every person who'd walk the face of the Earth. Unfortunately, stories and paintings passed down through the centuries often portray Jesus' death as much more pristine and much less heroic than the sacrifices of a prisoner who is unmercifully executed or soldiers who shield members of their unit from the bullets of enemy troops at the cost of their own lives. In fact, what Jesus endured for us was every bit as noble.

During the last few hours of Christ's earthly existence, He suffered excruciating pain and humiliating verbal abuse as He allowed Himself to die on the cross to pay the penalty for our sin. Jesus was arrested in the Garden of Gethsemane as He prayed passionately about His upcoming execution. As the authorities took Him away, all His followers fled, concerned only for their own safety. Peter, one of His closest disciples, three times denied he knew Jesus. Christ was then marched back and forth between Caiaphas (the high priest), Pilate (the Roman governor), and King Herod in a series of mock trials and insulting interviews that finally resulted in His being sentenced to death.

Prior to Jesus' execution, Pilate had Him scourged. We usually picture this as a whipping, but it was far more brutal. The instrument consisted of a wooden handle with several leather straps, each embedded with nails or pieces of bone. The victim was tied to a post or laid across a table, and the person administering the flogging struck him just below the base of the skull along the shoulders and dragged the leather straps slowly down his back. The sharp objects pulled off the skin and tore the muscle. Many died from this torture.

After Jesus was scourged, a crown made of thorns—possibly up to two inches long—was shoved onto His head and a purple robe draped across His bloody shoulders. In sarcastic tribute, the soldiers shouted, "Hail, King of the Jews!" as they struck Him on the face and spat on Him. They then tied part of the cross weighing more than 100 pounds to Jesus' battered shoulders and made Him carry it toward Golgotha, the site of His crucifixion. After the earlier beating, the weight of the cross was too much, and a man in the crowd was pressed into service to carry it the rest of the way to the hill outside Jerusalem where Jesus was crucified.

Crucifixion was used by the Assyrians and Persians in the 6th Century BC. It became common 200 years later during the rule of Alexander the Great and was adopted by the Romans in the 3rd Century BC. It was reserved for slaves or offenders of the worst class. In the case of Christ, the cross was assembled, and Jesus was laid upon it. Nails were driven through His wrists and feet, and then the cross was raised upright and dropped into a hole in the ground. The jolt of this procedure resulted in tremendous pain as skin, ligaments, and bones pulled against the nails.

Those who were crucified usually died by suffocation. As the victim hung on the cross, he'd push up with his feet to raise himself high enough to inhale. As he dropped down to the hanging position, he'd exhale. This continued until he was too weak to push up and was unable to breathe. Jesus, however, was spared that agony. Modern-day doctors who have studied Christ's crucifixion have concluded He died of heart failure.

God Awaits Our Response
Why did Christ endure such pain? Why did the Father allow His only Son to undergo such brutal treatment? Because God, in His wonderful love, had determined the only way sinful man would be able to come into a relationship with Him was for His Son to die in our place. Jesus paid a debt He didn't owe because we owed a debt we could never pay!

Through His sacrifice on the cross, Jesus gave each of us the opportunity to be saved from the punishment we deserve because of the many ways we've disobeyed God. We must choose to believe Jesus is the Savior for all mankind, sent from God the Father in heaven, and ***we must receive Jesus as our Savior***, giving Him complete reign in our lives. We do this through sincerely believing and then praying something like this:

> Father, I acknowledge I've fallen short of being the person you want me to be, and my rebellion separates me from You. Jesus, thank You for taking on the penalty for my sin by dying on the cross for me. I now open my heart to You and receive You as my Savior. Lord, thank You for forgiving me and allowing me to become part of Your family. Holy Spirit, through the strength and wisdom you provide, help me to become more and more like Jesus in this life and to rejoice in the certainty that I'll spend eternity in heaven when my days on Earth end. In Jesus' name I pray. Amen.

Of course, it's not just saying these words that makes someone a Christian. Through the years, many have prayed (or often simply read aloud) something like this without completely understanding what they were getting themselves into. They haven't grasped and been totally committed to making the dramatic changes involved in becoming a follower of Jesus. When Satan attacks, this lack of understanding and commitment causes them to quickly run up the white flag of surrender and return to the enemy's camp.

When young men and women begin the transition from civilian life to serving in the military—whether they get out after an initial hitch or stay in for a full career—they turn control over their lives to their commanders. They sacrifice much of the freedom they previously enjoyed as their daily schedules are subject to what their superiors require.

After they've completed training, they can be sent into combat at a moment's notice. Some may have to make the ultimate sacrifice, giving their lives in the service of their nation. Nothing short of a total commitment will enable them to faithfully complete their time in the armed forces.

When we sincerely pray to receive Jesus as Savior, we acknowledge we're giving control of our lives to God until our days on Earth come to an end. We agree to allow Him to begin a complete makeover of our lives, changing us from what we were before into what He wants us to be: present-day copies of His Son. We promise to let Him change our thoughts, words, actions, and desires so they reflect those of Jesus. We pledge to deny ourselves some of the pleasures we previously enjoyed, realizing the instant gratification we receive from doing our own thing is far less satisfying than the blessings He'll provide—in this life and for eternity.

Receiving Jesus as Savior means we'll be called on to be 100 per cent faithful to God, putting our reputations on the line, giving up some of our earthly comforts, and possibly sacrificing our lives in the cause of Christ. We commit to being unafraid of being dramatically different from those who've yet to decide to follow Jesus and courageous in returning to the hostile territory where they reside to boldly tell them about our Savior and to encourage them to become warriors in God's army.

Choosing to become a follower of Christ is definitely not the easy, comfortable, self-satisfying path through life that most would prefer. We may never possess what many other people try so hard to achieve or accumulate. But if we make this commitment understanding what it truly means and serving God with passion, our reward is a joyous, eternal relationship with the Creator and Sustainer of the universe!

The moment we make this commitment, our spiritual transformation is under way. We begin to do battle as soldiers in God's army against the adversarial force in which we previously served. Upon establishing allegiance to God, we're:

- ***Saved***: rescued from Satan's power over us.[31]
- ***Redeemed***: released from the punishment of separation from God we deserve because of our rebellion against Him; Jesus paid the penalty on our behalf.[32]
- ***Justified***: declared innocent and free of guilt before God.[33]
- ***Reconciled***: restored to a loving relationship with God.[34]

And all this happens in the first few seconds of our existence as followers of Jesus! Our new lives as Christians include several additional blessings.

- We're adopted into a ***new family*** and granted privileges as God's sons and daughters.[35]
- We receive ***new citizenship*** as eternal residents of God's kingdom.[36]
- We're blessed with ***new freedom***, exempted from Satan's previous domination.[37]
- We gain ***new character***[38] and ***new perspective***[39] as God's Holy Spirit takes up residence within our hearts.
- We're given ***new jobs***. Recreated in the image of Christ, God calls us to do good works that He prepared for us even before we received His Son as Savior.[40]

When I started life as a cadet at the Air Force Academy, the initial changes were visible primarily in my appearance. Little on the inside was different. When we turn from darkness to light through receiving Christ as Savior, the most immediate transformation is invisible. Our standing in the eternal, spiritual domain is dramatically altered. What follows these early changes, though, is the same for military troops and members of God's army. New soldiers and new followers of Christ begin a rigorous training program that enables them to become warriors who will be well prepared to defend their countries or their newfound faith.

Lessons Learned

- We enter life following Satan's command as soldiers of his forces of evil.
- To establish an allegiance to God, we must sever ties with our wicked leader.

- God calls us to make this transformation because, in His infinite love, He desires to have an intimate, everlasting relationship with us.
- Our evil nature makes it impossible to come into the presence of a holy God.
- Jesus died on the cross in tremendous pain and humiliation as a perfect sacrifice for our rebellion.
- Only through placing our faith in Christ as Savior can we make the transition from loyalty to Satan to allegiance to God, from darkness to light, and from everlasting separation from God to eternity in His presence.
- This shift in allegiance results in our becoming warriors in God's army, and for the remainder of our lives on Earth, we'll be engaged in spiritual battle against the forces of His wicked adversary.

Unit Analysis
To download Unit Analysis and Personal Battle Plan material, please go to www.forwardintobattle.com.

Whether we want to admit it or not, no one begins life as a child of God. As a consequence of the failure of Adam and Eve to follow God's instructions, we all start our earthly existence under the command of Satan. Fortunately, God loves us more than we'll ever fully understand this side of heaven. This is evident in the tremendous ransom He paid—the death of His beloved Son—so we could become members of His family. Jesus endured the pain and agony of the cross—in obedience to His Father and because of His great love for us—that we might escape the devil's control and become loyal followers of Christ. Through His sacrifice, Christ took upon Himself the penalty for our rebellion. When we place our faith in

Jesus, the Father looks upon us as worthy to spend eternity with Him, and He begins a lifelong process of helping us to become more like His Son.

1. Throughout our lives, we're constantly faced with situations that require us to make significant changes: leaving home for the first time, entering a profession after our formal education ends, adjusting to a new lifestyle following marriage or the arrival of children. What is the toughest transition you've had to make? What emotional highs and lows did you experience as you made this dramatic change in your life? How did you get through the challenges you experienced during this period?
2. The world under Satan's rule is filled with darkness that obscures the path God wants us to take. Read John 8:12 and 12:35-36, 46. What source of light does the Father provide to followers of His Son? How does Jesus help us to see where we're headed? What do you think this means in practical terms in our day-to-day lives?
3. Jesus' secret meeting with Nicodemus helps us to understand mankind's need to be transformed. How does Christ describe this change in John 3:1-6? What are the differences between physical birth and spiritual birth?
4. In John 3:16, how does Jesus say a person can be born again? The word ***believe*** in this verse means much more than a simple intellectual assent that Jesus really walked the Earth or that He was the Son of God. As we see in Matthew 7:21-23, true belief in Christ as Savior goes beyond doing significant works in His name. What do you think is involved in the belief Jesus mentions to Nicodemus?
5. If, in answer to the previous question, you described ***belief*** as complete trust that Jesus is the only way humans may enter into an eternal, loving relationship with God ***and*** a total commitment to

live one's life as God's word commands and in keeping with the example Jesus provided, you're on target! How do Jesus' words in John 14:1-6 illustrate the only path to God? According to John 14:21 and 23, how will our love for and commitment to Christ be measured?

6. When we truly believe in Christ in this way, our citizenship is transferred from Earth to heaven. Read Ephesians 2:1-10 and 19. Prior to receiving Christ as Savior, what is the evidence that our allegiance is to Satan rather than to God? What two elements of God's love motivated Him to allow us to become residents of His kingdom? According to verses 8 and 9, what must we do to experience adoption into the Lord's family? Once we've become citizens of heaven, what's our responsibility? (See verse 10.)

7. God expresses His love to mankind through His grace and mercy. Read Psalm 145:8 and Hebrews 4:16. Although many people believe these terms mean the same thing, they actually are quite different. God's grace is His unmerited favor, the blessings He bestows upon us when we don't deserve them. The Lord demonstrates His mercy when He withholds the punishment we deserve because we fail to meet His standards. How does God's grace reveal His love for mankind? Why is it necessary that He treats us with mercy?

8. What do the following verses reveal about God's love for us? Which of these descriptions—you may select more than one—mean the most to you? Why?
   a. God's love is unconditional – I Timothy 1:15
   b. God's love is undeserved – Romans 3:10
   c. God's love is unlimited – I John 3:1
   d. God's love is unsurpassed – Romans 5:8
   e. God's love is unending – Psalm 100:5
   f. God's love is unbreakable – Romans 8:35
   g. God's love is unable to be comprehended – Ephesians 3:19

9. In addition to His love, God possesses a number of other supernatural attributes. What impact does the fact that God is love have on the following elements of His character?
    a. God's omnipotence – He's almighty; His power is unrestrained
    b. God's omnipresence – He's present everywhere at once
    c. God's omniscience – He knows everything and is the source of all wisdom
    d. God's holiness – He's perfect, pure, and without fault
    e. God's righteousness – He does only what's right
    f. God's justice – He judges with total impartiality based on the standards He's set
    g. God's sovereignty – He reigns over the universe He created
    h. God's faithfulness – He always keeps His promises and carries out His purposes
10. Read Mark 15:15-39. How do the torture, humiliation, and execution of Jesus reflect His Father's grace and mercy? How do they demonstrate Jesus' love for us?

Prayer Points

- Praise God for His extravagant love, grace, mercy, compassion, and forgiveness
- Thank Jesus for His sacrificial death: He paid a debt He didn't owe because we owed a debt we could never pay
- If you have not done so previously, consider praying to express trust in Jesus as your Savior. (See the example prayer in number 7 under the Personal Battle Plan for this chapter.)
- Ask God to help you to fully appreciate that when you make this commitment to Christ, He forgives you, adopts you into His family, and transfers your citizenship from Earth to His kingdom
- Commit to serving faithfully as a soldier in the service of the Lord

Personal Battle Plan

1 **Evaluate your relationship with God:**

	Strongly Disagree	Somewhat Disagree	Neither Agree nor Disagree	Somewhat Agree	Strongly Agree
a. I have a great desire to appreciate the difference between God's light and Satan's darkness.					
b. I'm consistently loyal to God, obeying Him and refusing to allow Satan to trip me up.					
c. I regularly and sincerely express my gratitude to God for all He's done for me.					
d. I've committed my life to Christ and am trying my best to become more like Him.					

2. In Jesus' role as the One Who brings light into a dark world, He helps us to see our shortcomings much more clearly than we have in the past. **Note three to four areas of your life you want to review in the light of His perspective.** If you discover changes in your conduct are necessary, ask God for help in this transformation.
3. Often Christians can be among the more patriotic citizens in a nation. Apostle Paul reminds us, though, that Christ's followers are no longer citizens of Earth; we're residents of heaven on assignment here in the service of our Lord. **Evaluate the passion with which you represent your country and the passion with which you represent the Lord**. If you're more devoted to accomplishing your patriotic duties than you are to assuming your role as a citizen of heaven, pray the Holy Spirit would help you to give first place to your allegiance to God.
4. Define grace and mercy in your own words. Consider how these aspects of God's love are similar and how they're different. **List a few ways in which God has treated you with grace and a few examples of the mercy He's shown you,** and then express to Him your gratitude on both counts.

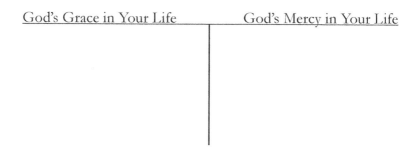

5. Over the next week in your prayers, **praise God for one attribute of His extravagant love each day**. It's unconditional, undeserved, unlimited, unsurpassed, unending, unbreakable, and unable to be comprehended. For the rest of your life, thank God daily for sending His

Son to pay the penalty for your rebellion, thus allowing you to receive salvation through faith in Christ.

6. **Assess the sacrifices you've made for others.** Determine the impact these acts of kindness have had in your life and the blessings others have received through your actions. Consider Jesus' tremendous sacrifice at Calvary, and invest your time, talents, and treasure in the lives of others with the attitude that led Christ to give up His life for all mankind.

7. To fully experience God's love and to joyfully express your love for Him, you must **receive Christ as Savior.** If you haven't done so, your first action must be to pray this simple prayer (or one very much like it):

Father, I acknowledge I've fallen short of being the person you want me to be, and my rebellion separates me from You. Jesus, thank You for taking on the penalty for my sin by dying on the cross for me. I now open my heart to You and receive You as my Savior. Lord, thank You for forgiving me and allowing me to become part of Your family. Holy Spirit, through the strength and wisdom you provide, help me to become more like Jesus in this life and to rejoice in the certainty that I'll spend eternity in heaven when my days on Earth end. In Jesus' name I pray. Amen.

The next step is to **tell a Christian you know and respect you've made this commitment** and to ask for help in becoming the follower Jesus wants you to be.

8. **Prepare for the next session** by considering how you, as a follower of Christ, should give Him the respect He's due.

Training in the Basics: Foundation for Service

THE INITIAL COUPLE of days of basic training at the Academy were quite civilized compared to what followed. Upper-class cadets were genuinely helpful, pointing us in the right direction so we were able to settle into our new environment. Occasionally, they engaged us in casual conversation, most often asking about our hometowns. I was proud to respond I was from Fresno. It's obvious to me now that few of the upperclassmen had ever heard of it.

This calm beginning became a distant memory unexpectedly one evening after dinner. We'd marched to the dining hall led by the caring upperclassmen who'd monitored vaccinations, uniform distribution, and campus orientation. When the relaxed meal ended, our leaders were replaced by insult-spewing ogres masquerading as veteran cadets. Lined up along the two-hundred-yard path from the dining hall to the dorms, they shouted abusive remarks at my trembling classmates and me as we hurried back to what we thought would be the sanctuary of our rooms.

Along this gauntlet, clusters of two or three upperclassmen pulled aside unsuspecting basic cadets. As one asked a question he really didn't want answered, his companions took up positions within an inch of their victim's ears, hurling abusive remarks that drowned out the weak response of the young man who was being bullied: "Get your chin in, Smack!

Shoulders back and down!" "I can't hear you, Doo-wad!" "You'd better look at Cadet Johnson when he's speaking to you!" "What's that mess on your shirt? Don't you know how to eat without spilling food all over yourself?!"

This was the start of a six-week program designed to drop 1,000 young men who'd been told they were "the cream of the crop" of American youth to the bottom rung of the military ladder. Before we'd learn how to lead, we'd have to learn how to follow. This, we discovered, was important for two reasons. First, we had to understand how to obey orders steadfastly. No matter what rank we eventually attained, we'd always report to a higher authority. Additionally, we'd develop empathy for those we'd ultimately lead. While the logic is flawless, it was quite a challenge for hundreds of teens with fairly high opinions of themselves to be harassed unmercifully, not only for the initial month and a half but through the entire first year.

Basic training was split into two roughly equal segments. The first was largely academic—a series of lectures on the Air Force, the Honor Code, and similar lessons, all held in classrooms or massive lecture halls. We also experienced rigorous physical training, running several miles each morning at the challenging altitude of 7,250 feet above sea level—far, far above that of West Point and Annapolis, as we learned in a quote we were required to memorize.

During the following three weeks, we moved to a tent city in the foothills. The program became even more physical as we scrambled through assault courses, trekked across the hilly countryside on land-navigation expeditions, and ascended obstacles up to 40 feet high during confidence-building exercises. These activities helped us learn what we could do individually as we pushed our bodies to the max and also enabled us to appreciate what we could accomplish as a team.

When we begin the transformation into full-fledged followers of Christ, we have a lot to learn. We must first gain an appreciation for our new leader. When we enter God's army, ***Jesus becomes our***

Commander. No longer can we choose what to do and what not to do, what to say and what not to say, what to believe and what not to believe. We're no longer in control of our lives; our divine Leader is calling the shots. The better—and more quickly—we understand Jesus' role as Commander and our position as His subordinates, the sooner we'll advance in our Christian lives.

Christ had a lot to say about how His disciples should respond to His leadership. Three times during His final meal with the 12, Jesus linked love for Him with obedience to His commands.[1] He also instructed the disciples to abide in Him, to forge a closeness that would allow them to accomplish extraordinary feats in His service.[2] As we become warriors for the Lord, we must first respect Christ as our divine Commander and must then create and maintain intimacy with our heavenly Leader.

Jesus emphasized that after He returned to heaven, His disciples wouldn't be alone. As soldiers in God's army, **we work as a team** with others who are dedicated to serving Christ. Our strongest ally—a partner Who'll never leave our side—is the Holy Spirit. Christ explained the Spirit would consistently teach us what we need to know to serve honorably and effectively, bringing to mind the truth Jesus shared during His time on Earth.[3] Additionally, the Spirit would convict people—especially followers of Christ—of spiritual truth.[4]

Our unit also is composed of angels who battle alongside us. During the church's early days, Jewish religious leaders imprisoned the apostles for spreading the gospel. God dispatched an angel to free them from jail and to encourage them to continue their ministry.[5] Similarly, an angel rescued Peter after Herod had thrown him into prison.[6] In addition to the angels, a vast group of Christians who've passed from this life to the next cheer us on from heaven.[7]

We also serve with others who've put their faith in Christ. As Jesus taught His disciples, He stressed the unity necessary among warriors in God's army. We're to love our fellow soldiers with the same love He demonstrated. This love, Jesus said, would identify us as His followers in the eyes of enemy forces.[8] Additionally, Christ commanded those who serve Him to love one another even to the point of laying down our lives for our fellow soldiers.[9] Our unity, explained Jesus, would serve as a strong witness to those not yet committed to Him.[10]

When Christ finished His instruction of the disciples, He sent them into the world.[11] Once we appreciate the basic concepts that Jesus is our Commander and that we serve with hundreds of thousands of warriors in a powerful army, we're ready for combat. Before we dash ahead onto the battlefield, we'd better make sure we've got the basics firmly in mind.

CHAPTER 3

Becoming a Follower

We refuse to present a picture of "gentle Jesus, meek and mild," a portrait that tugs at your sentiments or pulls at your heartstrings. When your heart is being wrung out like a sponge, you don't want a thin, pale, emotional Jesus. You want a warrior Jesus. You want a battlefield Jesus. You want his rigorous and robust gospel to command your sensibilities to stand at attention. You want mighty. You want the strong arm and unshakable grip of God who will not let you go—no matter what.

Joni Eareckson Tada[1]

THE FIRST STEP in making the transition to military life is basic training. Young recruits are immersed in a demanding routine—physically, mentally, and emotionally—designed to transform them from independent civilians to members of a "lean, mean fighting machine." Many lessons learned during their first 18 years must be unlearned. At the same time, they must absorb what it means to serve in the armed forces. Among the most important of these concepts is respect for authority.

Throughout my 33 years in the military, I was exposed to many leaders. At the Academy, some upper-class cadets subscribed to the theory that the best way to develop followers was to hassle them relentlessly. They used a number of tactics to put down first-year students.

During our initial six weeks, basic cadets were subjected to name-calling that included words I'd never heard. In addition, our leaders chose colorful—and often abusive—phrases to describe our tiny minds, our physical incompetence, and our inability to learn or to do the simplest things. While I could see a few new cadets with huge egos needed to be dropped a peg or two on the pride ladder, I couldn't imagine why the humble majority should be subjected to such vicious treatment.

Verbal abuse was accompanied by physical demands far beyond the more constructive group runs and competitions used to correct minor mistakes—or no mistakes at all. Many times I rounded a corner in the dorm to come face to face with a fire-breathing, upper-class demon. The following conversation often took place as I tried to scurry past the cadet who, with a sinister grin, was blocking the route to the safety of my room or the nearest latrine.

"Wait a minute, Smack Jazz! Who are you?"

"Sir, I am Basic Cadet Tyrrell, John T., 726404K!"

"Oh, so ***you're*** Tyrrell. I've heard a lot about you," he lied. "Do you know who I am?" As often as not, the questioner was not from my squadron but was just passing through the hall on his way to the mailroom.

"No, sir!"

"Why not?"

"No excuse, sir!"

"You know, Tyrrell, you're a sorry excuse for a cadet. Get down and give me 10 [pushups]!"

This process repeated itself every few yards until I finally reached my room. I'm pretty sure I did more pushups between June 26 and August 7, 1968, than I've done over the rest of my life combined!

Equally frustrating were the mind games our leaders played. During meals basic cadets took part in a round-robin question-answer session prior to being allowed to eat. We were required to memorize passages from *Contrails*, a little blue book with a silver, embossed cover. We'd be tested on the Oath of Allegiance to the United States, the Mission of the United States Air Force Academy, the Purpose of the Fourth-Class System, the "Air Force Song," and "The Star Spangled Banner." Thrown in for good measure were quotes by several distinguished people and the cheers that would be used at intercollegiate football games.

As we sat at attention, upperclassmen asked each "doolie" (a term derived from the Greek word for slave) to recite an item from *Contrails*. If he presented the information without error, he was allowed to begin eating. If he made a mistake, the table commandant instructed the basic cadet to pass his plate to the waiter. The unfortunate basic then either sat in silence while his mates inhaled their food, or he responded to a series of questions hoping multiple correct answers would earn him dessert.

This style of leadership continued when the academic year began. Once a couple of cadets in their second year at USAFA trapped me in their dorm room during mandatory study time. They asked me to run through required definitions and quotes, keeping my voice to a whisper. After 10 minutes of this harassment, I responded with a loud and hearty "Yes, sir!" Within seconds, the pair hurried me off toward my room, just as the cadet commander burst out of his room next door to determine the cause of the commotion.

I was later assigned to a flight—a unit of around 30 cadets—commanded by a Christian in his final year at the Academy. Cadet First Class Gary Combs didn't pressure first-year cadets. Instead, he treated us with dignity, encouraged us when we'd done well, and suggested how we could improve.

After my graduation, I worked for a wide range of commanders. One was a foul-mouthed, cigar-chewing colonel who inspired fear among all who worked for him. Another—who'd been a Rhodes Scholar—was down to earth despite his lofty education at Oxford. A third seemed to be afraid he'd make the wrong decision, so he made no decision at all. One of my commanders appeared to be more concerned with his next promotion than with the welfare of his subordinates. I also worked for a Navy admiral who often tapped into my 24 years of experience as our unit prepared for a challenging combat mission. I seldom heard from the Marine Corps general who replaced him.

Unit success wasn't always dependent on the commander's style. Most of these leaders were effective in ensuring the mission was accomplished. Although their followers might not have enjoyed working for some of these men, those being led carried out their duties as professionally as they could so the organization would succeed.

Jesus Is Our Commander

As we serve in God's army, we're led by a Commander Who always has our best interests in mind, Who always provides the encouragement we need, Who always ensures we're equipped for combat, and Who fights alongside us in every battle with the enemy. As Christians, we report to Jesus Christ, the Commander of our unit. This title is not a manmade term for our Savior; it comes straight from God's word.

As Joshua and his army approached Jericho, a man holding a sword confronted him. Joshua's response was similar to the more modern "Halt! Who goes there? Friend or foe?" The leader of the Israelites asked, "'Are you for us or for our adversaries?'" The reply sent Joshua rapidly to the ground in respect: "'No, rather I indeed come now as captain of the host of the LORD.'"

With great reverence, Joshua—probably the most powerful man on the planet after being called and strengthened by God—asked what his surprise visitor had to say. "'Remove your sandals from your feet, for the place where you are standing is holy.'" Joshua did as he was told. The Captain then presented the Jewish leader a very unorthodox plan for conquering the great, walled city. By following these directions, Jericho fell to the Jewish army through a few blasts on some trumpets and the shouts of the traveling band of immigrants.[2]

Who was this mysterious Person? Bible scholars agree the Captain of the host of the Lord is none other than the Lord Himself. The reason the ground was holy was because God was standing on it! Now, we know God the Father is a spirit, and certainly the Holy Spirit is a spirit. This leaves only Jesus as the divine visitor that day.

Portrayals of God as a warrior appear in both the Old and New Testaments. Isaiah reveals the Messiah will be a leader and commander for the peoples.[3] Earlier, following the Israelites' escape from the Egyptians, Moses and the sons of Israel sang, "'The LORD is a warrior; the LORD is His name. ... Thy right hand, O LORD, is majestic in power, Thy right hand, O LORD, shatters the enemy. And in the greatness of Thine excellence Thou dost overthrow those who rise up against Thee.'"[4]

The book of Revelation provides a picture of Christ's final battle with Satan. In Apostle John's vision, heaven is opened, and Jesus approaches Earth seated on a white horse to wage war. From His mouth comes a sharp sword He'll use to destroy the nations. And He's not alone! Right behind Jesus, also astride white horses, are the armies of heaven, clothed in white linen. This heavenly army crushes its adversaries, dispatching the evil leaders into a lake of fire that burns with brimstone and annihilating their soldiers.[5]

In describing the spiritual warfare between those who are soldiers in His army and those who aren't, Christ explains He didn't come to bring peace on the Earth but a sword.[6] According to John, Jesus' earthly mission was to destroy the works of the devil.[7] Apostle Paul tells us Christ's divine crusade against evil will continue until He has conquered all His enemies.[8]

By what right does Jesus assume command over the forces of good? Paul tells us God the Father placed all things in subjection to His Son when He commissioned Jesus as head over the church.[9] The apostle amplifies Christ's credentials to command by reminding us He created everything in the heavens and on the Earth—including the leaders of the armies that oppose Him! Jesus is Head of the church and Head over all rule and authority.[10] The apostle leaves no doubt about our Commander's supremacy over His troops.

So, back in Joshua's day, God sent His Son into the world even before His birth at Bethlehem to lead His chosen people in their victory over Jericho. In addition, Jesus will command the forces that will defeat Satan at the "end of the age." This divine Commander leads our unit, and He makes available to us His power and His wisdom so we may be victorious in our battles in His service.

Loving Our Leader

Joshua demonstrated high regard for his Commander when he met Jesus while on the way to Jericho. The great Jewish general fell on his face in awe as Christ informed him he was standing on holy ground. Modern-day warriors can take an example from Joshua. We're to love Jesus with all our heart, all our soul, and all our mind. Christ calls this the great and foremost commandment.[11]

Many years ago, I attended a talk by a guest evangelist at our church. He was particularly well known through his travels around the country and a weekly television program. I remember vividly the thrust of his sermon. He pointed out that words such as all, every, none, and never were exactly what God intended when He inspired them in the writers who put pen to paper.

When the Son of God calls something great and foremost, there can be nothing more important. More than any other spiritual requirement, we're to love God—Father, Son, and Holy Spirit—with every ounce of our being. Therefore, our primary response to our heavenly Commander is to love Him above all others.

Love as it's described in the New Testament comes from two Greek words. *Phileo* is an ardent affection, an impulsive love. *Agapao* is a deeper form of love. It signifies high regard or esteem and is the word for the love of the Father for His Son, for mankind, and for followers of Christ. It's also the type of love God desires humans to have for Him and for one another. Jesus' chat with Peter after His resurrection illustrates we're to love as the Father loves. He twice asked His disciple, "'Do you love Me?'" In both cases, Christ used the word *agapao*. In both cases, Peter replied in the affirmative, but he used the word *phileo*.

In his expanded translation of the New Testament, Kenneth Wuest suggests the conversation went something like this: "'Do you have a love for Me called out of your heart by My preciousness to you, a devotional love that impels you to sacrifice yourself for me?'" "'Yes, Lord, as for You, You know positively that I have an emotional fondness [or a friendly feeling] for You.'"

Peter's answers prompted Jesus to ask a third time, but He used the term *phileo*. Peter responded with the same word. Again according to Wuest: "'Do you have a friendly feeling and affection for Me?'" "'You know from experience that I have a friendly feeling and affection for you.'"[12]

The disciple's answers weren't too far off the mark, and Jesus restored him to a position of leadership among His closest followers. But what response do you suppose Jesus would have preferred? I'd have to go with "Yes, Lord, I have a love for You called out of my heart by Your preciousness to me, a devotional love that impels me to sacrifice myself for You." It's this higher, *agapao* love Jesus desired, and today God longs for His children to develop this same deep love for Him.

Making Jesus Lord

This degree of love is required if we're to make Jesus, our Commander, the Lord of our lives. We often hear new Christians say, "I've accepted Jesus as my Lord and Savior." These eager believers are only half right. While Christ is our Savior from the very instant we sincerely place our faith in Him and allow Him to begin to transform us into what He wants us to be, we seldom give Him complete control of our lives until months—even years—later when we realize He wants us to hold nothing back in our love and obedience.

Making Jesus Lord involves creating intimacy between God and us. The human equivalent is the relationship between two people in love. Intimacy begins to develop during dating. When a young man and young woman realize they're "meant for each other," they want to move beyond physical attraction and awareness of the activities and interests they both enjoy. They want to be together constantly, spending hours discussing every aspect of their lives. As the relationship develops, they reveal more about themselves than they've ever told anyone else.

The best way to develop intimacy to is share with one another in person. When I played basketball in high school, my first "true love" and I finished our classes more than an hour before my practice began. She lived less than two miles from the school, and I calculated I could walk her home, spend five minutes at her house, and run back to the gym—all in 65 minutes. We had wonderful chats as I carried her books along the way, and I got to know her very well.

After our time together, I'd sprint back to school, change into my basketball gear, and report to practice—usually just as the coach was blowing his whistle for the players to assemble. He took roll and then sent us to run laps around the court. Between the two miles I ran to get back to school and another mile at the start of practice, I was exhausted before I touched a basketball. It was worth it, though, because of the 45 minutes I'd spent with the "girl of my dreams."

Of course, we can't always be in the physical presence of our dearest friends, and that's why Alexander Graham Bell invented the telephone. In the old days, a couple probably racked up more time on the phone while dating than all their other calls put together. Today young lovers can communicate more often and more easily via the cell phones they carry with them. And if the pair can't speak to each other, they can text messages back and forth.

Our budding love doesn't stop at talking or texting. We're also eager to demonstrate our affection by presenting fabulous gifts to our beloved. Well, let's put that another way. It's the responsibility of the male to give these gifts, while the female has to develop the skill—she already has the desire—to receive them.

The most intimate human relationship we experience is between husband and wife. Theoretically, the desire for deep communication and gift giving and receiving developed during courtship continues—though these often tend to dwindle as a marriage progresses. Whether this is a result of over-familiarity, competition for attention when children arrive on the scene, or other reasons, when all is said and done, we know our spouses better than any other person.

Our experiences in dating and marriage are very similar to those in our relationship with God. We start out a bit awkwardly, unsure of Who this other Person really is but feeling we'd like to get to know Him better. As we discover more about Him and begin to communicate with Him, we find we very much enjoy being in His presence. We tell others about Him and can't imagine what it would be like to be without Him. We eventually pledge ourselves to Him, promising to love, honor, and obey for the rest of our lives.

The honeymoon is pure ecstasy; we're inseparable. Our intimacy with Him grows stronger until, suddenly, we realize the relationship is beginning to slip a little. Whether it's taking Him for granted ("He'll always be around; I'll talk with Him later"), the urge to engage in some other very important or exciting things we'd like to do, or any number of other excuses, we allow our time with God to be crowded out. The Person Who'd been the center of our universe is now little more than a casual acquaintance.

This isn't the way God intends for it to be.

Building Intimacy with Christ

I once heard intimacy defined as "into me see." God certainly sees into us. He knows everything about us and loves us anyway—as the sacrifice of His Son demonstrated. His greatest desire, as illustrated by His greatest command, is that we see into Him, that we know Him better than we know any human, and that we love Him with all our heart and soul and mind.

During Jesus' final meeting with His disciples before His arrest, the concept of intimacy—in several directions—was on His agenda. Christ said He's preparing a place for us in His Father's house, and He'll come to take us to where we'll be ***together***. He also disclosed He was in the Father, the Father was in Him, and the Father abiding in Him spoke through Him. Jesus said that when He departed Earth, the Father would send His Spirit to be with us, to ***abide in us*** forever. A time was coming, Jesus said, that He'd be in His Father, we'd be in Christ, and Christ would be in us.[13]

Jesus explains how love fits into intimacy between the Father, Son, Spirit, and us. He says if we love Him, we'll obey His commandments, we'll be loved by the Father and the Son, and God will abide in us.[14] Ten times in the first 10 verses of John 15, Jesus uses the word "abide." In John 17, the idea forms the basis for Jesus' prayer to His Father just prior to His crucifixion. As one of my USAFA professors used to say, anything repeated this often is a "foot-stomper." We can be sure we'll have to know this for the exam!

The word *abide* means to take up residence, stand fast, await, or submit to. In the context of following Christ, we're to love God so deeply that we can feel His constant presence within us. We're to stand firm in His love, His strength, His wisdom. We're to wait on Him to reveal His perfect love, direction, and peace. We're to experience a two-way love relationship more consuming than any relationship we'll have with any human partner at any time.

In the mid-1600s, a monk in a small abbey in France understood what Jesus meant by loving God above all else, of abiding in Him. Nicholas Herman was an uneducated man who grew up in Lorraine. After doing time as a footman and a soldier, he entered the Carmelite order in Paris in 1666 and was given the name Brother Lawrence. His role was to keep the kitchen clean, but his communion with God was so deep that visitors to the abbey often bypassed the abbot to spend time with the monk.

Although Brother Lawrence wrote no books, a Cardinal published a collection of conversations the monk had with visitors and notes he'd written to those who'd asked for help in drawing nearer to the Lord. Though less than a quarter inch thick, *The Practice of the Presence of God* has provided excellent advice for followers of Christ for more than three centuries.

Brother Lawrence once advised a visitor that one must make a "hearty renunciation of everything which ... does not lead to God. That we might accustom ourselves to a continual conversation with Him, with freedom and in simplicity. That we need only to recognize God is intimately present with us, to address ourselves to Him every moment, that we may beg His assistance for knowing His will in things doubtful, and for rightly performing those which we plainly see He requires of us, offering them to Him before we do them, and giving Him thanks when we have done. That in this conversation with God we are also employed in praising, adoring, and loving Him incessantly, for His infinite goodness and perfection."[15]

It's often said we can tell people's devotion to God by looking at their calendars and checkbooks. As we see how others spend time and money, we discover how intimately they're related to God. Brother Lawrence probably had no money, working in a monastery kitchen. But if we were to look at his calendar, it must have had only a single entry repeated throughout the day: Draw closer to God and praise His holy name!

As far as investing our worldly wealth in ways that demonstrate our love for God, we can turn to the story of an immoral woman's encounter with Jesus for inspiration. As Christ dined at the home of a well-to-do

Pharisee, the sinful woman entered the dining room, wet His feet with her tears, wiped them with her hair, kissed them, and anointed them with costly perfume. Jesus commended this extreme demonstration of love, forgiving her many sins and granting her salvation through her act of faith—much to the surprise of the more "religious" guests at the meal.[16]

Some contend the world today is more fast-paced than it was in the 1600s. Others suggest it's much more challenging to make ends meet financially than when perfume was selling for much less per ounce. While this is all relative, God desires that all of us make our relationship with Him ***the*** top priority in life, devoting time and money to deepening the bonds between us and the God Who loved us enough to sacrifice His Son on our behalf.

As we love Jesus and establish intimacy with Him, we can become more faithful warriors in His army by remembering the ways in which a soldier ***respects*** his or her commander. A follower:

- **R**epresents
- **E**xamines
- **S**ubmits
- **P**roduces
- **E**xtends
- **C**ooperates
- **T**rusts
- **S**acrifices

The Spiritual Follower Represents

During my time in the Air Force, I occasionally traveled away from my home base on temporary duty. I was sent by my commander as his representative, and I knew my hosts would form opinions of my boss and my organization based on the quality of my work. My goal was to do the best job I could so those watching would know I came from a superb unit.

When Jesus sent out His disciples to minister in His name, people on the receiving end drew conclusions about Christ based on the words and deeds of His followers. On one occasion, He dispatched His dozen ambassadors after giving them authority to cast out demons and heal diseases. The disciples' orders also included preaching that God's kingdom was near. They'd witnessed Christ perform these tasks, and now it was their turn to represent Him by accomplishing the work they'd seen Him do.[17]

Jesus' final act on Earth was to direct His disciples to go into all nations to draw people to God.[18] Since that day, everyone recruited into God's army has been tasked with representing our Commander among all we interact with, helping them on their journeys of faith.

The Spiritual Follower Examines

Throughout my military career, I attended a variety of schools. Most included classes on leadership. Others featured lessons on the most advanced techniques of completing my day-to-day duties. While this classroom instruction was helpful, I learned much more from my leaders. As I observed their performance, I picked up valuable pointers on what to do—and what to avoid—as I advanced in rank.

To represent Christ to others, we have to know Him deeply and personally. Jesus' disciples were with Him around the clock. No one before or since has had the opportunity to learn about the Master and from Him as did those 12 men. They listened to His lessons. They observed Him in action. And throughout their close relationship with Jesus, the disciples came to appreciate His character and His actions.

We, too, must examine the life of Christ. While we can't do this in His presence, through the pages of scripture we're able to "'know [the Father], the only true God, and Jesus Christ Whom [He] hast sent.'"[19] God has provided a wonderful biography so we can observe our Leader in action, learning valuable lessons on how to conduct our spiritual operations and the traits and values we must possess to be effective in our duties.

The Spiritual Follower Submits

Through the first 18 years of our lives, we're being prepared to be independent, to take charge of our own destinies. It's not surprising, then, that submitting to a higher authority is one of the most difficult aspects of being part of any group.

As we examine the life of Christ so we can represent Him faithfully, one of the key traits we discover is His humility. At no time was this more evident than in Jesus' passionate prayer in Gethsemane just prior to His crucifixion. As the Son agonized over His approaching execution, He let His Father know He wasn't looking forward to dying. In an act of total submission, however, Jesus said He was ready to do whatever His Father required.[20] Apostle Paul tells us Christ humbled Himself by becoming obedient to the point of death on the cross.[21]

We submit to Christ as our Commander in two ways. First, we acknowledge His supremacy. The Father has given Jesus **all** authority in heaven and on Earth.[22] Therefore, His soldiers are to give Christ first place in everything.[23] In addition, we obey His commands. The Lord desires our total submission, and He promises to bless those who humble themselves under His mighty hand.[24]

The Spiritual Follower Produces

By definition, followers don't sit on the sidelines telling others what to do; they make a valuable contribution to achieving the goals of their organizations. Followers create a product or perform a service. Group effectiveness depends on how well they execute their duties. In combat, the unit will emerge victorious only if its soldiers accomplish the tasks they're assigned.

When Jesus sent out 70 of His followers to minister in the cities He was planning to visit, they returned and reported with joy they'd cast out demons in His name.[25] Apostle Peter gave a sermon in Jerusalem, and 3,000 in the crowd enlisted in God's army.[26] Peter and John then healed a man who'd been lame since birth. Those who heard of the miracle were amazed, and we can assume some may have received Christ as Savior.[27]

Apostle Paul traveled throughout the Mediterranean by land and sea to share the love of Jesus with anyone who'd listen. All these disciples—and others who've followed Christ though the centuries—produced. In some cases, the results were astonishing in the physical realm. Often, they produced spiritual results, helping others grow in their relationships with God.

As followers of Christ, we must produce results pleasing to our Commander. Jesus told His disciples He'd chosen and appointed them to bear lasting fruit,[28] and He calls His present-day followers to be similarly fruitful. Paul echoes Christ's instruction. Warriors in God's army are to walk in a manner worthy of the Lord, to please Him in all respects, and to bear fruit in good works.[29] Our fruit is to touch the lives of others so they know Jesus and draw closer to Him.

The Spiritual Follower Extends

One of the reasons leaders take on followers is because the task at hand is larger than what the person in charge can accomplish single-handedly. In combat, a company commander would never rush headlong into battle on his own. His troops would be right behind him, and the entire unit would fight to the best of its ability to accomplish the mission. Similarly, serving alongside our Commander, we can have a great impact in extending God's kingdom on Earth.

Prior to His crucifixion, Jesus told His disciples that when He was reunited with His Father, those who believed in Him would do even greater works than He had done.[30] He knew His time on this planet was coming to an end. He knew, too, that many generations of His followers would continue His ministry after He returned to heaven.

Christ's wisdom has been confirmed as millions of His followers have continued to build a global movement in every corner of the world upon the foundation He laid in a small country in the Middle East. Like the initial cadre of Jesus' soldiers, it's now our turn to help extend His Father's kingdom to the remotest part of the Earth.[31]

The Spiritual Follower Cooperates

Jesus taught an important lesson in the way He "deployed" those 70 troops mentioned above. He sent them into ministry two by two.[32] His disciples learned this concept well as—after His death—many pairs of Christ's followers traveled the countryside to set up the early church. Peter and John worked together in Jerusalem. Paul and Barnabas joined forces in Antioch for a year and then set out on a missionary journey into what today is Turkey. Sadly, a serious disagreement caused Paul and Barnabas to part company, but the importance of teamwork held fast as Paul set out to minister with Silas in Syria, and Barnabas and John Mark sailed for Cyprus.

Occasionally, those serving in a combat unit compete rather than cooperate. They may become rivals for the attention of the commander. They may seek to be rewarded for their dedicated efforts and promoted well before their contemporaries. While this can be constructive, it may jeopardize unit success if it's carried to an extreme. As we'll see in the next chapter, it's crucial we respect those in God's army. We must be aware of the important contributions they make as together we seek to carry out the Lord's orders. We can accomplish much more working as a team than if we proceed in isolation or at odds with other followers of Christ.

As we fight alongside other warriors, our Commander is always with us. Jesus told His followers, "'Where two or three have gathered together in My name, there I am in their midst.'"[33] In addition to working well with the troops in our spiritual units, we must cooperate with Jesus by seeking, discovering, and acting on His direction and following His battle plan. He won't desert us, and His supernatural strength will enable us to stand firm in the fiercest attacks.

The Spiritual Follower Trusts

In order for followers to carry out each of the tasks above, they must believe in the integrity and ability of their leaders. Over more than three decades in the military, I served under commanders I was willing to follow into war, trusting they would lead our unit to victory. On the odd occasion, however, I had grave reservations over whether or not the boss would be able to lead us out of the parking lot at the end of the duty day. Those in the second group seemed to be short either on honesty or competence—or both!

Jesus inspired trust in those who followed Him. Despite constant harassment from Jewish religious leaders, His 12 disciples didn't abandon Him through His years of ministry—at least not until the night of His arrest. Jesus' followers walked by His side and followed His direction because they trusted Him. They understood Jesus was much more than simply a wandering preacher or someone out to make a name for Himself. When Christ questioned Peter about Who he thought He was, he responded that Jesus was the Son of the living God.[34]

Christ has earned our trust by instruction that is as true and relevant today as it was when He spoke it. We know we can rely on Him because He not only talked the talk, but He walked the walk. We can find no evidence that Jesus said or did anything wrong; He was faultless in word and deed. Throughout His time on Earth, Christ reflected the glory of His Father, and this went well beyond the charisma of human leaders. Finally, we can trust Jesus because He died to pay the penalty for our rebellious attitude toward His Father, and He returned to life—just as He said He would.[35]

The Spiritual Follower Sacrifices

Not all soldiers in God's army are called to give their lives in the service of our Commander. We may, however, be required to make some sacrifices as we carry out our duties. Jesus' disciples left their jobs and, in some cases, their families to follow Him. Apostle Paul took more than a few stones to the body for the sake of Christ and eventually gave up his freedom (but not his testimony, even to the guards who kept him in custody).

When a well-to-do young man wanted to join Jesus' ragtag band of followers, Christ laid out the entrance requirements. The man would have to sell his possessions and give the profits to the poor. This would assure him treasure in heaven, and then nothing would hold him back from following Jesus. One of the saddest verses in the Bible tells us he went away in grief because he was very wealthy.[36]

In our modern world, a number of things might hinder us from pledging total allegiance to Christ. Like the young man, it may be our present prosperity—or our quest for riches. Perhaps we prefer relaxing comfortably in the background to stepping into the firing line of possible rejection or ridicule for following Jesus. Maybe we'd rather spend time satisfying our own desires than ministering to others. Whatever the distraction, whatever we might have to lay aside as we follow our Commander, we must remember service in God's army will be rewarded by treasure in heaven that far surpasses anything we might accumulate on Earth.

This isn't to say there are never casualties among those serving as warriors for the Lord. Every day, followers of Christ around the globe are persecuted for their faith. Some lose their jobs. Others lose their homes. Still others lose their lives because they refuse to renounce their allegiance to Jesus. These valiant soldiers remind us that the closer we get to the frontlines of spiritual warfare, the greater the likelihood of sacrifice becomes.

In the service of their country, members of the armed forces are to respect their leaders and obey their orders. Spiritual warriors are to ***love*** and ***respect*** our Commander and ***obey*** His commands. We do this in a one-to-one relationship with Christ, but we don't do it alone. As we serve Jesus, we fight alongside a host of others who have enlisted in God's army through faith in His Son. Together, we can achieve much more than any of us could accomplish individually.

Lessons Learned

- Following our recruitment into God's army, we must undergo an extensive basic training regimen designed to prepare us for spiritual battle.
- As warriors serving the Lord, Jesus is our Commander.
- Christ—as Captain of the host of the Lord—visited Earth before His birth in Bethlehem, confronting Joshua prior to his siege of Jericho.
- Jesus will repeat His military role when He returns to the planet to deal Satan his final defeat.
- In response to Christ's leadership, we must love our Commander with every ounce of our being, making Him Lord of our lives and creating an intimacy with Him that is characterized by our constantly experiencing His presence within us.
- Soldiers in God's army respect our commander as we represent Him, examine His life, submit to His authority, produce spiritual fruit, extend His kingdom, cooperate with Him and others in His forces, trust in His integrity and ability to help us in our duties, and make any sacrifices He requires of us.

Unit Analysis

To download Unit Analysis and Personal Battle Plan material, please go to www.forwardintobattle.com.

As we begin our service in God's army, we start with basic training. Among the most important lessons we must learn is the composition of our unit. First, we must appreciate Jesus' role as our Commander. He leads us into every spiritual battle we experience on Earth. Because God has bestowed upon Christ the authority to lead us, we must render Jesus the highest respect. We do this by loving Christ just as He loves us and creating a deep intimacy with Him. As we make Jesus the Lord of our lives, the Holy Spirit abiding in our hearts will produce in us the desire and the ability to obey the Lord's commands.

1. Think back on some of the teams you've belonged to. They may have been businesses, athletic clubs, church groups, military units, or other collections of people working toward a common goal. Consider the groups' leadership, teamwork, dedication, and other characteristics. What separated good units from bad ones? How did the leaders set the pace in successful groups?
2. Christ promised to be with His disciples always, and He's with His followers today. While we have no problem thinking of Him as a great teacher, a miraculous healer, a loving friend, and the Savior of all who place their trust in Him, we may find it difficult to consider Jesus as our Commander. Read Joshua 5:13 – 6:5. What do you learn about Christ's role as Commander from this passage? How does it reinforce the prophecies found in Isaiah 55:4 and Revelation 19:11-21?
3. Many people are driven by pride to seek the highest rank, the most powerful position, the greatest wealth they can attain. Read Matthew 4:8-10. After his first couple of temptations failed to cause Christ to turn His back on His Father, what was Satan's final assault? How did Jesus defeat this and the devil's earlier attacks?
4. How are you required to interact with human leaders who've been placed above you in various groups? According to Ephesians 1:19-23, what is the source of Jesus' power? How should we respond to His authority? From these verses and Paul's instruction in Colossians 1:18, do you have any doubt about Jesus' credentials to command God's army?
5. In Chapter 2, we discovered that when we receive Christ as Savior, we're saved (delivered from the power of sin), redeemed (released from

the punishment of death), justified (declared righteous before God), and reconciled (restored to fellowship with the Lord). How should these changes motivate us to "love the LORD your God with all your heart, and with all your soul, and with all your mind" as Jesus instructed in Matthew 22:37?
6. One of the ways God desires that we demonstrate respect for our heavenly Commander is through developing a deep, personal relationship with Him. How is intimacy among the Father, Son, Holy Spirit, and soldiers in God's army illustrated in John 14:1-3, 10-11, 16-17, and 20? In a practical sense, how do we draw closer to the Lord?
7. Read John 14:15, 21, and 23 and John 15:1-10. What's the link between love, abiding in Christ, and obedience?
8. Apostle Paul's service in God's army as he summarizes it in II Corinthians 11:16-27 was filled with challenges. How does his willingness to endure such hardship reflect his respect for Jesus?
9. Discuss how Christ's followers are called to represent, examine, submit, produce, extend, cooperate, trust, and sacrifice. What hope does II Corinthians 4:7-10 provide as we respect our heavenly Commander today?

Prayer Points

- Praise our mighty and eternal God that His Son is our Commander and that the Father has placed all things in subjection to Christ
- Thank Jesus that He fights alongside us in all our spiritual battles; He never leaves us on our own
- Ask God to help you develop an intimacy with Him so His love will become more real to you
- Commit to demonstrating your love and respect for Christ by obeying His commands

Personal Battle Plan

1. God the Father has commissioned His Son to serve as our Commander. Think about how you respond to your earthly leaders, and then **assess your allegiance to your heavenly leader.**

   <u>Never   Sometimes   Often   Always</u>

   a. I follow Christ with great reverence and respect.
   b. When I receive His direction, I respond completely, immediately, courageously.
   c. Nothing sidetracks me as I seek to accomplish the duties He lays out for me.
   d. I am able to follow His example consistently.

2. Based on the evaluation above, **list areas in which you need to be more responsive to Jesus' leadership.** For each, jot down one specific action you'll undertake over the next month. Pray for God's help, and make this an agenda item when you meet with another Christian for prayer and accountability.

3. **Review your love for God**.
   a. Do you consistently love Him with *all* your heart, soul, and mind? If not, what's holding you back? Indicate what you'll do to **break down these barriers**:
   b. In the words of Kenneth Wuest, "Do you have a love for God called out of your heart by His preciousness to you, a devotional

love that impels you to sacrifice yourself for Him?" Or "Do you have an emotional fondness [or a friendly feeling] for Him?" If the former, press on! If the latter, indicate what you'll do to **move to a deeper love for the Lord**.

4. Determine whether or not your **actions reflect your love for God**. Do you obey His commands consistently? List specific areas in which you're having the greatest problems obeying God's instructions, pray daily for His help in overcoming these challenges, and tap into His power to make the changes required to show Him you love Him.

5. **Check your day timer and checkbook** to determine whether they adequately reflect your love for God. If you were on trial in a court of law for possessing a deep and unshakeable love for the Lord and the judge and jury were to review these documents, would they find enough evidence to convict you? Indicate what you'll do to ensure the time you spend in the activities of life and the way you manage your finances demonstrate your love for God.

6. A follower of Christ respects his or her Commander. **Assess how well your daily words and deeds reflect your respect for Jesus** by placing an "X" on each of the lines below. Pray for God's direction in areas that require improvement, and make a note of what He leads you to do. Talk to a mature Christian friend if you need practical advice.

Openly represent_____Keep my faith
Jesus in all my   in Christ a
relationships   secret from others

Regularly examine the_____Already know everything
example of Jesus as   I need to know about Christ
revealed in scripture

Continually submit to Jesus and obey His commands	Resist Christ's direction when it conflicts with my desires
Consistently produce spiritual fruit in the lives of others	Don't want to rock the boat by talking about religion with others
Frequently extend God's kingdom by leading others to Christ	Leave the conversion activities to church leaders and evangelists
Constantly tap into help from human and supernatural members of God's army	Handle my spiritual duties by relying on my own strength and wisdom
Totally trust Jesus in all aspects of life	God can help with some of the big issues, but I just can't turn over everything to Him
Willingly sacrifice in my service to the Lord	Carve out a bit of time for spiritual activity after getting everything else done

7. **Prepare for the next session** by considering how well you work alongside other members of God's army.

Chapter 4

Working on A Team

As much as we admire solo achievement, the truth is that no lone individual has done anything of value. The belief that one person can do something great is a myth. There are no real Rambos who can take on a hostile army by themselves. Even the Lone Ranger wasn't really a loner. Everywhere he went he rode with Tonto!

John C. Maxwell[1]

THE TOP PRIORITIES during our basic training as God's warriors are creating an intimate relationship with our Commander and learning how to be good followers. We also must develop respect for the others on our side so we'll be prepared to fight our spiritual battles as a unit.

Warfare is a team effort, not an individual event. As the children of Israel journeyed to the Promised Land, the Lord instructed Moses to take a census. God was very specific about how Moses was to record the total number of Jews headed toward Canaan. He was to count every male 20 years old and older who was capable of going out to war in Israel. When the tally was completed, the Jewish army numbered 603,550 soldiers! (See Numbers 1.)

Undoubtedly, this massive force was divided into smaller units of men who trained and fought together. As we engage in spiritual warfare, to our right and to our left, in front and behind—and even above—are other members of God's army. If we're to fulfill our various roles, it's crucial we know and appreciate those who serve with us.

Thousands of years ago, Jesus—the Captain of the Lord's army—gave Joshua directions before the Israelites' great victory at Jericho. Today He commands His forces in the continuing battle between good and evil. It's easy to spot a major difference between Christ's involvement then and now. Joshua didn't take instruction from a spirit. Jesus was there in the flesh, and the Hebrew general immediately deferred to One greater than himself. Likewise, as the prophecy outlined in the book of Revelation runs its course, Christ will be physically present to crush Satan and his followers.

The Role of the Holy Spirit

In our daily spiritual combat, we can't expect to see our Commander out in front of His troops. Scripture contains no evidence Jesus will return to Earth prior to the events recorded in the book of Revelation. How does He lead us today? How can we tap into His direction and strength? As Jesus told His disciples prior to His crucifixion, the Holy Spirit—the third Person of the Trinity—is a powerful member of our unit.

Football teams have a thick book that contains diagrams of individual assignments for hundreds of plays. In the old days, the quarterback would select a play and tell his teammates. All 11 men then executed their tasks to the best of their abilities. Somewhere along the line, a head coach decided he needed more influence in the decision, so he developed an elaborate system of hand signals to instruct the quarterback which play to run. As technology developed, one bright coach realized he could insert a miniature radio receiver into the helmet of his quarterback and, over a secret frequency, transmit a play to his leader on the field.

Wouldn't it be great if we could insert a receiver into our spiritual helmets so we could pick up instruction and encouragement from God? Well, long before a pig's hide was fashioned into an oblong ball for the first time, the Lord had devised this capability. It has absolutely nothing to do with transmitters or receivers, electromagnetic waves or micro-miniaturization.

The Father simply chose to insert His Holy Spirit into the hearts of all who receive Christ as Savior.[2] The Spirit within us enables us to tap into God's direction, and He also gives us the strength we need to carry out what He instructs us to do. And because God's "transmitter" is operational 24 hours a day, we never go into battle without His wisdom and power—unless we short-circuit the system by ignoring the Spirit's leading.

The Holy Spirit is the least-understood Member of the Trinity. Although this term doesn't appear in scripture, several passages link God the Father, God the Son, and God the Holy Spirit. After His resurrection, Jesus instructed His disciples to help people far and wide to become His followers, "'baptizing them in the name of the Father and the Son and the Holy Spirit.'"[3] Apostle Paul mentioned the Three in the closing of his second letter to the church at Corinth.[4]

Among the evidence for the Spirit's being included in the Trinity was an event in the early church. The husband-wife team of Ananias and Sapphira sold some land and donated a portion of the proceeds to the work of Jesus' apostles. In a blatant lie, they passed off their gift as representing the entire profit they'd received. Peter, though, wasn't fooled. He initially condemned Ananias for lying to the Holy Spirit. The apostle then rebuked the greedy man with these words: "'You have not lied to men, but to God.'"[5] As Jesus is fully God, so is the Holy Spirit.

God's word illustrates the divine nature the Spirit shares with Father and Son. The second verse of the Bible reveals the Holy Spirit participated in the creation of Earth.[6] His existence preceded this amazing cosmic event. Like Father and Son, the Spirit is eternal.[7] The sovereignty of God also is evident in His Spirit. The Father allows the Spirit to select and then distribute spiritual gifts—special abilities to carry out our God-given duties—to all who've put their faith in Christ.[8]

The Spirit possesses the same almighty power as the Father. We see this displayed not only in the world's creation, but also as the Spirit came upon Mary to conceive God's Son.[9] The Spirit also is all knowing. Only He is aware of the thoughts of God.[10] Finally, God's Spirit exists at the same time at every location in the heavens and on the Earth.[11]

Soldiers in God's army can take confidence knowing this divine member of our unit constantly stands alongside us in battle. He provides the supernatural strength and wisdom we need to defeat every attack of our evil adversary. Unlike our human compatriots—who occasionally are sidelined through injury, battle fatigue, or simply distraction—the Spirit is always with us. It's impossible for Satan to separate us from this powerful Ally.

Prior to His crucifixion, Christ promised His disciples He'd ask the Father to send the Spirit to aid them throughout their earthly lives. Jesus said the Spirit wouldn't simply come upon them from time to time as He did during Old Testament days when God set out special duties for His people, but the Spirit actually would live within believers. Christ also explained the Spirit would:

- Teach His followers about spiritual things and would help them remember what Jesus had taught.[12]
- Bear witness to Christ—Who He is and what He's done on behalf of mankind.[13]
- Guide His followers in the truth, disclosing to us what the Father and Son desire for us to know.[14]
- Convict the world concerning sin, righteousness, and judgment. In other words, the Spirit would make it clear that we'd fallen far short of what God wants us to be, that God's standard is perfection, that the Lord would judge all, and that only those who put their trust in Christ would receive eternal life.[15]

This is very good news for us on the frontlines of spiritual combat day in and day out. Why? Because if the Spirit convicts people, we don't have to labor under the pressure that this is our responsibility. Our task, in the words of Dr. Bill Bright, founder of Campus Crusade for Christ, is to share the gospel in the power of the Holy Spirit and to leave the results to God. Of course, although this duty may be stated very simply, accomplishing it isn't easy. We can take heart, though, in knowing that as we work to accomplish our orders, both Jesus and the Holy Spirit are members of our unit. With them leading the way, we can be victorious.

Angels Serve Alongside Us

In addition to God the Son and God the Holy Spirit, legions of angels join us to battle Satan and his evil forces. Far from the cute, chubby little characters depicted on greeting cards or in cartoons, angels make up the supernatural fighting force Jesus commands. We're not talking about a platoon here. Myriads—a huge number—of angels worship the Lord in the heavenly realms and patrol the Earth, at God's command engaging in battle with the troops of Satan.[16]

These fierce spiritual warriors first appear in their military role when God passes judgment on Sodom. The wickedness of its residents prompted the Lord to dispatch two angels to destroy everyone in town except Lot, his wife, and his daughters.[17] God sent an angel on a similar mission in the days of King David. Burning with anger against Israel, the Lord instructed an angel to strike the people, and 70,000 men were killed.[18]

God sometimes sends out His angelic forces in large numbers. When the king of Aram ordered a great army equipped with horses and chariots to capture Elisha, the prophet was not alarmed. And why would he worry? As Elisha gazed upon the nearby mountain, an even more powerful force composed of horses and chariots of fire stood ready to protect him.

The Lord used this component of His heavenly army to save the prophet from certain death and to put an end to the raids Aramean troops had been making into Israel.[19]

We learn in God's word that angels are spiritual beings who do not die, and they delight in praising God.[20] They're powerful and obedient as they carry out God's orders.[21] While these duties may require them to wreak havoc among large groups of those who oppose the Lord, angels also minister to individual followers—and future followers—of Christ.[22]

Angels guide us as we complete our mission as an angel directed Abraham's servant on his quest for a wife for Isaac.[23] An angel guided Philip to travel along the road from Jerusalem to Gaza so he'd meet and share the gospel with an official of the queen of Ethiopia.[24] These heavenly messengers also have guided people to seek out Christians, as an angel led Cornelius, a Roman centurion, to send for Peter so the officer, his family, and his servants could hear the good news about Jesus. (See Acts 10.)

Additionally, angels provide for our needs as an angel supplied food and drink for the prophet Elijah as he fled from evil Queen Jezebel when she threatened to kill him.[25] Angels ministered to Christ after His 40-day fast in the wilderness and Satan's three temptations.[26] They also protect and deliver us in times of trouble as an angel prevented lions from mauling Daniel[27] and another rescued Peter from prison.[28] God's messengers comfort us as they strengthened Jesus as He was praying in the Garden of Gethsemane[29] and encouraged Paul just prior to a shipwreck.[30]

As we battle the forces of evil, the angelic contingent of God's army is just a prayer away. Peter learned this lesson as he awaited God's deliverance from prison. The Lord dispatched an angel to carry out a rescue mission that took the apostle past a pair of guards, through the prison's iron gate—which opened by itself—into the city streets, and to the home of his fellow believers, who were deep in prayer for Peter's release.[31] The freed apostle may well have called on the words of King David to praise God: "The angel of the LORD encamps around those who fear Him, and rescues them."[32]

Encouragement from Heaven

The writer to the Hebrews mentions another component of our unit: a great cloud of witnesses that surrounds us. This phrase follows immediately after the author lists the names of faithful Christians from the past. Their commitment to Christ should strengthen our resolve as we "run with endurance the race that is set before us."[33] Their encouragement—through their sacrifice and service as well as their cheering us on from heaven—should help us to overcome the attacks and distractions that would prevent us from accomplishing our orders.

The greatest cloud of people I've been a part of was a group of 100,000 who packed Wembley Stadium in London in May 1986 to watch the English Football Association Cup Final. So many people wanted to see this match that thousands of forged tickets had been produced and sold, and several young men who'd purchased neither real nor counterfeit tickets tried to enter the grounds by climbing up ropes or bed sheets that had been tied together and lowered by friends who had legally entered the venerable stadium.

The competitors that day were players from two teams from the same city. Liverpool supporters were dressed in red and were waving red and yellow scarves; Everton fans sported blue and white attire for the most important match of the year. A festive atmosphere invaded the stadium as spectators sang rousing fight songs and taunted those cheering for their adversaries. Because a significant percentage of those at the match were from Liverpool or nearby, opposing factions occasionally joined forces in singing sarcastic choruses aimed at Manchester United, a despised rival that didn't make it to the final.

Throughout the match, none of the spectators sat bored. Liverpool fans loudly urged Ian Rush to put the ball into the net; Everton supporters were equally vocal in calling on Gary Lineker to score. The fans may have issued more prayers that Saturday afternoon than did the congregations in all the churches in Liverpool the following day! Everyone at the game was engaged; all played a role in the result (a 3-1 win for Liverpool) as they cheered for their favorite team.

Similarly, many of God's faithful who've preceded us are cheering us on. From what we read in Hebrews 11, Abel, Enoch, and Noah are in the crowd. Abraham and Sarah are there, too. Jacob, Joseph, Moses, and Rahab are looking on with great interest. Gideon, Barak, Samson, Jepthah, David, Samuel, and the prophets are urging us to victory. Also on hand are all the other martyrs on this list of spiritual warriors.

Many more make up this throng in heaven. Early church leaders Tertullian, Augustine, Bede, Anselm, Becket, Francis of Assisi, and Thomas Aquinas are shouting their encouragement. Martin Luther and John Calvin are focused on how we're doing. Jonathan Edwards, John and Charles Wesley, George Whitefield, and William Carey are supporting our efforts. Charles Finney, George Muller, C. H. Spurgeon, D. L. Moody, Dietrich Bonhoeffer, and C. S. Lewis are excited to see us succeed. And sitting right there next to them are my Sunday school teacher when I was eight years old, the cadet who led me to the Lord in 1968, and the Christlike pastor of the little church we attended in England in the mid-1980s.

Famous and unknown. Martyrs and those who died naturally after long lives of sacrifice. Powerful leaders and those who shunned the limelight. Great writers and those unable to read. Well-known orators and those whose contributions came more through actions than words. Men and women from every continent, every ethnic background, and every age throughout history.

All are worshiping the Savior they loved and served. They're also closely watching every move we make, every word we speak in our efforts to glorify the King of kings and Lord of lords during our short service in God's army on Earth. We'll meet them one day in heaven, but until then, we can be strengthened by their constant encouragement. In fact, if you sit silently for several minutes when you next pray, I'll bet you'll hear them cheering!

Service with Current Warriors

In addition to the divine and departed members of our unit, we also serve with all the living soldiers who've placed their faith in Christ and are engaged with us in spiritual warfare.

At the end of our first year at the Academy, my classmates and I endured what probably was the most demanding training in the four-year program: Survival, Escape, Resistance, and Evasion. The initial phase involved three days in a simulated prisoner-of-war camp tucked away in the foothills of the Rocky Mountains. It was the summer of 1969, and thousands of young American military men were fighting and many were dying in the jungles of Vietnam. SERE was designed to prepare us for the challenges we might face in hostile territory during combat.

Following classroom training, we boarded trucks for the trip to the camp. After what seemed like an hour's drive, upper-class cadets acting as enemy soldiers ambushed the convoy. They quickly rounded up the startled group of younger cadets, and in very humiliating fashion, assigned each of us a prisoner number. Although I went through the training nearly five decades ago, I still remember my number: 343!

To confuse us, our captors placed cloth bags over our heads for the remainder of the journey to the prison compound. The next several days were filled with interrogations and physical activity that left us exhausted. At least once or twice, we had to endure solitary confinement in tiny, wooden boxes. We were fed a bit of rice occasionally and were allowed to sleep only a few hours each day.

At the conclusion of this phase—hungry, thirsty, and worn out physically and mentally—we were deposited deeper into the mountains with two partners. Our task was to evade capture by the enemy for three days. We were to hide during the day and move to various checkpoints by night, living off a bit of food we'd been provided and anything else we could scavenge in the woods.

Our trek began at about 10 p.m. Within 15 minutes walking through the dense forest under an overcast sky, I was separated from my partners! To make matters worse, the air became misty, and the mist turned to rain. I found a small cave, spread out my sleeping bag, and laid down. As I pondered alternative courses of action, any temptation to doze off vanished as I realized my field jacket and sleeping bag had been drenched by rainwater dripping from the roof of the cave.

I've never felt so alone as I did that night. With little food, only a canteen of fresh water, and a uniform and sleeping bag saturated with rain, making it to the first checkpoint seemed impossible. If only I'd not lost my teammates, I'd have been much more hopeful. If I'd been able to plot out strategy with a couple of others facing the same challenge, I'd have had a much more positive view of what I could accomplish. When the rain eventually turned to snow (in June!), I almost gave up. Fortunately, I found a couple of classmates who'd lost the third member of their team, and we completed the trek together.

We sometimes live our spiritual lives in isolation. We convince ourselves we can follow Christ without the help of others. We believe Satan's lie that we're smart enough and strong enough to get by on our own. And then we're surprised when we make little progress in carrying out our Commander's orders.

In God's word, we see many warnings about forsaking the help of others in our unit. We're told, "Two are better than one because they have a good return for their labor. For if either of them falls, the one will lift up his companion. But woe to the one who falls when there is not another to lift him up. ... And if one can overpower him who is alone, two can resist him."[34]

Jesus must have had these words in mind when He rounded up 70 of His followers and sent them out two by two to minister. After issuing a warning about the hostility they'd face and instructions on the logistics of their travels, Christ gave them their orders. They were to heal the sick and proclaim the kingdom of God.[35]

What a comfort it must have been to have another person to talk with on their journeys. You can imagine their initial anxiety as the groups fanned out through the countryside. "Can we really heal people?" "Will we be able to come up with the right words to glorify the Father?" "Have we picked up enough from watching Jesus to do these miracles ourselves?" "How much faith do we need to accomplish all He's given us to do?" "Where will we stay?" "What if we don't find food and lodging?" "Can the two of us resist an angry crowd?"

These and many other questions must have raced through the minds of each member of the nearly three-dozen pairs as they traversed the dusty, lonely roads of Israel. But because they had someone else to talk with, these anxious thoughts became the focus of a dialog that, eventually, dispelled their fears and filled them with strength.

As the 70 disciples trusted God for the help they'd need, He blessed them incredibly. Their faith increased by leaps and bounds, and they couldn't wait for their next opportunity to heal or to preach. You can picture them eating dinner after a full day's ministry rejoicing as they considered all the Lord had done for them the past several hours.

"Did you see the joy on that crippled man's face when he took his first few steps?" "Can you imagine what it must have been like for that little woman to hear again after being deaf for more than a decade?" "How could I have felt such peace as I spoke about God's love in front of so large a crowd?" I'll bet it wasn't easy getting to sleep as they reviewed the miracles they'd been a part of that day. And as they talked with one another well into the night, they most certainly gained new strength and determination for the following day's activities.

Imagine, too, the excitement the partners shared as they approached Christ at the end of their travels. Giddy with joy, almost in unison they reported the demons had been subject to them in Jesus' name. These men who'd become so close as they served God together must have warmly embraced one another as Jesus reminded them He'd given them authority over the power of the enemy and had been watching Satan fall from heaven like lightning.[36]

Though it's not recorded in scripture, it's unlikely these men hugged each other at the end of Jesus' congratulations, returned to their homes, and never again saw each other. Odds are the same pairs ministered together on other occasions, eagerly searching for folks who needed physical and spiritual healing. In the same way, we're to be strengthened and encouraged by being plugged in with other followers of Jesus. As we worship, as we study God's word, as we pray together, and as we hold one another accountable, the Father will build us up for service. Then He'll look across our unit and select teams to send into action ministering to others in His name.

Teamwork Is Crucial
Another part of our training at the Academy provides an excellent parallel on how the body of Christ is to pull together. Hidden away on the vast campus is the Leadership Reaction Course: a series of exercises in which cadets are given what seem to be a few inadequate tools to accomplish nearly impossible tasks.

For example, one station involves getting an injured aircrew member across a river in enemy territory after a helicopter has been shot down. A seven-person team is given a stretcher and five planks of wood between four and six feet long. A pool of water represents a river, and in it are three wooden pilings that simulate all that remains of a bombed bridge. Portions of each of the pilings and the river are contaminated. Team members have 15 minutes to get the injured crewman—a 145-pound mannequin—and their boards across the water. One of the cadets is selected to lead the expedition.

The seven eager cadets tackle their initial obstacle thinking the upper-class evaluator is interested in whether or not the group is successful. This, as team members learn during a debrief following their first effort, is only a secondary concern of the cadet reviewing their performance. The primary measure of success is how well the group works together.

Actions of different groups vary dramatically. Some leaders want to earn high marks for their tactics, so they outline what they want the others to do without asking for input. Other leaders are so indecisive that the horn signaling the end of the obstacle blares only a few minutes after team members begin to carry out their strategy. Leaders occasionally assign followers the wrong roles in what would be excellent plans. Have you ever seen a 140-pound weakling try to maneuver a 55-gallon drum on his own as a 220-pound football recruit stands nearby holding a length of rope? Not the best use of team members!

It usually takes a group of cadets only a failure or two to develop a pattern for tackling the remainder of the obstacles. When given the scenario, the leader calmly reads it to the group, pointing out the tools the team has received. The leader then presides over a quick discussion in which each team member is allowed to present suggestions, and the group agrees on a plan.

The leader checks physical attributes and assigns each member a task. All this takes only a few minutes, and the remainder of the time is allotted to accomplishing the plan. Of course, not every group comes up with solutions for all the obstacles, but the probability of success increases significantly when members consider their strengths and limitations and work together as a team, each performing with excellence the assigned role.

My adventures on the Leadership Reaction Course remind me of Paul's comparison of the human body and the body of Christ.

> For even as the body is one and yet has many members, and all the members of the body, though they are many, are one body, so also is Christ. ... For the body is not one member, but many. If the foot says, "Because I am not a hand, I am not a part of the body," it is not for this reason any the less a part of the body. And if the ear says, "Because I am not an eye, I am not a part of the body," it is not for this reason any the less a part of the body.
>
> If the whole body were an eye, where would the hearing be? If the whole were hearing, where would the sense of smell be? But now God has placed the members, each one of them, in the body, just as He desired. If they were all one member, where would the body be? But now there are many members, but one body.
>
> Now you are Christ's body, and individually members of it. And God has appointed in the church, first apostles, second prophets, third teachers, then miracles, then gifts of healings, helps, administrations, various kinds of tongues. All are not apostles, are they? All are not prophets, are they? All are not teachers, are they? All are not workers of miracles, are they? All do not have gifts of healings, do they? All do not speak with tongues, do they? All do not interpret, do they? But earnestly desire the greater gifts.[37]

When I was assigned to an Air Force fighter wing in England in the mid-1980s, I saw this teamwork reflected day in and day out. For a mission to be successful, a host of airmen with various skills had to combine their efforts with great precision. A group of mechanics tuned jet engines in a huge maintenance hangar at the same time a cadre of computer specialists in another building upgraded software for the "black boxes" they'd later reinsert into the aircraft. As intelligence officers briefed aircrews on the threats they'd face on the way to and over their targets, munitions experts transported huge bombs from ammunition bunkers and loaded them onto the jets, and fuel-loaders pumped gallons of JP-4 into the aircraft.

When all was ready, the pilot and weapons system officer climbed on board. Air traffic controllers in the tower issued take-off instructions, and the pilot responded to the directions he received. As the pilot flew the jet to its destination, the WSO ensured it remained on course. When the crew arrived over its target, the WSO launched the ordnance, and the pilot reversed direction and headed for home. If anyone in this chain failed to perform with excellence, the mission might well have been aborted; the target would have survived.

As many people perform with precision to ensure a successful military mission, we must pull together as a unit to accomplish our spiritual mission. And as we carry out our orders, each of us has a role to play. Gifts and abilities vary among the followers of Christ, but what is consistent is God's desire that we work as a team. If any of us fails to perform with excellence, our unit will be less effective in making an impact for Christ. If we work well with one another—following the direction of our Commander, tapping into the power and wisdom available through the Holy Spirit, and being encouraged by the saints who have preceded us—God will give us the victory!

Lessons Learned

- As warriors in God's army, we serve alongside a host of supernatural and human compatriots in our battle against Satan and his evil forces.
- God's Holy Spirit reveals to us the Father's perspective and gives us the strength to carry out our spiritual orders.
- Myriads of angels stand ready to provide for our needs, deliver us in times of trouble, direct our spiritual activities, comfort us, and protect us.

- The vast cloud of Christian warriors who preceded us provides great encouragement, cheering us on as they witness our efforts from their vantage point in heaven.
- The soldiers serving in God's army today build up one another prior to combat and protect one another during our spiritual battles.
- We can find confidence in the assurance that with Christ as our Commander and a strong cadre of others serving in our unit, we can defeat our wicked adversary.

Unit Analysis

To download Unit Analysis and Personal Battle Plan material, please go to www.forwardintobattle.com.

We carry out our duties as soldiers in God's army confident that we haven't been assigned to a remote outpost where we serve Him on our own. The Holy Spirit within us, the angels who surround us, and the great cloud of believers who now reside in heaven make up the supernatural component of our unit. At the same time, we labor among fellow followers of Jesus who've been called, equipped, and sent out by the Lord. We're truly members of the greatest fighting force that has ever been assembled, and this fact should give us great strength and courage as we take on Satan and his evil troops.

1. What's been the most effective group in which you've served? What were its aims, and how effectively did the group achieve its goals? How did the relationships between members of the team ensure success?
2. What do we learn about the Holy Spirit from these verses?
    a. Genesis 1:2
    b. Psalm 139:7-13
    c. I Corinthians 2:10-11
    d. Hebrews 9:14

3. According to John 14:16-17, where does the Holy Spirit abide with respect to those who've received Christ as Savior? How do the following verses tell us the Spirit will come to our aid as we engage in spiritual warfare?
   a. Acts 1:8
   b. I Corinthians 2:16
   c. John 14:26
   d. John 16:8-15
   e. Matthew 10:16-20
   f. Romans 8:26
4. Read the story of Elisha's confrontation with the Aramean army in II Kings 6:8-23. How does the activity of God's heavenly forces in coming to Elisha's defense give you confidence for your daily battles against Satan and his evil troops?
5. How does the involvement of angels in the lives of early Christians provide encouragement that these powerful, spiritual beings continue to help modern-day saints in the age-old struggle against evil? According to the following passages, what help can we expect angels to provide us?
   a. Acts 8:26-39
   b. Acts 12:7-10
   c. Acts 27:22-26
6. As you read Hebrews 12:1-3, recall some of the saints who've gone before you. Some may have been giants in the history of Christianity; others may be relatively insignificant folks who had a tremendous influence on your life. Discuss those now in heaven who helped you to grow in your faith. How has their impact in your life continued even after their deaths?
7. Apostle Paul's description of the body of Christ in I Corinthians 12:12-14 and 25-27 reinforces the need for teamwork as we carry out the orders the Lord has given us. It also provides encouragement

that as we concentrate on our individual roles, the Lord will work through us to help us accomplish our mission. Think back to occasions when you tried to serve Christ on your own. What were the results? Now consider how others have ministered to you and with you. Share the differences between your isolated and your team experiences.

Prayer Points

- Praise God that His powerful Holy Spirit dwells within the hearts of all who put their trust in Christ as Savior and that His angels stand ready to come to our aid in battle
- Thank God for those wonderful saints who've served and preserved the church through the centuries, those now in heaven who had a significant impact in your life, and those with whom you're privileged to labor today
- Ask God to help you to follow faithfully Jesus' leadership, always conscious of all He's doing in and through you and the company of saints you serve with
- Commit to enter courageously the spiritual conflict that will continue until Christ returns, totally devoted to excellence in accomplishing your duties as part of a team and never lagging behind as others put their lives on the line for our Lord

Personal Battle Plan

1. **Evaluate the role of the Holy Spirit in your life and ministry.** If you don't know much about Him and how He can help, make an appointment with a Christian you respect, and ask how to tap into the Spirit's assistance. Prayerfully jot down a couple of actions through which the Spirit can take on greater prominence in your life, and then commit these changes to the Lord.

2. Do you consider angels as mythical beings created by people with an overly developed imagination, or are they truly emissaries God sends to aid us in our labor on His behalf? **Describe your honest feelings about angels**. If you have trouble believing the reality and role of angels, commit to learning more about their existence and purpose by studying God's word, reading other Christian literature, and discussing the topic with followers of Christ you respect.
3. Perhaps some wonderful saints who helped you draw closer to God are now watching your progress from heaven. Alternatively, you may have been touched by the stories of biblical or historical men and women who've served the Lord faithfully. **List the names of two or three people whose spiritual lives have been an inspiration to you,** briefly jot down their impact, and thank the Lord specifically for all they mean to you. Pray, too, that your life might be an inspiration to others with whom God brings you into contact.
4. In your current ministry for the Lord, **list those with whom you are working most closely**. For each, describe the greatest benefit you've derived from your partnership. Plan to personally thank these folks for all they've done for you. Consider what you've done and will do to help your co-laborers to grow in Christ, and ask for God's help in taking these actions.
5. **Assess how well you work alongside other followers of Christ**.

Strongly Disagree	Somewhat Disagree	Neither Agree nor Disagree	Somewhat Agree	Strongly Agree

a. I consider myself to be a team player in ministry with other Christians.

	Strongly Disagree	Somewhat Disagree	Neither Agree nor Disagree	Somewhat Agree	Strongly Agree

b. I prefer to work quietly in the background by myself rather than to labor on the frontlines with others.

c. I often find myself in strained relationships with other members of God's army.

d. I like nothing better than to encourage other Christians and to see them rewarded, even if my actions go unnoticed.

Make a note of improvements you'll work on as a result of your responses above.

6. The following list contains duties performed by the human members of God's army. For as many as you can, **write the name of someone in your Christian community who carries out these tasks**. Don't

forget to include your name. If you have trouble determining where you fit, ask a Christian mentor for his or her thoughts. When you've listed as many people as possible, pray God will continue to bless you and the others as you carry out your duties for His glory.
   a. Communicating a special message from God
   b. Having insight in how to apply God's word
   c. Knowing the Bible
   d. Teaching others about God's ways
   e. Sharing the gospel with others
   f. Having extraordinary confidence in God
   g. Leading others
   h. Encouraging others
   i. Praying for others
   j. Healing others
   k. Performing miracles
   l. Caring for God's people as a pastor
   m. Helping those in need
   n. Being compassionate
   o. Being hospitable
   p. Giving generously
   q. Analyzing & planning
   r. Serving God in another culture
7. **Prepare for the next session** by listing what you believe is God's primary mission for your days on Earth.

Anticipating Combat: Preparation for Conflict

AFTER WE GAIN an appreciation for our unit, Christ commissions us to take up our important responsibilities in God's army. In preparing us for the battle, Jesus gives us a glimpse of His expectations. "'I chose you, and appointed you, that you should go and bear fruit,'" He explains.[1] Like Christ's disciples, we have a challenging role to play in the spiritual conflict that has raged since Satan attacked Adam and Eve in the Garden of Eden.

Before we enter combat, *we must understand our mission*. Since the days Christ walked the planet, many valiant Christian warriors have been confused about our primary objective. Our mission is to become like Jesus. God calls us to be conformed to the image of His Son.[2] If we become who the Lord wants us to be, we'll do what He wants us to do. The actions will follow as our character is transformed to mirror that of Christ.

Jesus set out this mission for us when He washed His disciples' feet as the group observed Passover. After He completed this humble act, He encouraged his followers to follow His lead. "'If I then ... washed your feet, you also ought to wash one another's feet. For I gave you an example that you also should do as I did to you.'"[3] Jesus' example, of course, wasn't just washing feet. He spent three years demonstrating ways in which His disciples could become more like Him. Christ reinforced this call to action when He commanded the 12 to love each other just as He'd loved them.[4]

Not only did Jesus instruct His disciples to become like Him, He also suggested how this could occur. We become more like Christ as we spend time with God. In fact, Jesus said eternal life was all about getting to know Him and His Father.[5] Time and again in His final meeting with those who would establish His church, Jesus stressed the importance of intimacy with the Lord. Christ discloses Himself to us, abides in us, and answers our prayers.[6] He also calls on us to abide in Him.[7] When we conform to the image of God's Son, our actions will bear much fruit,[8] we'll do even greater works than Jesus did,[9] and we'll experience a joy that comes from Christ Himself.[10]

As we set out on our mission, we must be aware of the challenges we'll meet along the way. Intelligence gathering starts early and continues throughout our lives. Even before we learn to speak, we possess an inquisitive nature that prompts daily reconnaissance through our surroundings. As individual words become phrases and phrases stretch into sentences, we pose a flurry of questions to Mom and Dad. "What's that?" "Where's it live?" "What's it eat?" "Why's it green?" Our curiosity is never satisfied.

We carry this same desire for information into our school days. "How'd they cross the ocean in that boat?" "What happens if I mix these two chemicals?" "Who came up with that idea?" "Why do we have to learn this?" "Who's that girl?" "Is she going out with anyone?" "Can you get her phone number for me?"

Competitive athletes know the importance of gathering intelligence. Their coaches tell them the strengths of opposing offensive and defensive units, whether or not the pitcher usually starts a hitter with a fastball or a curve, or where the best scorer typically shoots. Awareness of their foes' abilities and patterns is crucial in defeating them.

Competition is not limited to sports. As university graduates step into business, they quickly learn about the operations of companies that compete with them for profit, market share, customer loyalty, and all the other indicators of corporate success. In fact, intelligence gathering in the business world occasionally involves undercover efforts to determine how a competitor creates its products with an eye to copying materials, procedures, or plans.

In the armed forces, intelligence takes on significance well beyond its importance in other walks of life. Knowing what to expect from a potential aggressor can mean the difference between life and death. Military leaders must design strategies to counteract the enemy's strengths and exploit its weaknesses. An accurate analysis of the firepower and tactics a foe will employ is vital to victory.

Spiritual warriors must understand how our adversary will seek to defeat us. Satan has been on the offensive for a long time and has built up a strong arsenal he can use against God's army.

Christ illustrates Satan's power in the titles He gives him. He calls him the ruler of the world and the evil one.[11] These descriptions make it clear that the devil is not simply a mysterious force floating around the planet. He's a personal being who has recruited followers of his own. The Lord has allowed him to rule the Earth—which God created, sustains, and owns—at least for a while. Satan has great power, which he uses to carry out evil deeds among those who follow his command and those who don't.

Satan "entered into" Judas, exerting his power in convincing the disciple to betray Christ. The devil had control over Judas when he helped the chief priests and Pharisees to arrest, try, and eliminate Jesus.[12] It's sobering to realize Satan had this powerful influence over someone who'd walked with Christ for several years.

Jesus warned His band of the seeds of hatred Satan had sown, directed at Father, Son, and all who enter God's army.[13] The natural consequence of this intense hatred is that the evil one would direct his forces to persecute the followers of Christ, just as they persecuted Jesus.[14] When Christ prayed for His disciples—present and future—He acknowledged again that Satan would lead his troops to hate all those who put their trust in Him as Savior,[15] and He also identified the devil's ability to deceive men and women so they cannot know God.[16]

Satan employs an assortment of evil schemes to maintain the allegiance of his human troops and is often successful in misdirecting worship toward him. Jesus, however, gives hope to His followers as He assures us that despite the tribulation we'll endure in this life, He'll provide eventual and eternal victory.[17] We can take courage in this and in knowing the Father is answering His Son's prayer that He'd protect us from our evil foe.[18]

CHAPTER 5

Understanding the Mission

A Christian should be a striking likeness of Jesus Christ. If we were what we profess to be and what we should be, we would be pictures of Christ. We are to imitate Him so closely that the world will have no doubt we have been with Jesus.

Charles Haddon Spurgeon[1]

IN THE VERY early hours of June 7, 1972, around two dozen cadets in their early 20s gathered in the social center at the Air Force Academy. Twenty-two sets of bleary-eyed parents, siblings, grandparents, aunts, uncles, fiancés, and girlfriends joined these young men. The occasion? The commissioning ceremony for Cadet Squadron 13, which took place 10 hours prior to graduation.

After speeches that were much too long by officials I have long since forgotten, it was time for each cadet to be sworn into the active-duty Air Force. This was done in alphabetical order, so my moment of glory was at the tail end of the event. This did not dampen my pride as I finally stepped forward with retired U.S. Air Force Reserve Colonel A. R. Tyrrell—Uncle Ray—to recite my oath of office.

As he slowly read the phrases of the statement that was to govern my service for the next 28 years, seven months, and 24 days, I repeated them to the obvious delight of my mother, father, uncle, and cousin. In much the same words I'd spoken four years earlier, I pledged to defend the United States against all enemies. I announced I was taking the oath without reservation, and I promised to faithfully discharge my duties as a second lieutenant. With these words, I concluded four years as a cadet and began a career as a commissioned officer.

Fast forward to the summer of 2002. British missionaries who had lived in the United States for about eight years—a retired lieutenant colonel in the British Army and his wife—invited me to share a milestone in their lives. In a large crowd at the Federal Court House in Norfolk, Virginia, I witnessed them and several dozen others being sworn in as U.S. citizens. As a U.S. District Court judge administered the oath of allegiance, the group of new citizens repeated with differing proficiency in English:

> I hereby declare, on oath, that I absolutely and entirely renounce and abjure all allegiance and fidelity to any foreign prince, potentate, state, or sovereignty of whom or which I have heretofore been a subject or citizen; that I will support and defend the constitution and the laws of the United States of America against all enemies, foreign and domestic; that I bear true faith and allegiance to the same; that I will bear arms on behalf of the United States when required by law; that I will perform noncombatant service in the armed forces of the United States when required by law; and that I take this obligation freely without any mental reservation or purpose of evasion. So help me God.

The judge then pronounced these former residents of nations on several continents citizens of the United States of America.

The two oaths bear strong similarities to one another. Each includes a statement of allegiance to the U.S. constitution and a pledge to defend the United States. Both declare nothing has clouded the judgment of those making these promises and acknowledge the importance of God's help in carrying out the duties that might be required of them. Finally, both launch those making these pledges on a new phase of life. The major difference in these oaths is striking. To become a U.S. citizen, one must reject allegiance to any former ruler while agreeing to be bound by the leadership of a new sovereign.

God Commissions His Warriors
When we receive Jesus as Savior and are trained in the basics involved in following Him, He commissions us to serve in God's army. Our commission reminds us that when we changed allegiance by receiving Christ as Savior, our citizenship changed. Apostle Paul wrote to the Ephesians that those who aren't Christians are aliens with respect to God.[2] During His days on Earth, Jesus said much the same thing. While being questioned by Pontius Pilate, the Roman governor of Israel, Christ explained His kingdom was not of this world.[3]

When we choose to follow Christ, we become citizens of heaven and members of God's household.[4] Like new U.S. citizens, Christians reject our former allegiance to Satan—the ruler of the world[5] and the prince of the power of the air[6]—and pledge our service to God—the King eternal.[7]

God's word tells us of many who were commissioned to serve the Lord. Early in the history of mankind, God became frustrated with the evil in the world. He was disgusted with the wickedness of the human heart and sorry He'd created people. The Lord's plan to remedy this situation was to eliminate virtually everyone on the planet. Because Noah had found favor in God's eyes, though, He commissioned him and his immediate family to carry on the human race following His destruction of everyone else.[8]

Similarly, God commissioned Abram, who later became known as Abraham, to be the father of a great nation. The loyal servant obeyed without hesitation. (See Genesis 12.) The Lord also commissioned Moses, but He had to resort to fireworks to get the attention of the future leader of the Israelites. Moses received his call to duty as God spoke to him from a burning bush. (See Exodus 3.) When his life ended, Moses passed the mantle of leadership to his top general. God commissioned Joshua and filled him with a spirit of wisdom.[9]

Many years later, God used another fantastic event to commission Isaiah. The prophet was allowed a glimpse into heaven prior to learning what God required of him. It must have been quite a scene: "… the Lord sitting on a throne, lofty and exalted, with the train of His robe filling the temple. Seraphim [angelic beings, literally "fiery, burning ones"] stood above Him, each having six wings; with two he covered his face, and with two he covered his feet, and with two he flew. … And the foundations of the thresholds trembled at the voice of him who called out, while the temple was filling with smoke."[10]

Jesus recruited His first few disciples during a walk along the Sea of Galilee. He initially chatted with Simon and Andrew, who were fishermen. Strolling a bit farther, He came across another set of brothers—James and John—who were mending their fishing nets. Christ invited the four to follow Him.[11] He met Philip as He walked through Galilee, offering him the same opportunity: the chance to serve with Him in His earthly ministry.[12] Jesus would later commission these five and His other disciples to make disciples far and wide.

In addition to those Christ called to service, many people came seeking His help. He deemed some of them worthy to minister in His name. One was a rich ruler who asked how to receive eternal life. When Jesus told the inquisitive young man of the importance of keeping God's commandments, the brash fellow suggested he'd always obeyed them. Christ then instructed the man to sell his possessions, give to the poor, and become His follower, but he turned down the Lord's commission. He was more interested in preserving his wealth than in following Jesus.[13]

Perhaps the most dramatic commissioning into God's army was that of Saul. As he persecuted everyone he could find who'd placed their trust in Christ, Saul wanted a dramatically different commission. Filled with hatred, "breathing threats and murder against the disciples of the Lord," Saul asked the high priest for permission to arrest followers of Christ in Damascus. His request granted, he began his northward journey, only to be stopped by a heavenly roadblock.

A great light knocked Saul to the ground, Jesus addressed him, and his life took a 180-degree turn. God commissioned Saul to bear His name before Gentiles, kings, and the sons of Israel. A few days later, the Lord came to a Christian in Damascus named Ananias in a dream. God commissioned him for a most unlikely task: to go to the aid of Saul, the persecutor of those who'd become followers of Christ.[14]

God has commissioned a vast number of people over the centuries. The writer to the Hebrews catalogues the service of several courageous Christians, all called by God and commissioned to act on His behalf in the evil world around them. (See Hebrews 11.)

Knowing Our Mission
After we've been called to service, trained, and commissioned by God, we're poised for action. However, before we step onto the spiritual battlefield, we need to make absolutely sure we understand the mission the Lord has for us.

Warfare today is vastly different from what it was like decades ago. Gone are the days when massive armies, navies, and air forces slugged it out in wars that lasted many years. Today's armed forces are lean and agile, able to respond quickly and powerfully to the spread of terrorism around the globe. This poses a tremendous challenge for leaders of peace-loving nations of the world. They've determined that if terrorism isn't preempted, tens of thousands of innocent people could be killed by those wishing to advance their evil causes. Within this unsettled environment, imagine the following scenario.

After months of training, the commander of a military unit informs his soldiers they'll be deployed into a "classified" area of operations, but he's not allowed to tell them where. All he can say is that in 24 hours, they'll be airdropped into the battle zone. The commander directs his troops to pack their wartime deployment kits, bid farewell to their loved ones, and report to the airfield in six hours for the flight into hostile territory.

As the troops board the huge cargo aircraft that will transport them halfway around the world, soldiers are noticeably shaken as they think about being thrust into combat. Even the most self-assured have been reduced to anxiety by not knowing where they're headed or what they'll find when they get there. They hope the commander will reveal all the details once the plane is airborne. The monstrous jet lifts off the runway, and minutes turn into hours with no sign of a briefing. Finally, the commander stands up and slowly walks to the front of the aircraft. Over the public address system, he speaks to the brave warriors assembled before him.

"We'll be over the drop zone in 30 minutes. I'm completely confident the months of rigorous training we've undergone have prepared us for this challenge. The forces of evil in this world cannot—must not—be allowed to destroy free societies. We must stop their efforts to kill the innocent, to breed fear in the hearts of those who don't agree with their radical philosophies. When you step out of this aircraft and begin your descent toward the land below, you're representing not just our great nation, but all those countries that have banded together to put an end to terrorism around the world.

"As in all combat, some of you won't return from this battle. Be assured, though, that you won't have died in vain. Our countrymen, as well as those whose land we now seek to protect, will revere you for your sacrifice. I count it the greatest honor of my two decades in uniform to go into this battle with each of you. We will be victorious!"

With that, the commander walks casually back to his seat, exchanging high-fives with some of his troops and slapping others on the back. As the aircraft begins to circle over a city shrouded in darkness, its residents totally unaware of the presence of a fighting force from outside their borders, soldiers in camouflaged gear and carrying sophisticated weapons line up at the jump doors. A few pray; others simply stand in silence. At the appointed time, the jumpmaster instructs an aircrew member to open the door, and one by one, brave warriors step out and plummet toward the ground.

Let's stop here for a reality check. What's wrong with this picture? It shouldn't take you too long to determine that these soldiers are now descending into what will be a hostile environment in an unknown country with absolutely no idea what their mission is. They've had some training in tactics and techniques, but in the absence of direction on what they're to do in the upcoming battle, they can't possibly know what's expected of them and how their success will be measured. They might employ their combat skills extremely well, but if, in their ignorance, they seek to accomplish the wrong goals, they'll fail in the mission they were sent to perform.

Fortunately, no military leaders would send their forces to engage the enemy without ensuring the troops fully understood the mission. Unfortunately, all Christians are engaged in spiritual warfare, but many of us, although we've learned some tactics and techniques, aren't totally sure what our mission is. God doesn't want us to enter battle unprepared, and He's laid out in His word what He wants us to accomplish.

Our primary mission is described in a short phrase tucked away in the eighth chapter of Paul's letter to the Romans. Believers who are struggling find great comfort in the assurance that God causes all things to work together for good to those who love Him and are called according to His purpose.[15] But what is that purpose? As followers of Christ, we're to be ***conformed to the image of God's Son***.[16] That's our mission. You see, this was the Lord's plan even before Adam and Eve arrived on the scene. God the Father, God the Son, and God the Holy Spirit agreed to "'make man in Our image, according to Our likeness.'"[17]

We Can't Do It Alone

While our duties as we seek to accomplish this mission may be different, we're all charged with becoming like Jesus. And if we are what God wants us to be—conformed to the image of Christ—we'll do what He wants us to do. Of course, if we're to become more like Jesus, we must leave the transformation to God, Who'll accomplish this change as His Spirit works in and through us.[18]

When our children were young, their artwork constantly decorated our refrigerator door. In early drawings, Dad, Mom, sister, and brother were stick figures, hair-covered round heads sitting atop single-line bodies, sometimes wearing clothes but often with their stick-like arms and legs totally bare. The difference between what we can be and do in our lives if we insist on shaping ourselves rather than allowing God to mold us into the image of Christ corresponds exactly with our children's drawings compared to what would've been created had we posed for Rembrandt. Left to our own devices, we become at best a very crude approximation of Jesus. If we allow the Holy Spirit to work in and through us, others will see Christ in us.

Apostle Paul warns us that if we rely on our own strength and intelligence, we'll be conformed to something, but it won't be the image of God's Son. He encouraged the Romans not to take on the likeness of the world, but to be transformed into people who reflect God's good and acceptable and perfect will.[19] In other words, we're to be changed so others hear Christ in our words and see Him in our deeds. As we become more like God's Son, the Father will work through us to share His love with those around us.

Of course, to become like someone, we must know about the person we're trying to copy. Those who want to become great military leaders study the lives of Alexander the Great, Napoleon, Patton, and Montgomery. Those who want to become great soccer players review tapes of the skills and tactics of Pelé and Messi. Those who want to become great artists read about what inspired Monét or Renoir and spend hours viewing their masterpieces.

This type of study may help us become like the masters, but it's not as effective as spending time in the presence of those who have been most renowned in their fields. We could follow the lead of those we admire much better if we were somehow able to become their apprentices, studying at their feet, getting to know them personally as we serve them in some small way.

Paul had both types of learning in mind when he wrote to the Romans. To be transformed from the world's model and conformed to the image of Christ, we must experience a renewing of our minds. This involves studying about Jesus as He is revealed in scripture and knowing Him more deeply as He reveals Himself to us in the day-to-day activities of life. And how do we see Him at work around us? Christ explains that if we obey His commandments, we demonstrate our love for Him. In return, He promises the Father and Son will love us, and Jesus will reveal Himself to us.[20] Through diligent study and keen observation, and with the help of the Holy Spirit, we can achieve the mission God lays out for us.

If we're to become more like Jesus, we must live by the priorities He demonstrated and taught. When a Pharisee asked Him the greatest commandment, Christ responded it was to love God with all our heart, soul, and mind. Then He added some bonus advice, quoting from Leviticus 19:18. We're to love our neighbors as we love ourselves.[21]

Priority 1: Love for God

Because Jesus loved His Father, He spent a great deal of time in prayer. Christ prayed alone on a mountain after His miraculous feeding of 5,000 men and countless women and children,[22] and He prayed in a lonely place one morning while it was still dark.[23] Jesus often made a habit of slipping away to the wilderness to pray.[24]

When making important decisions or in times of extreme challenge, Christ's prayers intensified. Jesus spent all night seeking the Father's direction before selecting His 12 disciples,[25] and He prayed so intensely in the Garden of Gethsemane the night of His arrest that His sweat became like drops of blood.[26]

The gospels also reveal Jesus regularly gathered with others to worship the Lord. On a visit to Nazareth, where He'd been brought up, Christ entered the synagogue on the Sabbath—as was His custom—and stood up to read.[27] It was important to Jesus to spend time praising His Father publicly, not just praying to Him privately.

If we want to become more like Jesus, we must develop an intimate relationship with His Father. God desires that we love Him with all our hearts. One way we can establish and maintain a greater intimacy with the Lord is found in the refrain of an old hymn written by C. Austin Miles in 1912. Titled simply "In the Garden," the chorus is:

> And He [Jesus] walks with me, and He talks with me,
> And He tells me I am His own,
> And the joy we share as we tarry there
> None other has ever known.[28]

It Starts with Prayer

Our intimacy with God grows as we walk and talk with Him. Jesus encouraged His followers to ask in His name, and He'd answer their requests so the Father would be glorified.[29] He said those who abide in Him could ask whatever they wished, and it would be done for them to glorify the Father.[30] As what we ask in Jesus' name is granted, we'll be filled with joy.[31] The asking Jesus describes in these verses is spending time with God in prayer.

In our hectic lives, how can we apply Jesus' instruction to pray? First, we have to know what prayer is. We often describe it as talking with God. This is true, but it's also a bit simplistic. In fact, our typical conversations with God are nothing like the chats we have with our human friends and relatives. Take marriage, for example. Can you imagine a husband conversing with his wife like this one morning?

"Oh, my darling wife. Thank you for being all a wife should be! I'm sorry I haven't always been the husband you deserve.

"Today I'd like you to wash the dark clothes, put them out on the line, and when they're dry, take them down and fold them neatly. Please, my dear wife, iron my two white dress shirts and the gray and blue plaid shirt I bought last week. I've noticed the furniture is in dire need of dusting and polishing, so would you please do your best to spruce it up today. After you're done, it would be wonderful if you'd vacuum downstairs.

"I confess I should have planted those new flower bulbs and shrubs over the weekend, but the men playing ahead of us on the golf course must have been beginners. They thrashed around all over the course, and that really slowed us down. At any rate, the weather this afternoon is supposed to be excellent, so please do the planting. While you're at it, the grass along the fence is a bit out of hand, so please clip it. As long as you're doing that, you might as well mow the lawn—another chore I couldn't get to because of those novice golfers Saturday.

"Have I mentioned how much I love you!

"Thanks for the great breakfast and packing my lunch. I'll be home about 7 p.m. and will want to eat right away because at 8, I want to watch the big baseball game on TV. Let's see, roast beef, boiled potatoes, green

Understanding the Mission

beans, and a salad would be excellent. And if possible, would you throw in a nice apple—no, check that, cherry—pie. My mouth is watering already!

"Jonathan told me he's having trouble in math. I'm not so special with the numbers, so would you do a bit of tutoring when he gets home from school. And don't forget Jessica's science fair project. Gee, I remember when I was a kid, we had to do those projects ourselves. It's amazing that today the parents do the projects while the kids are texting their friends. If you need ideas, let me know.

"Well, that's about all I can think of for today. Thanks, honey; you're the greatest!"

"Dear, I ...," his wife replies.

"Sorry, hon. I've enjoyed our conversation, but my carpool is here. I'll talk with you tomorrow morning—same time, same place. Bye!"

How long do you think this marriage would last? Frankly, I'm surprised it lasted long enough for the couple to have school-aged children! Sadly, this is how many Christians approach prayer. It's become largely a one-way session in which we outline for the Creator and Sustainer of the universe what we'd like Him to accomplish for us, carefully inserting an occasional "I love you" or "I'm sorry." A conversation like this is virtually useless—in marriage and in our relationship with God.

Prayer is a two-way exchange between the Lord and us. The husband's words above actually contain four elements we should bring to God's attention. Our prayer should begin with adoration, ***revering God for Who He is and what He's done*** for mankind, disregarding what we want and what He's done for us (we'll get to that later). The Book of Psalms contains some wonderful examples.

Having expressed our praise, we then spend time ***restoring our relationship with God***. We confess we've fallen short of what the Lord desires for us to be and to say and to do. We acknowledge these failures have disappointed God and erected a barrier between Him and us. We agree with God that what we've said and done was wrong. And then we experience the joy of His forgiveness and cleansing as we draw back into a closer relationship with Him.[32]

We then enter into a period of ***responding to all God has done in our lives***. We thank the Lord very specifically for the wonderful way He's cared for us and those we love. As we do, we must be aware that one of Satan's great deceptions is to try to get us to think we—in our strength and wisdom—have accomplished what, in reality, God has done in, for, or through us.

After revering God, restoring our relationship with Him, and responding in gratitude for all He's done, we come to the point of ***requesting His assistance***. First, we ask for God's help in resolving challenges being faced by others (this prayer is called intercession). Then we ask for help with issues we're confronting (this is referred to as petition).

An important part of prayer—one the husband in our illustration missed and one we often fail to experience—is ***receiving what God has to say***. This comes as we listen to the Lord. He doesn't speak to us aloud, but His Holy Spirit within us guides us with the Father's direction, comforts us in times of trouble, and helps us understand things that would be beyond our comprehension without this divine assistance. The process of listening requires that we slow down, that we not allow our fast-paced lifestyle to distract us from focusing on the Lord and what He's trying to communicate.

As we humbly approach the Lord, we can be certain He's listening. We also can be sure that—100 per cent of the time—He'll answer our prayers according to what He considers to be in our best interest. Of course, we may not always see things from God's perspective. We're restricted to a view that includes the finite past, the present, and the short-range future. God's timetable is eternal; He knows all about our past, what we're facing now, and what will happen to us for the rest of our lives. As our relationship with the Lord deepens, we'll view our circumstances from His perspective and discover our desires more closely match His desires.

We often cram so much activity into each day that we fail to take time to be alone with the Lord. He encourages us to cease striving, to be still and know He is God.[33] If we don't spend time in prayer daily—serious prayer, not superficial chatter in which we assign God His to-do list— we'll fail to discover His guidance and tap into His strength, which are crucial for victory in spiritual warfare. We'll also miss out on the intimacy God intends for us to experience with Him, and we'll be ineffective in sharing His love with others.

Followers of Christ in the church's early days recognized the value of earnest prayer. After an overnight jail stay, Peter and John were hauled before the religious authorities and commanded not to teach others about Jesus. The apostles refused to comply with these orders and, when released, returned to their Christian companions. The small band called on the Lord to grant them power in spreading the gospel. Their prayers were answered in a unique way. The place where they'd gathered was shaken, they were filled with the Holy Spirit, and they began to speak the word of God boldly. (See Acts 4.)

God Communicates through His Word

In drawing close to the Lord, we also must spend time in scripture. Solomon reminds us that God said, "'I love those who love Me; and those who diligently seek Me will find Me.'"[34] One of the best ways to find Him is through the pages of the Bible. God's word reveals Him to His children. We learn of His creation of the world and everything in it. We see how He's acted on behalf of His people through the centuries.

Through the pages of scripture, Christ reveals God to us. Although the Father is a spirit, we can appreciate Him through Jesus' reflection of His character. The writer to the Hebrews tells us how this is possible. "He [Christ] is the radiance of His [the Father's] glory and the exact representation of His nature."[35] If we really get to know Jesus, we'll also know His Father, Who sent Him to minister on Earth. Christ confirms this during His last gathering with His disciples as He explains, "'If you had known Me, you would have known My Father also. ... He who has seen Me has seen the Father.'"[36]

The Bible also guides us in the way God wants us to go. The Psalmist said, "Thy word is a lamp to my feet, and a light to my path."[37]

Months before their first game, football players begin to learn their individual assignments for each play. As we saw earlier, coaches provide them a large notebook with every play diagrammed with arrows showing where each player will go when the ball is put into play. During practice the coaches hold up the diagrams, and players execute the plays, first walking slowly into position and then picking up the pace until they can run through the maneuver.

After weeks of rehearsal, the team is able to carry out each play with precision—and without looking at the diagram. In the huddle, the quarterback calls a play, and the team runs it as they have so many times during practice. It would look ridiculous if 11 men trotted onto the field with huge notebooks tucked into their skin-tight football pants. It also would be extremely awkward. By game time, each player has memorized the actions he'll be called upon to perform.

Christians also have a playbook that tells us what we should do in the game of life. It's been developed by a veteran Coach who is very knowledgeable about the game, not through observation from afar, but because He created the players, invented the rules, constructed the strategies, and spent more than three decades on Earth living out what He'd designed.

Our task now is to learn the playbook—the word of God—so thoroughly that the lives we lead bear a striking resemblance to the life His Son lived 2,000 years ago. Initially, we'll have to refer to the playbook often. Over time and with practice, we'll be able to execute our plays flawlessly because we've studied and memorized God's instructions.

Knowledge of scripture is crucial for soldiers in God's army. It prepares us for battle, sustains us in combat, and restores us following the fighting. Members of military units spend hours studying intelligence reports before they enter conflict. Their lives—and the lives of others in their units—depend on their knowing what's contained in these documents. As we engage in spiritual battle, God's warriors should study His word just as thoroughly. Familiarity with scripture is a tremendous aid in achieving our mission of becoming more like Christ.

Jesus told His disciples God's word is truth.[38] He'd spent a good deal of time studying and memorizing the scriptures. This was evident during His confrontation with Satan after He'd fasted for 40 days in the wilderness to prepare for His ministry. Three times, Satan attempted to entice Christ to do something inconsistent with what the Father wanted. Each time, Jesus defeated His adversary by quoting a passage from the scriptures.[39]

Paul encouraged his young protégé, Timothy, to handle accurately the word of truth so he could gain God's approval.[40] The apostle also reminded Timothy that God inspired all scripture so followers of Christ may be well equipped to serve the Lord.[41] During a stop in Berea on Paul's second missionary journey, the apostle observed local residents studying God's word with great eagerness and diligence.[42] The Lord expects the same wholehearted review and application today.

We mustn't take our time in the scriptures lightly. We should read God's word regularly, studying it so we better understand what the Lord is saying. We should meditate on it, going over it in our minds so we grasp its application in our lives. We can do this throughout the day and as we lay in bed at night.[43] We should memorize passages of scripture so we can share them with others when God brings the weary or confused into our paths. We also can combine prayer and time in the word in regular devotions with God.

Worship with Gratitude

Another way we experience intimacy with God is through worshiping with others. Many of us, however, have a distorted view of the hour or so we spend at church each Sunday morning. You may have heard people say, "Oh, we don't go to that church any more. It just didn't meet our needs." Unfortunately, some Christians rate worship in the same they evaluate other activities in their lives. "I didn't get much from that class. The professor was a bit boring." "That movie wasn't very entertaining. I wouldn't recommend you see it." "The service in that restaurant was terrible! We waited an hour to get our meals." "The pastor's sermons are O.K., but those old hymns from the 1800s have got to go!"

Worship, though, is not about what we get from it. It's not a matter of whether or not the preacher is a first-class orator, as persuasive as a charismatic political leader and as entertaining as a standup comedian. It doesn't matter whether or not we find the music stimulating or that the worship sticks rigidly to a timetable that will get us out of the building at precisely the same time each Sunday.

Our worship is primarily a matter of what we put into it. It's praising the Lord for Who He is and for all He's done through the ages. We must put off the selfish distractions that demand satisfaction of our perceived needs and spend time exalting the Father, Son, and Holy Spirit.

When the children of Israel weren't rebelling against God or ignoring His leading, they seemed to grasp the essence of worship. In one of many examples from the Old Testament, as the Levites led worship, they broke out their harps, lyres, cymbals, and trumpets for a time of festive praise and thanksgiving. In I Chronicles 16, the priest's words recognize God's might and express joy for all He'd done for His people.

> Give thanks to the LORD. Call upon His name. ... Sing to Him, sing praises to Him; speak of all His wonders. Glory in His holy

name; let the heart of those who seek the LORD be glad. ... Seek His face continually. Remember His wonderful deeds which He has done.

Sing to the LORD, all the earth. ... Great is the LORD, and greatly to be praised; He also is to be feared above all gods. ... The LORD made the heavens. Splendor and majesty are before Him.

Ascribe to the LORD the glory due His name. ... Worship the LORD in holy array.

God's chosen people held nothing back as they worshiped the Lord. The people who spoke these words were filled with passion. This was a huge celebration, and our modern-day worship should reflect the same excitement, awe, and gratitude.

The people of Judah discovered a link between worship and victory in battle. In the days of King Jehoshaphat, forces from three nations set out to make war on Judah. The king led a prayer that doubled as a pep talk, and a prophet announced victory for God's people was at hand. Then "all Judah and the inhabitants of Jerusalem fell down before the LORD, worshiping the LORD. And the Levites ... stood up to praise the LORD God of Israel, with a very loud voice."

The next morning, Jehoshaphat's army assembled on the battlefield. Rather than engaging their adversaries, they once again broke into worship. Miraculously, as the forces of Judah lifted their voices in praise, God Himself routed their adversaries. (See II Chronicles 20.) As modern-day warriors in God's army worship the Lord, we call on the same almighty power to defeat our satanic foes.

Jesus had an interesting conversation concerning worship with a Samaritan woman during a rest stop on His travels. Although the Jews doubly despised the woman for her gender and her religious beliefs, Christ initiated contact with her. After a short exchange, the topic of worship came up. "'You worship that which you do not know,'" explained Jesus. "'We worship that which we know, for salvation is from the Jews. But an hour is coming, and now is, when the true worshipers shall worship the Father in spirit and truth; for such people the Father seeks to be His worshipers. God is spirit, and those who worship Him must worship in spirit and truth.'" Having completed this brief lesson, Jesus told the woman He was the long-awaited Messiah.[44]

As we worship in spirit, we humbly come before God, allowing the Holy Spirit to help us praise the Father for His divine attributes and thank Him for what He's done in our lives. As we've seen, Jesus told His disciples God's word is truth.[45] He'd previously equated His own words, inspired by His Father, with truth.[46] Therefore, a significant element of worship must be gaining a better appreciation for scripture and exalting God for revealing His truth to us through His Son.

It's important we do this among other believers so we may draw strength and encouragement through our collective worship. While we can experience meaningful worship alone in our homes, in the midst of God's beautiful creation, and as we serve Him through serving others, the Lord Himself calls us to join with Jesus' followers in offering Him the praise He is due.[47]

For 24 years, Henry Francis Lyte served as a pastor at Lower Brixham in Devonshire, England. Because of failing health, he was advised to give up his ministry. In September 1847, within a few months of his death, Lyte preached his final sermon. That evening, he gave a short hymn he'd written to a member of his family.[48] In the first stanza of "Abide with Me," he calls on the Lord to be with him during dark times, "when other helpers fail and comforts flee." Lyte then asks God to abide with him as he approaches his final days on Earth. In the third verse, the writer issues a plea all of us should echo every minute of every day of our lives.

I need Thy presence every passing hour;
What but Thy grace can foil the tempter's power?
Who like Thyself my guide and stay can be?
Through cloud and sunshine, O abide with me.[49]

As we develop a greater intimacy with the Lord—as we abide in Christ—through prayer, spending time in God's word, and worship, we begin to take on the image of His Son. Others see Jesus in us. And as our relationship with God grows more intimate and we love Him more each day, we'll discover we also possess a greater love for those around us.

Priority 2: Love for God's Family

Jesus also loved those who became part of God's family. The best example of this is the time He spent with His closest followers. He gathered His disciples specifically to learn from His example so they'd be ready for the work He'd later commission them to do.[50] Sometimes Christ took the disciples aside after teaching the crowds with parables and explained the meaning of these stories to His closest followers.[51] In addition, His teaching took the form of instruction, as when Jesus prepared the 12 for field training exercises. (See Matthew 10.)

Christ also taught by demonstration, healing the sick, casting out demons, and washing the disciples' feet. He ensured they rested,[52] comforted them,[53] and prayed for them. (See John 17.) Finally, Jesus gave the disciples authority and sent them into service doing what they'd seen Him do.[54]

Jesus' discussion with His disciples before His arrest illustrates the relationship we should develop with those who serve alongside us. Christ commanded them to love one another, and He explained their love for each other was to match His love for each of them. He told them the greatest expression of love is to lay down one's life for his friends.[55] That's a pretty tall order. Occasionally, though, our allegiance to God may require that we put others—in or outside God's army—ahead of ourselves through this supreme sacrifice.

Among the more than 900 troops who boarded the SS Dorchester on a dreary, winter day in 1943 were four chaplains. World War II was in full swing, and the ship was headed across the icy North Atlantic where Nazi U-boats lurked. On the morning of February 3, a German torpedo ripped into the ship. "She's going down!" the men cried, scrambling for lifeboats. A young soldier crept up to one of the chaplains. "I've lost my life jacket," he said. "Take this," the chaplain said, handing the soldier his jacket. Before the ship sank, each chaplain gave his life jacket to another man. The heroic chaplains then linked arms and lifted their voices in prayer as the Dorchester went down.[56]

Few of us will be called upon to die for our compatriots in God's army. All of us are called on every day, however, to love and to live for our fellow soldiers.

Several New Testament writers have much to say about love. Paul encouraged the Corinthians to pursue love, and he instructed the Ephesians to "walk in love, just as Christ also loved you."[57] John, who refers to himself as the disciple Jesus loved, obviously learned a great deal from observing Christ's love. In I John 4:7-21, he mentions love 27 times. As we read this passage, we learn that:

- God is love, and love is from God. In His love, He sent His Son into the world to die for our sins.
- We're to love one another. If we do, God abides in us, and His love is perfected in us.
- Those who love are born of God and know God. Those who don't love don't know God.
- There's no fear in love; perfect love casts out fear.

- We love because God first loved us.
- We can't love God, Whom we haven't seen, if we hate our brother, whom we have seen.

If the only reasons for us to love others were obedience to God's command and conformity to Jesus' example, that should be enough motivation. However, Christ provides another reason. As we love other Christians as Jesus loves us, all who observe this love will know we're His disciples.[58] This permits us to be great witnesses to others—even before we say anything to them about Jesus. They'll see a difference in our lives compared to those who aren't Christians, and they'll want to know why believers demonstrate such love for one another—a love many of them don't know. This will lead to opportunities to tell them such love is possible only through faith in our loving Savior.

Priority 3: Love for Those outside God's Family

In addition to His love for the Father and those who became part of His family, Jesus' love prompted Him to spend time in the world drawing people to God. He taught, proclaimed the gospel, and healed the sick.[59] He cast out demons and evil spirits[60] and brought the dead to life.[61] He performed a variety of other signs and miracles, pronounced blessings on people,[62] and challenged unrighteousness.[63] All these actions had exactly the same motivation: to bring men and women, boys and girls closer to the Lord.

Jesus' ministry knew no limits based on age, nationality, religious background, or character. Christ reached out to adults and children, Jews and Gentiles, political and religious leaders, those who did good and those who did evil, family and friends and complete strangers. He healed the blind, the deaf, the dumb, the lame, the demon-possessed, and many others suffering from a host of illnesses. He was equally at home in Jerusalem or in the villages that dotted the countryside.

As we seek to follow the example Jesus left for us, a very important lesson emerges from the time He spent with others. For Him, a request for help was never an interruption. When approached by someone in need, Christ looked upon the situation as an opportunity to share God's love with the person. He responded graciously, through the power, wisdom, and love the Father had nurtured in His Son's heart during Jesus' intimate and extended times of prayer.

Paul recognized the importance of loving those who don't share our faith in Christ. The apostle encouraged Jesus' followers to serve one another in love, and he added they should also serve all people.[64] Usually it's not difficult for us to love other Christians. Loving and serving those who haven't placed their trust in Christ, however, is a bit more challenging.

Often the best we're able to do is to serve unbelievers because of our love for God and obedience to His commands, but we go through the motions without truly loving the people on the receiving end. If this is true of us, we're failing to live by the spirit of the Lord's instruction. We must deeply and sacrificially love those we serve. After all, this is what Jesus did!

Today some Christians withdraw from the company of people who don't follow Jesus. True, we're around people at work, and we may say hello to folks we pass on the street. In many cases, though, we know the characters in our favorite weekly television series better than we know our neighbors. We can tell others the joys and challenges of a half dozen fictional officers on a police drama, yet we don't know the names of the members of the family next door.

One way to gauge whether or not we love others as God intends is to compare our love to the description Paul provides in I Corinthians 13. After describing the importance of loving others, the apostle summarizes what love is and what it isn't, what it does and what it doesn't do.

On the positive side, love is patient and kind. It's pleased when the truth comes out. Love bears up under the most trying circumstances and believes in what's good and right. It hopes for the best and endures, no matter what challenges it faces.

On the other hand, love is never jealous, boastful, or arrogant. It doesn't produce indecent or improper actions, and it doesn't lead to demands by one party who believes his or her way is the only way. Love doesn't allow one to lapse into anger when provoked or to sink into frustration or depression when wronged. It doesn't find pleasure in what's evil or perverse. Paul's conclusion is that true love never fails.

When we receive our commission from God, our mission is to be conformed to the image of His Son. Jesus gives us the model for achieving this goal in His life and teaching. We're to love God, and we're to love others. As we seek to achieve our mission, Satan is using all his wicked power to prevent us from conforming to the likeness of Christ. We need to gather intelligence on our adversary—learning his strategy and tactics—so we can defeat him in battle as Jesus did during His days on Earth.

Lessons Learned

- God commissions soldiers in His army to battle a powerful and devious foe and gives us the mission of being conformed to the image of our Commander—Jesus Christ, His Son.
- The Holy Spirit works in and through us to help us become more like Christ.
- We learn how to conform to Jesus' image as we study His life in the pages of scripture and as we observe Him at work in the world today.
- Jesus models the life we're to live in the time He spent with His Father, a few close followers, and all the others He interacted with in the world.
- To become more like Christ, we must develop intimacy with God through frequent and fervent prayer; regular time in God's word; and focused, meaningful, individual, and corporate worship.
- As we more closely follow the example of Jesus in developing intimacy with His Father, we will—like Christ—more fully love those God brings across our paths.

Unit Analysis

To download Unit Analysis and Personal Battle Plan material, please go to www.forwardintobattle.com.

After becoming acquainted with our Commander and the troops who fight alongside us, we're ready to be commissioned into service and to make our final preparations for combat. But what is it we'll be trying to achieve as we enter the battle against Satan and his evil forces? It's easy to confuse our individual duties with the overall objective, but we must focus on the "big picture" if we're to pull our weight in this unit. Simply stated, the mission for followers of Christ is that we become more like Him. In following Jesus' example, we must spend time with God, with a few close followers of Christ, and with the larger group of people with whom we come into contact. As we draw closer to the Lord, we'll begin to love others as He loves them. This will take us well beyond the comfortable, shallow relationships we usually experience, and we'll begin to reflect God's glory so others may draw closer to Him.

1. Think back to your own or a close friend's graduation, commissioning, promotion, or similar ceremony. Describe the emotions and sense of excitement that prevailed as one phase of life came to an end and another began. How should this enthusiasm and expectancy be evident in our spiritual commissioning?
2. We read in John 18:36 that Jesus considered Himself a citizen of heaven, not of this world. According to Ephesians 2:19, how does Apostle Paul describe our citizenship prior to joining God's army? What two changes take place when we become followers of Christ?
3. Take a look at II Corinthians 3:18. Paul tells the followers of Jesus in Corinth our mission is to be transformed so we display the Lord's image. Briefly share your thoughts on what aspects of Jesus' character and actions our lives should mirror.

4. The foundation for everything Christ did on Earth was laid through spending time with His Father. One of the ways we develop and maintain intimacy with God is through prayer, which has four main components.
   a. As we **revere** the Lord, we focus solely on his character and His universal blessings—not on how He's dealt with us individually. Review Psalms 146-150. How do these expressions of adoration provide a model for your prayers?
   b. We know from Romans 3:23 that all of us have missed the mark. Apostle John provides some wise counsel on **restoring** our relationship with the Lord. Read I John 1:5-10. What does the Lord require of us when we recognize we've fallen short of what He wants us to be and to do? The word "confess" actually means "to say the same as." God desires that we see our inappropriate actions from the same perspective He views them. When we sin, we must not try to justify our actions, excusing them as correct or inconsequential. We must agree with God that what we've said, done, or thought doesn't measure up to the standard He's set for us. When we agree with God, what two responses can we expect from Him? What confidence should this inspire in us?
   c. Our **response** to God in prayer focuses on those purely personal blessings we've received from His hand. It's amazing how often Christians pray for God's help and then fail to thank Him for what He does in answer to our requests. Incredibly, we sometimes take credit for the Lord's actions. What are some specific examples of how you may have done this in the past? How can you better express your gratitude in prayer and in conversation with others—Christians and those who haven't yet come to faith?
   d. As Jesus discussed prayer with His disciples, He mentioned conditions for and results of making **requests** of the Lord. Read

John 14:13-14, 15:7-8, and 16:23-24. How are we to ask the Father to take action in our lives and the lives of others? If we pray according to Christ's instructions, what will happen? Consider the effect on those we've prayed for and the impact on God's reputation among those who observe His response to our requests.
5. Share some practical ways you've found to maintain a regular prayer life. Read Psalm 46:10 from various translations of the Bible. How have you been able to step away from the hectic pace of life—job demands, family duties, responsibilities at church, and action-packed hobbies and vacations—to *receive* what the Lord is trying to communicate to you?
6. Proverbs 8:17 reminds us that if we seek God, we'll find Him, and one of the ways He reveals Himself to us is through the timeless message of scripture. In the following verses, how can God's word aid us in our day-to-day lives?
   a. Psalm 119:105
   b. Matthew 4:1-11
   c. II Timothy 3:16-17
7. Satan loves to distract followers of Christ during worship. How have you experienced this, and how have you overcome the devil's evil schemes?
8. According to I John 4:21, Ephesians 5:1-2, and John 13:34-35, why should we love others? In Matthew 22:39, Jesus tells us to "love your neighbor as yourself." How well do you know your neighbors? Do you really know the people you work with? How can you love those around you as much as you love yourself? And how can you demonstrate this love to others?
9. In addition to spending time with His Father, Jesus spent time with a few close followers. Every warrior in God's army should be involved

in a mentoring relationship—being encouraged by a more mature Christian, helping a new believer to grow, or preferably both. How did Jesus mentor His disciples in Mark 4:33-34? What approach did He adopt in Matthew 10:1-15? How can you help others in their spiritual journeys through instruction, demonstration, and providing opportunities for service?

10. Matthew 9:35-38 tells us Jesus also spent time among the multitudes teaching, preaching, and healing. To what types of people did He minister? To what types of people do you minister? Read Galatians 6:10. Do you think you should broaden the scope of those you serve in Jesus' name? Are you frustrated when people interrupt you seeking help, or do you view these events as opportunities to share the love of Christ with those who approach you?

Prayer Points

- Praise God for providing and preserving the example of His Son in the pages of scripture
- Thank the Lord for considering us worthy to follow in the footsteps of Christ, despite the many ways we fall short of what He wants us to be and do
- Ask God to help you to learn more about His Son and to be conformed to the image of Jesus through the strength and wisdom only He can provide
- Commit to following the example of Christ and moving beyond your comfort zone in:
  - Prayer, time in God's word, and worship
  - Helping a few other men or women grow in their faith
  - Ministering to larger, more diverse groups than you have in the past

Personal Battle Plan

1. We often tend to evaluate how we're doing in our spiritual lives by comparing ourselves to others around us. Actually, the yardstick we're to use in measuring our growth as a follower of Christ is the person of Jesus Himself. Thinking about how Christ lived His life, **meditate on these questions**: Do you feel a greater loyalty to the kingdom of heaven or to the kingdom of Earth? Does how you spend your time reflect this loyalty? Are you consistently allowing God to transform you from being a citizen of this world to conforming to the likeness of His Son?
2. **Assess your current prayer life and the time you spend in God's word**.
    a. How much time do you spend in prayer daily? How well do you incorporate the elements of revering, restoring, responding, and requesting into your prayers? Are you slowing down enough to allow God to communicate with you as you listen? Do you feel closer to God as a result of the time you spend in prayer? Are you simply repeating the same prayer to God day in and day out, or is your time with the Lord fresh and vibrant each day?
    b. How much time do you spend reading the Bible daily? Do you pray before you read, asking the Lord to reveal what He'd have you understand and apply? Do you meditate on what you read, or are you happy to skim quickly through the verses for the day? Do you consult other sources that might help you better appreciate what you find in scripture? Do you memorize verses that will help your faith grow and that you can share with others?
3. **Make an appointment with God for prayer and Bible reading daily**. Decide how much time you'll spend on these disciplines each day. You may wish to start with a manageable amount of time—say 15 minutes on weekdays and half an hour on weekends—but plan to see your time with the Lord grow as He blesses you during your prayers

Understanding the Mission

and reading. Pray for God's strength as Satan tries to keep you from meeting with the Lord.

Sunday:	Time_____	Duration_____
Monday:	Time_____	Duration_____
Tuesday:	Time_____	Duration_____
Wednesday:	Time_____	Duration_____
Thursday:	Time_____	Duration_____
Friday:	Time_____	Duration_____
Saturday:	Time_____	Duration_____

4. **Develop a prayer log**. Update it each time a new prayer topic arises, and enter a note when God responds to your requests. **Keep a notebook handy when you read and pray**. It's amazing how often God will transmit a thought to you as you're engaged in these spiritual activities. It may be a verse He wants you to look up later or an action He wants you to take. More often than not, if you fail to jot it down, you'll forget to do it.

5. **Focus totally on God as you worship**. Forget about grading the music or the sermon. Don't worry about what time the service will end. Resist the temptation to view the experience in terms of what you get out of it. Simply pray at the outset that the Lord would help you to defeat any distractions, and give your full attention to what every song, prayer, and spoken word reveals to you about our awesome God. At the same time, praise Him for Who He is and for all He's done, is doing, and will continue to do—for all eternity!

6. You may be a relatively new soldier in God's army, or you may be a longtime follower of Jesus. In either case, you can benefit from the direction and encouragement of someone with a bit more experience. Have you found a seasoned veteran with a lot of time on the frontlines who can help you grow in your faith? **Assess the time you spend**

with your mentor. If you're making steady progress, make sure to express your gratitude. If not, talk about what you can do to get the most out of your relationship. If you haven't discovered someone who can assist in this way, pray for God's provision of a mature Christian, approach the person with an offer to get together regularly, and pray for the Lord to richly bless this relationship.

7. **Evaluate the impact you're having on the spiritual lives of a few other people.**

	Thinking About It	Praying About It	Just Getting Started	Making a Difference
a. Have you prayerfully sought out some other Christians you can disciple?				
b. How well are you teaching them—by word and by deed—how they should be growing closer to the Lord?				
c. Do you comfort them as needed and pray for them regularly?				
d. Have you helped them to engage in ministry among others?				

If you are not currently involved in this type of discipleship, list the names of two people you feel God wants you to approach, and ask Him to use you to help these folks grow in their faith. If you're a new Christian, pray that God will reveal to you when He feels you're ready to take on this role.

8. **Evaluate your love for others.** List the people with whom you have most frequent contact in each of the groups below. Make sure to include some folks who are not yet Christians. Now honestly assess whether or not what you say to them and what you do for them is motivated out of a deep love for them. If your words and deeds are more a function of your love for God or are prompted by a sense of duty, list what you will do to develop a greater love for these folks—and how they'll be able to see this love being worked out in and through you.
   a. Family:
   b. Co-Workers:
   c. Neighbors:
   d. Targets of Ministry:

9. **Prepare for the next session** by contemplating Satan's goals and tactics as he and his troops try to keep you from fulfilling your mission.

CHAPTER 6

Gathering Intelligence

If you know the enemy and know yourself, you need not fear the result of a hundred battles. If you know yourself but not the enemy, for every victory gained you will also suffer a defeat. If you know neither the enemy nor yourself, you will succumb in every battle.

Sun Tzu[1]

DURING MY TIME in the Air Force, I was twice assigned to joint commands composed of U.S. soldiers, sailors, airmen, and Marines. In the first, American forces were complemented by troops from our host nation: the Republic of Korea. The headquarters of U.S. Forces Korea was located at Yongsan Army Barracks in Seoul, a mere 30 miles south of the Demilitarized Zone that separates North and South Korea.

My year at Yongsan coincided with one of the more volatile periods since the conflict that split the country. At regular intervals, the North Korean government issued threats against the U.S. and ROK forces stationed along the 151-mile border between the nations. Generals south of the DMZ considered an attack unlikely, but they always took the warnings seriously because of the massive size of the enemy force—said to number a million men in uniform—and because Seoul was so close to the border. Claims that the North Koreans had access to weapons of mass destruction also caused concern. Tensions rose, too, when North Korean navy vessels periodically entered waters off the Republic's west coast.

Within the USFK command center at Yongsan, a huge intelligence staff constantly monitored military activity across the border. With predictions that 500 North Korean multiple-rocket launchers could rain hundreds of thousands of artillery shells on Seoul every hour, the intelligence community remained vigilant for any signs that our potential enemies would attempt to overrun South Korea. Obviously, the more time U.S. and ROK forces had to prepare, the greater the odds we'd repel an attack and save lives in the capital.

Anticipating what might occur was all the more challenging because the North Korean leader, Kim Il-Sung, revered as a god by many in his country, didn't make decisions with the mindset of Western leaders. It was virtually impossible to determine what he might do in various situations. Despite several heightened alerts during my year in Korea, the Supreme Leader never followed through on any of his numerous, angry threats.

My next tour of duty took me to the U.S. Atlantic Command. Within a month of my arrival, I was deep into planning for an operation in which American troops would be sent to liberate Haiti, a nation being controlled at the time by Raoul Cedras, a dictator who cared little for the welfare of his people. As the planning and conduct of the operation spanned several months, USACOM was successively led by two four-star officers, the first a Navy admiral and the second a Marine Corps general. Each placed significant demands on the command's large intelligence staff.

Our leaders wanted to know everything they could about what U.S. forces would face in battle. This included the hardware enemy troops could throw into the fight and the strategies and tactics they'd employ against U.S. forces. The goal for the admiral and general was to know the enemy so well that they could anticipate and preempt his actions so the U.S. operation would succeed.

Fortunately, combat was averted as a diplomatic solution was accepted at the eleventh hour. U.S. aircraft carrying paratroopers had departed their bases headed south when the agreement, brokered by former-President Jimmy Carter, was signed in Port-au-Prince. Rather than American warriors entering the country in the midst of hostile fire, they landed peacefully at the city's airport with the mission of rebuilding the poor nation.

Knowing Our Enemy

In the furious spiritual battle surrounding us, it's crucial we know as much as we can about our adversary. As Apostle Paul reminds us, "Our struggle is not against flesh and blood, but against the rulers, against the powers, against the world forces of this darkness, against the spiritual forces of wickedness in the heavenly places."[2] We face fierce opposition. And Satan's evil troops are always on the prowl, seeking to devour Christians who don't know how to tap into God's power to defeat them.

One reason the devil's attacks are often successful is that we have a distorted view of our rival. Many years ago, a group of touring Christian actors and actresses visited our church. On Saturday afternoon, the troupe put on a play for children. We had no stage, so the youngsters were arranged in a semicircle on the floor about 10 feet away from where the actors performed. The younger children sat in front, and the older children sat behind them.

The play was about good and evil. Several minutes into the performance, it was time for the devil to make a grand entrance. A large prop representing a boulder stood to one side, and an actor representing Satan was positioned behind it. On cue, he jumped out to within a few feet of the five-year-olds in the front, lifting his arms in a menacing arch and snarling at the audience. His red and black make-up; sharp, fang-like incisors; muscular physique; and hissing voice should have been enough to send 50 frightened children scrambling in all directions.

Confronted by such a grotesque beast when I was their age, I'd have been first out the rear exit. To my amazement, the children remained in position, not demonstrating any sign of fear. In fact, a few had the nerve to chuckle as the prince of the power of the air gazed upon them with hatred. The play continued, and the troupe received a standing ovation at its conclusion.

As my wife and I later assessed what we'd witnessed, we decided panic was averted because, by the late 1980s, children had been so conditioned by what they'd seen on television and in video games that they were desensitized to something that a generation earlier would have scarred a youngster for life. To children over the past few decades, Satan is a lot less frightening than the villains who superheroes defeat on television and computer screens every day.

Public opinion research confirms that children in the U.S. have grown into adults with no fear and little understanding of Satan. In 2007, the Barna Research Group discovered nearly three in five American adults (57%) believed Satan is not a living being but is a symbol of evil.[3] In a study two years later, 59% of ***professing Christians*** in the U.S. denied Satan's existence. In 2009, only 35% of those who identified themselves as followers of Christ believed the devil is real, and 6% said they weren't sure.[4]

More recent studies suggest opinions may be shifting. Commissioned by the True Life in God Foundation, Survey Monkey discovered in May 2013 that 56% of Americans believed in the existence of Satan.[5] Four months later, YouGov research concluded 57% of people across the U.S. thought the devil exists.[6] Of course, belief in the existence of Satan doesn't necessarily mean survey respondents comprehend the impact the devil has in their lives.

The Bible leaves no doubt about the reality of our adversary. We know he's a personal being rather than a concept by the various names he's given, deeds he's done or will do, and actions taken against him. We learn very early in scripture that Satan, called a serpent, deceived Eve in the Garden of Eden.[7] Through this evil act, the devil became the world's first military recruiter. By enlisting Adam and Eve to join his army in rebellion against God, Satan ensured all mankind would begin life in his service.

By the end of the Bible, Apostle John tells us God will send an angel from heaven to lay hold of "the dragon, the serpent of old, who is the devil and Satan," bind him for 1,000 years, and seal him in an abyss so he'll be unable to deceive the nations.[8]

Between these references, most of what we discover about the personal nature of the devil comes from the New Testament. When the Pharisees accused Jesus of casting out demons in partnership with "the ruler of demons," Christ explained His authority came from God and not from the prince of demons.[9] In explaining the parable of the sower, Jesus tells us the "evil one" steals the gospel from many who hear it.[10]

Christ also brands the devil a murderer who doesn't stand in the truth and "a liar, and the father of lies" who speaks deceitfully.[11] Acknowledging Satan's power, Jesus warned His disciples, "'The ruler of the world is coming, and he has nothing in Me.'"[12]

In letters to the Corinthians and the Ephesians, Paul labels the devil "the god of this world." The apostle charges that Satan "has blinded the minds of the unbelieving, that they might not see the light of the gospel of the glory of Christ, Who is the image of God."[13] Furthermore, Paul suggests Belial—a name that referred to Satan's corruption, lawlessness, perversion, and rebellion—has no ties with Christ.[14]

Paul told Jesus' followers in Ephesus "the prince of the power of the air" was at work in all who disobeyed God. As the leader of the "world forces of darkness," says the apostle, Satan oversees a great struggle against Christians.[15]

Apostle Peter warns that the devil, our adversary, prowls about like a roaring lion, seeking someone to devour.[16] Peter's fellow disciple John suggests "the angel of the abyss"—Abaddon in Hebrew and Apollyon in

Greek—rules over the forces of evil.[17] These names refer to the devil's desire to destroy all that's good, all that's of God. John also explains that in Satan's role as "the accuser," he brings the shortcomings of Christians before God day and night.[18]

From this list of names, titles, and evil deeds, it's clear Satan is a personal being. He hates God and wants control over the universe. The devil will do everything in his power to damage the Lord's reputation and keep his troops from shifting their allegiance to God.

Satan's Objectives and Tactics

In his constant struggle against mankind, the devil has two primary goals. His greatest desire is to ***keep people from receiving Christ as Savior***. Satan doesn't want human soldiers born into his forces to desert in favor of service in God's army. When he fails at this objective, his desire is to ***prevent Christians from conforming to the image of Christ*** and helping others to know Jesus. He wants to rob God's warriors of the love, joy, peace, and other character traits the Holy Spirit is seeking to produce in them.[19] And make no mistake about it: Satan is a very strong opponent. "The whole world lies in the power of the evil one."[20]

Satan employs several tactics to keep us from what God wants us to be and to do. In a parable Jesus told about a farmer, He describes how the devil ***seeks to undo God's work***. As the Lord sows His word, Satan comes immediately to snatch the truth of God from those who hear it. In other cases, he creates affliction or persecution that causes people to fall away from God. The devil also plants desires for wealth and magnifies anxieties about the challenges of life to prevent others from fulfilling their spiritual responsibilities.[21]

In addition, Satan ***preys upon men's hearts and minds***. Even before Jesus observed the Last Supper with His closest followers, the devil convinced Judas to betray Christ. During the meal, Satan entered into Judas, who then went to the authorities to launch the events that led to

Jesus' crucifixion.[22] Similarly, the evil one twisted the hearts of Ananias and Sapphira to lie to the apostles, and the pair paid for this with their lives.[23]

These incidents reveal Satan can turn followers of Christ against the Lord. Paul recognized the danger of the devil's attacks on the minds of Christians. He warned believers in Corinth that Satan would try to lead their minds astray from the simplicity and purity of devotion to Christ.[24]

Satan also ***produces physical and emotional affliction*** to turn people away from the Lord. With God's permission, the devil destroyed Job's family, health, and possessions as he tried to get this blameless man to curse God. (See Job 1-2.) When Jesus healed a woman who'd been ill for 18 years, He explained that Satan had caused this suffering.[25]

The devil uses a variety of evil tricks. We first encounter him in the Garden of Eden, where he ***introduces doubt*** into Eve's thinking. Satan subtly twists the words of God to transform their meaning. As a result of his psychological warfare, Eve does the opposite of what the Lord had commanded.[26]

The Bible also tells us Satan ***disguises himself*** as an angel of light,[27] gaining people's acceptance because they don't see him as the source of all that is contrary to God's design. In addition, he ***uses various schemes*** to overcome his human prey.[28]

In late 1990 and early 1991, as coalition forces prepared to launch an attack on Iraq, amphibious exercises along the Persian Gulf were visible to friend and foe. Major television outlets provided daily updates on operations along Kuwait's east coast, speculating where and when an attack might come. This coverage prompted some former military leaders to criticize the news media, questioning whether or not journalists had committed treason. The concern was that broadcasts on potential battle plans would lead to defeat and the deaths of hundreds of coalition troops.

When Desert Storm kicked off, those who'd followed the "offensive" television coverage were amazed to discover the focal point of the operation was on the opposite flank. Coalition forces took no action along the Persian Gulf. Their rehearsals had been designed to distract the attention of Iraqi forces from the region where the actual attack would be conducted. And the scheme worked! Allied troops quickly emerged victorious, thanks in large measure to the deception of the earlier exercises. In much the same way, Satan uses deceptive schemes to distract us, and then he hits us with a powerful attack in another area.

In an attack on the Son of God, Satan **_misused scripture_** in an effort to cause Jesus to sin. Three times the evil one came to Christ after He'd fasted 40 days in the wilderness. He tempted Jesus to satisfy His hunger by turning stones into bread, to satisfy His curiosity by throwing Himself off the temple to see if the Father would rescue Him, and to satisfy His desire for wealth and influence by worshipping him. In the second temptation, Satan manipulated the words of the psalmist.[29] Jesus' response to this trick—His reaction in each of the three temptations—was to quote the word of God correctly.[30]

Satan's disinformation campaign continues as he seeks to disarm modern warriors in God's army. We derive great power from scripture, so if the devil can entice us to believe half-truths and to ignore the Lord's encouragement and direction, he's much more likely to defeat us. As Jesus demonstrated, the more familiar we are with God's word, the less vulnerable we are to Satan's attacks.

Another tactic the devil uses is the classic military attempt to **_divide and conquer_**. Satan's attack on Adam and Eve illustrates this approach. First, the devil sought to drive a wedge between the pair and their heavenly Father. Additionally, Satan pitted the man and woman against each other. By convincing Eve to disobey God's command, the devil set the stage for the world's first marital spat. When confronted by the Lord about their failure, Adam was quick to blame Eve. Though she didn't retaliate against Adam in God's presence, you can imagine the earful he received as they were dressing in the clothes the Lord fashioned for them!

It's no wonder that in Jesus' final prayer before His death, the theme of unity figured prominently. Christ prayed fervently that His followers might be one, just as Father and Son are one: "'I in them, and Thou in Me, that they may be perfected in unity.'"[31] If we aren't united, we pose an easy target for Satan to isolate us and cut us off from the power we derive from God and our fellow soldiers.

Fallen Angels in the Forces of Evil
As powerful as the devil is, he is limited. He's neither almighty nor all knowing. He can't be present everywhere at once. Satan can command a number of potent attacks in many directions simultaneously, but he relies on a legion of demons to assist him in his wicked deeds.

The devil's troops are the angels who rebelled against God before the creation of the world. When the Lord banished Lucifer and his angelic rebels to Earth, they began to prepare for their wicked activity. Their goal is to create a barrier between people and the God Who loves them and Who desires to establish a personal, eternal relationship with them.[32]

These sinister forces are masters at special operations. They sneak in under cover to attack individual soldiers and units of God's army, often attempting to destroy their adversaries in a series of small-scale battles rather than a huge, frontal assault. They're happy to strike us while we're resting in the security of our garrison before we set out to engage in battlefield operations.

The devil's forces attack without warning; we don't realize they're near until they're upon us. And they strike where we're most vulnerable. While Satan isn't all knowing, he and his demons are aware of the temptations most likely to defeat us at our weakest points. They plan their assaults with passion and carry them out with ferocious intensity. If Christians ignore or underestimate our potent enemy, we'll walk into an ambush.

The Old Testament refers to demons as evil spirits. On some occasions, God uses them to achieve His purposes. Gideon's son, Abimelech, became king of Israel by murdering his 70 brothers. To punish Abimelech, God sent an evil spirit to anger men in the king's hometown so they'd take action against the ruler.[33] Similarly, as soon as Prophet Samuel anointed David to replace Saul as king, "the Spirit of the Lord departed from Saul, and an evil spirit from the Lord terrorized him."[34]

Demons Deceive

Scripture reveals demons actually have access to God. When Ahab, king of Israel, was considering taking on the forces of the king of Aram, he reluctantly called Micaiah to predict the outcome of the battle. Hopeful the prophet would join others who unanimously prophesied Israel would be victorious, Ahab expected the worst: "'I hate him because he does not prophesy good concerning me, but evil.'" The king was proved a prophet as Micaiah announced Israel would be crushed if Ahab pursued his plan.

Offering a bit of advice Ahab hadn't requested, Micaiah shared a vision of heaven with the king. God summoned an evil spirit who'd entice Ahab to fight—and fail. The Lord asked the spirit how he'd achieve this, and he replied, "'I will go out and be a deceiving spirit in the mouth of all his prophets.'" God approved the idea, and He sent the spirit off with these words: "'You are to entice him and also prevail. Go and do so.'"[35]

Paul cautioned Timothy that evil spirits will attempt to deceive Christians into placing their trust in false doctrines.[36] The apostle also instructed the Christians in Rome that demons can't separate followers of Christ from the love of God,[37] and he warned believers in Ephesus to use God's armor to defeat the attacks that are inevitable as we serve as spiritual warriors.[38]

Demons Introduce Alternate Gods and Idols

As Satan and his demons seek to prevent people from experiencing the love of God, one of their key tactics is to shift our focus of worship away from the Lord. While Moses met God on Mount Sinai to receive the Ten

Commandments, Aaron and the Israelites were the targets of a demonic plan to create and worship a golden calf. The people, unsure whether or not Moses would return to lead them, demanded a manmade god that would go before them on the remainder of their journey. The Israelites made sacrifices at the foot of the idol, claiming it was the god who had brought them out of Egypt. God wasn't pleased! (See Exodus 32.) We see later He was particularly angry with the Israelites' sacrifices to "goat demons."[39]

Later generations were just as eager to deflect their worship toward unworthy targets. Satan's henchmen enticed God's chosen people to take up the evil practices of other nations. Throughout the history of the kings of Israel and Judah, the Jews worshiped at the altars of other gods, served idols, and practiced fortune telling. (See II Kings 17 for a summary of the Israelites' submission to demonic temptation and the consequences when God's anger boiled against His people.) Evil practices through the years included parents sacrificing their children to demons.[40]

Demons Cause Pain and Suffering

Jesus encountered demons when He visited the country of the Gerasenes. A naked man who'd been entered by many demons greeted Him. Christ cast the demons into a herd of pigs, which plunged over a bank into the lake, and all the animals drowned. Jesus encouraged the healed man to tell others "what great things God has done for you."[41]

On another occasion, Jesus was introduced to a deaf and dumb boy who had no control over his actions. An evil spirit often threw the lad into the water or into a fire. Although the demon didn't respond when the disciples tried to remove him from the boy, Christ's rebuke healed the young man on the spot. Jesus used the incident as a lesson on the importance of faith, prayer, and fasting in defeating satanic forces.[42] Christ also cast out an evil spirit from a man who was blind and unable to speak and another from a woman who'd been bent over and unable to straighten up for 18 years.[43]

After Jesus removed another demon, He taught those who'd watched about the power and devious nature of these evil beings. If a person is able to repel a demonic attack, the defeated foe may recruit additional forces to mount a new offensive. If successful, the impact on their target is even more devastating than what the lone demon could have accomplished.[44]

Having demonstrated His authority over demons, Christ provided His disciples an opportunity to practice what they'd observed. Jesus gave them authority to cast out unclean spirits and to heal every kind of disease and sickness.[45] He also commissioned 70 others and sent them out in pairs to heal and to preach. They returned with great delight, reporting that "'even the demons are subject to us in Your name.'"[46]

Paul relied on experience as he taught young churches in Europe and Asia about demons. Annoyed by a demon who was controlling a slave girl's fortune-telling, the apostle rebuked the spirit, saying, "'I command you in the name of Jesus Christ to come out of her!'" The girl was healed immediately.[47]

Satan Will Not Prevail

Fortunately, the devil's reign of terror in the world is only temporary. God permits satanic forces to carry out their evil deeds, but a time is coming when the Lord will inflict His ultimate punishment upon Satan and his demons. Jesus tells us He's readying an eternal fire for these wicked forces,[48] and they'll be tormented there day and night forever.[49] This gives us great hope, but it also prompts us to consider how we're to engage enemy forces through the period leading up to this final victory. We can learn a great deal from what Christ and Paul did and taught.

God's warriors must acknowledge the existence of evil spirits who were once angels the Lord created to serve Him. They joined a rebellion led by Lucifer, were banished from heaven, and exist today to inflict suffering and confusion upon humans. Their desire is to separate us from God's love and provision and to exalt Satan as the focus of our worship.

Demons attack by seeking to influence people's thoughts and by entering them and causing pain from within.

As in the days when Christ lived on Earth, His modern followers can defeat demons in their wicked activities. Our authority over these evil spirits comes from our heavenly Commander. Paul cited the name of Jesus to command demons to cease their destructive tactics, and we can do the same.

The forces of evil gain strength from their powerful leader. Therefore, we must remember Jesus' instruction that our ability to defeat them can be assured only through unwavering faith in the strength we receive from the Father accompanied by consistent prayer and fasting. To engage these spiritual enemies in any other way is as hopeless as walking into earthly warfare unarmed.

Thousands of years have passed since Satan cast his initial spell of deception in the Garden of Eden and later sought to destroy Jesus' ministry before it got under way. Yet today he and his demons use the identical techniques we see described in the Bible as they try to separate people from God. We must be ready for the evil schemes we know Satan will unleash against us. Armed with this information, we're prepared to take on our powerful foe.

We're All in the Battle

Not every soldier in God's army is eager to rush to the battlefield when his or her preparation is complete. While most realize a great spiritual war is raging, many are perfectly happy to let other warriors carry out the fighting while they view the conflict from a distance.

In October 1944, less than a year before World War II ended, a 30-year-old Californian was looking forward to returning home following duty aboard a U.S. Navy seaplane tender in the south Pacific. Little did the artillery gunner know that he'd soon witness what later was called one of the most one-sided victories for the American forces in that theater of operations. Here's how my father described the memorable battle.

> The crew of the USS Half Moon felt like the proverbial "sitting duck" when the word came through that a Japanese task force was approaching Surigao Straits in the Philippines. We had been ordered several days before to proceed from Leyte and establish an advanced seaplane base for our squadron of PBY patrol bombers.
>
> I was sitting in the fire-control workshop, wondering how long we would be anchored behind this little island, when suddenly Ace Campbell burst in and said, "Hey, Ty, there's a Japanese task force bearing down on us. There's some 'wagons, flat tops, cruisers, and cans, and they're all coming this way, hell bent for Leyte."
>
> I had the mid watch that night, and Chuck Hodge and I met on the quarterdeck. We had been on watch for an hour or so when, suddenly off our starboard quarter, the sky lit up like noonday. "That's a Japanese starshell!" shouted Hodge. "Nothing else would light the sky up like that. Run and tell the old man."
>
> When I got up to the bridge, the captain directed that we sound general quarters and pass the word for all departments to make immediate preparations to get under way. At this time, we didn't know if there was an American ship within 50 miles of us. The gong, gong, gong of the general quarters alarm always put a little terror in your heart, especially in the dead of night. Men were soon pouring out of their sacks, and about a minute later, all guns were manned and ready.
>
> As all this was happening, our squadrons of PT (patrol torpedo) boats closed in to about half a mile to try to get their torpedoes

into one of the Japanese ships. Two battleships—the Huso and the Yamasiro—were accompanied by five cruisers and eight destroyers.

Unbeknownst to us, Rear Admiral Jesse B. Olendorf was lying in ambush with a powerful task force comprising several of our old pre-war battleships that had been damaged at Pearl Harbor, sent back to the States, and re-outfitted with the latest radar fire-control gear. The California, Tennessee, and Pennsylvania—all with 14-inch turrets—and the West Virginia and Maryland—mounting 16-inch rifles—opened fire with pinpoint accuracy and were getting hits from the first salvo on.

The Japanese hesitated as their leading ships were hit and caught fire, and panic overtook them. For the next 40 minutes or so, there was a seething inferno as cruisers and destroyers engaged in rapid, continuous fire. We sat, intrigued, as if in some gigantic football stadium, sitting on the 50-yard-line, watching two powerful teams try to annihilate each other.

As we continued watching, we cheered and screamed words of encouragement to our forces every time we saw a Japanese ship take a hit. The center of the action was an inferno. Tons of white-hot, high-velocity, high-explosive steel shrieked through the air.

As suddenly as the fighting started, it was over. We wondered who the victor was. As the sun broke over the eastern sky, we were all up topside in as high a vantage point as possible to see what had happened. Through smoke from burning ships miles down the straits, five grand old ladies—five that had been left for wounded or dead, who rose out of the rubble and disgrace of Pearl Harbor to live and fight again—had won!

From the decks of the USS Half Moon rose a mighty cheer, 220 voices full of acclaim for the great victory we had observed. There would never be another victory like the one we had witnessed.

Many of God's warriors—like the sailors aboard this small ship hidden by an island as a fierce battle raged on the horizon—seem content to observe our battle against Satan and his forces from a vantage point that's secluded and safe. They cheer when a prominent evangelist leads many to Christ or when a devoted missionary helps an entire tribe to comprehend the gospel. They pray for those engaged in various ministries and may be quick to write a generous check when a friend on the mission field needs financial support.

Soldiers in God's army, though, don't have the option to withdraw to a position of security to watch in awe as others engage in spiritual combat. Our potent adversary presses his attack on every one of us around the clock, and an ambush could come at any time. In addition, God desires that we take the offensive in this warfare, building up our fellow warriors and recruiting new members into His forces. Each of us has a role to play as we draw our weapons and contribute to the defeat of our evil enemy.

Lessons Learned

- Satan is a powerful foe, determined to do all he can to sever our connection to Almighty God.
- The devil's greatest desire is that people don't come to saving faith in Christ; failing this, he unleashes his wicked attacks at believers to disrupt our walk with the Lord and make us ineffective in sharing the good news of Christ with others.
- The Lord has given Satan rule over the Earth for an extended period, but this won't last forever.
- The devil employs a number of evil tactics to throw us off track as we try to follow Christ.

- Limited in power and range, the devil relies on an army of demons—other fallen angels—to assist him in his wicked deeds.
- Success in defeating the most potent attacks of Satan and his demons will come only through a deep and active faith accompanied by consistent and expectant prayer and fasting.
- Each of God's warriors is engaged in combat; none can opt to withdraw to safety.

Unit Analysis

To download Unit Analysis and Personal Battle Plan material, please go to www.forwardintobattle.com.

Before we step into the fierce spiritual battle around us, we must know our foe. Through the centuries, death and destruction have descended upon individuals and entire civilizations as Satan and his powerful army have overcome millions of people who were unaware of his evil schemes and their eternal consequences. As soldiers in the Lord's forces, we must carefully analyze our adversary, understanding fully his objectives and tactics. Only then can we meet our enemy head on, trusting in the Lord's power, not our own. This will enable us to be what God wants us to be and to do what God calls us to do with passion and excellence as we remember He will give us the victory.

1. In sports, business, and the military, how important is knowledge of one's adversary? In these fields, what information about the opposition is crucial in planning strategies and tactics?
2. Read the following verses and discuss what they reveal about the character and activity of Satan:
   a. Isaiah 14:12-20
   b. John 8:44

    c. II Corinthians 4:4
    d. I Peter 5:8
    e. Revelation 12:10
3. Jesus and the Pharisees discuss Beelzebul—another name for Satan—in Matthew 12:22-29. This word means ruler or prince of demons. Read other titles for the devil in John 14:30 and Ephesians 2:2. What do these descriptions tell us about the power Satan wields?
4. The devil's primary goal is to prevent humans from coming to know Christ as Savior. Next on his priority list is causing Christians to stumble in their walk with the Lord and in sharing the gospel with others. He started his evil schemes in the Garden of Eden when he attacked Eve. Read Genesis 3:1-7. How does Satan twist God's instructions in his efforts to get Eve to disobey?
5. In Matthew 4:1-11, how are the tactics Satan employed against Jesus similar to those he used in tempting Eve? How has Satan tried to throw you off course in the same way? How were you able to defeat him?
6. Mark 4:1-20 provides insight into other techniques our adversary uses. What do these verses reveal about how Satan attempts to achieve his objectives? Has he been successful in his attacks against you or others you know using these methods? What defenses can we use when he attacks in these ways?
7. Because Satan is limited in knowledge and cannot be present everywhere, he commands other fallen angels to carry out his dirty work. What does Psalm 106:35-39 suggest is one of the ways demons attack us? What present-day idols distract us from following God as He desires? How can we avoid giving in to this temptation?
8. According to I Timothy 4:1, what's another tactic of our demonic adversaries? How can you test various doctrines to determine what's true and what's false or deceitful?

Prayer Points

- Praise our almighty and eternal God that Jesus—through His death on the cross on our behalf—already has defeated Satan and his evil henchmen
- Thank God for revealing in scripture how the devil will attack us and for providing the means for us to overcome every temptation that comes our way
- Ask the Lord to help us recognize any attempts by satanic forces to get us to fall away from the paths He wants us to travel
- Commit to tapping into God's strength and wisdom immediately upon becoming aware of Satan's attacks so we won't give in to temptation

Personal Battle Plan

1. **Determine your view on Satan.** Is he a personal being or simply an evil force of some kind? How does scripture back your conclusion?
2. The devil's top priority is to blind people who are not followers of Christ to the good news that they can spend eternity with God through Jesus' sacrificial death on their behalf. **Reflect on your spiritual life.** Have you ever truly received Christ as your Savior? Are you sure you'll reside forever in heaven when your days on Earth end? If you haven't committed your life to Christ but would like to do so now, pray the prayer below. Then ask a more mature Christian for advice in how to grow in your faith.

Father, I acknowledge I've fallen short of being the person you want me to be, and my rebellion separates me from You. Jesus, thank You for taking on the penalty for my sin by dying on the cross for me. I now open my heart to You and receive You as my Savior. Lord, thank You for forgiving me and allowing me to become part of Your family. Holy Spirit, through the strength and wisdom you provide, help me to become more and more like Jesus in this life and to rejoice in the certainty that I'll spend eternity in heaven when my days on Earth end. In Jesus' name I pray. Amen.

3. Although the devil doesn't know everything, he has an excellent idea of where we're most vulnerable to his assaults. When he gets us to fall short of God's desires and expectations, he'll return to the scene of our defeat and tempt us again. **Review *where* Satan most often attacks you.**

	Never	Sometimes	Often	Always
a. At home				
b. At work				
c. At leisure				
d. At church				
e. In the car				

Ask God for His help in understanding Satan's attack history. Pray for the wisdom to discern quickly when Satan is trying to ambush you.

4. Satan's attacks may come more frequently in one or two locations than in others. He also knows the types of temptations most likely to defeat us. **Evaluate *how* the devil seeks to get you to turn away from God's desires.**

	Not a Problem	Sometimes Give in	Often Fall Short	Certain Defeat
a. Lust of the flesh: food, drink, sex, pornography, lethargy				

	Not a Problem	Sometimes Give in	Often Fall Short	Certain Defeat

- b. Lust of the eyes: greed, desire for money and possessions, cheating on taxes, envy, jealousy
- c. Boastful pride: position, power, prestige, status, acclaim, favor
- d. Affliction: pain, illness, emotional distress, worry, stress, sadness, isolation, guilt, persecution
- e. Spiritual attacks: lack of time devoted to spiritual pursuits

Circle the three specific areas in which you fail most often (for instance, food, greed, and guilt). Pray daily for God's wisdom in identifying each type of attack and for His strength to defeat it.

5. **Assess how Satan is attacking you in the spiritual dimension.**
   a. Getting you to dwell on your sin rather than confessing it and receiving God's forgiveness and cleansing.
   b. Distracting you from reading God's word and applying His truth in your life or creating doubt or confusion when you do spend time in scripture.
   c. Getting you to believe and act on spiritual doctrines inconsistent with the Bible.
   d. Convincing you God doesn't care about you or that He's unable to help you.
   e. Isolating you from God and other Christians.

f. Convincing you you're too busy with other priorities to spend time in spiritual pursuits.

   Ask God to help you to give Him first place in your life.
6. **Fortify yourself against future attacks.** Share your points of vulnerability with a trusted Christian friend, and ask for prayer for God's protection in these areas. Touch base with this person weekly to report your progress (successes and failures) and to provide specific areas of prayer for the coming week.
7. **Prepare for the next session** by considering how God helps followers of His Son to defeat Satan's attacks.

Engaging the Enemy: Operations on the Battlefield

Through the years, I've come across many devoted followers of our heavenly Commander who are well acquainted with the other members of God's army. They've received their commissions, understand their mission, and know the enemy.

Several of these believers try passionately to learn as many facts about following Christ as they can. If they were pursuing a secular education, they'd be close to earning a doctorate. While this is commendable, their efforts often lack one thing: They fail to carry the knowledge they accumulate onto the spiritual battlefield.

All who've received Christ as Savior are called to fight in God's forces. As we enter combat, our first stop is His arsenal, where ***we can draw from an array of weapons***. Protected by the armor of God, we're also blessed with spiritual vision that permits us to see the battlefield as God views it. We're empowered with the same divine strength Christ displayed during His time on Earth. In addition, the Holy Spirit issues each of us extraordinary gifts we can employ to accomplish our mission. Finally, God embeds into His soldiers the character of His Son so we can carry out our duties honorably. Armed with these weapons, we're ready for battle.

Before Jesus' arrest and subsequent crucifixion, He told His disciples the proof of their devotion would be what they achieved on His behalf.

"'He who abides in Me, and I in him, he bears much fruit,'" Christ explained. By bearing fruit in obedience to what Jesus called them to be and to do, they'd glorify His Father.[1]

Jesus also said His disciples' obedience would clearly demonstrate their love for Him.[2] He explained that those who believe in Him would do even greater works than He did.[3] If we truly love Jesus, we must be totally committed as we step into combat, employing the strategy He provides us to accomplish the orders He gives us.

During World War II, a cocky, young aviator from the Central Valley of California received his orders after completing flight training at Craig Army Airfield near Selma, Alabama. He was shipped to England, where he served at East Wretham Field in Norfolk, flying P-47 and P-51 fighter-escort missions when American bombers hit German targets on the continent. On one of his flights over enemy territory, Uncle Ray was shot down. He spent the next year in prisoner-of-war camps in Poland and Germany.

In Ray's later years, he was quick to share the knowledge he'd gained in his eight decades of life. Only one topic was off limits. No matter how hard we tried to learn details of his time as a prisoner, Ray was tight-lipped. He'd decided or had been instructed not to talk about his days as a POW. Perhaps he thought he might divulge top-secret information. Maybe he'd been so physically or emotionally abused that the memories haunted him for more than 50 years following his rescue. Whatever the reason, we learned very little about that year.

In our conversations, we discovered his confinement had laid the foundation for the driving philosophy of his life. On almost every occasion we spent with Ray, he reminded us of a speech Sir Winston Churchill gave at Harrow School in London on October 29, 1941. In those dark days of war, the Prime Minister instructed his audience, "Never give in, never give in, never, never, never, never—in nothing, great or small, large or petty—never give in except to convictions of honor and good sense."[4]

This is the total commitment we must possess if ***we're to fight and win our spiritual battles as soldiers in God's army***. Satan and his devious henchmen will do everything in their power to derail us from following our Commander. As spiritual war rages around us, we cannot, we must not give in. We must use the weapons God makes available to us to defeat Satan's attacks and to live a life that honors the Lord and helps others to draw closer to Him. Our orders call us to be missionaries and ambassadors, sent out by God to make a difference in the decaying world.

During my nearly 30 years in the Air Force, I often was asked what I did. "I'm a missionary," I replied. This always produced quizzical looks. How could a military officer be a missionary? I explained that as a Christian, my main job was to tell others about Jesus. I received orders to transfer from one base to another—throughout the United States and in Italy, England, and Korea—roughly every three years. Although an assignment officer in Texas was under the impression he was managing my career, I knew God was actually calling the shots, placing me at locations where I could best serve Him.

God's warriors are also ambassadors. When we were stationed in the United Kingdom in the mid-1980s, my wife and I were invited to attend an awards presentation at the home of the U.S. Ambassador. After being escorted on a short tour of the palatial buildings and beautiful gardens, we proceeded through a receiving line to be introduced to the ambassador. Not aware that the President often chose a major financial backer to fill such a prestigious role and in awe of the splendid surroundings, a lady in the line asked the high official, "How do you become an ambassador?"

The dictionary defines ambassador as an accredited diplomat sent by a state on a mission to a foreign country. In the same way, we represent the King of kings, sharing His positions on the issues of life with those in our homes, at work, and in our communities. Though His thoughts may at times be unpopular, we must be faithful to present His views precisely and passionately. And the most important message He's instructed us to convey is that there is salvation in no one other than His Son. Our orders require us to be "ambassadors for Christ, as though God were entreating through us; we beg you on behalf of Christ, be reconciled to God."[5]

Our training is complete. Our mission is clear. Now we must take up our weapons, receive our orders, and move out with passion as we step onto the battlefield.

CHAPTER 7

Drawing Our Weapons

If we fight the Lord's battles merely by duplicating the way the world does its work, we are like little boys playing with wooden swords pretending they are in the battle while their big brothers are away in some distant bloody land.

Francis Schaeffer[1]

OTHER THAN AN occasional trip to an Air Force firing range to maintain currency in shooting a pistol, the closest I ever came to actually using a weapon was during my assignment in the Republic of Korea. As I processed through various stations upon arriving at U.S. Army Garrison Yongsan, one of my stops was the armory. I was given a card to carry with me at all times. If we were ever attacked, I'd be directed to return to the building, show my card, and pick up my firearm. I never saw "my" weapon, but the soldier on duty assured me it would be there if needed.

With more than a million soldiers stationed across the border, North Korea posed a constant threat to U.S. and ROK forces. On my first visit to the Demilitarized Zone, we passed under a series of large bridges along the highway. My escort explained that in the event of an invasion, South Korean troops would detonate explosives positioned on the bridges to slow the enemy's advance into the Republic's capital.

For several weeks after the trip, this brought all kinds of disturbing visions to mind, usually in the middle of the night. I dreamed divisions of invaders would surge past the destroyed bridges and storm into Seoul. As I was serving in a desk job at the time, I pictured myself sitting at my computer armed with my pistol as a fierce North Korean soldier burst into my office. I hoped he'd allow me to log off and shut down the machine before opening fire.

Satan is a master of guerrilla warfare, and his attacks may come anytime, anywhere. If we know the weapons the Lord has issued to us, it's much less likely we'll be defeated when our evil foe catches us off guard. God's arsenal also contains the arms we'll need to take the initiative in reaching others for Christ. Whether we're defending ourselves when under attack or pressing the offensive against satanic forces, we must employ spiritual weapons to fight spiritual battles. "The weapons of our warfare are not of the flesh, but divinely powerful!"[2]

Shortly after David was anointed king over Israel, he assembled his military forces for their journey to Jerusalem. Day by day, fighting men enlisted "until there was a great army like the army of God." Some of David's troops were equipped with bows and arrows; others carried slings and stones, shields, and spears. Sons of Zebulun, Reuben, and Gad signed up to serve the king, bringing with them "all kinds of weapons of war." Not every soldier had a variety of weapons, but with the arms their leaders had distributed, the army was prepared to fight and win its battles. (See I Chronicles 12.)

When we receive Christ as Savior, one of our first stops in the transition from the forces of evil to the forces of good is the Lord's armory, where we're outfitted with weapons for defensive and offensive operations. God issues all of us some common weapons, and He also provides each of us unique armaments for the orders He'll give us.

Vision to See As God Sees
The Lord has blessed all His troops with the mind of Christ so we can detect the spiritual dimension of life, just as Jesus did 2,000 years ago.

Apostle Paul explains that before we're recruited into God's army, even the wisest people are unable to grasp the wisdom of God. We look at what God sees as foolishness and consider it great wisdom. When we become followers of Christ, the Holy Spirit reveals godly knowledge to us. What previously had been obscured now becomes crystal clear, all because God has blessed us with spiritual insight. (See I Corinthians 1-2.)

In Old Testament times, one man was singled out for his great wisdom. When Solomon assumed the throne following the death of his father—King David—God invited him to ask for whatever he wanted. Solomon didn't request a long life, great wealth, or victory over his enemies; he asked God to give him an understanding heart to judge the people of Israel and to discern between good and evil. Impressed with Solomon's humility, the Lord granted the new king wisdom and discernment superior to anyone who'd come before or after him. God also blessed Solomon with what he hadn't requested—riches and honor—so "'there will not be any among the kings like you all your days.'"[3]

Solomon displayed this godly wisdom in governing his people. In addition, the king wrote about wisdom in his book of Proverbs. He warned that fools despise wisdom and encouraged those who read his words to "make your ear attentive to wisdom, incline your heart to understanding."[4] Solomon explained the Lord is the source of wisdom, knowledge, and understanding for those who are upright and who walk in integrity.

The king went on to provide this instruction: "Trust in the LORD with all your heart, and do not lean on your own understanding. In all your ways acknowledge Him, and He will make your paths straight. Do not be wise in your own eyes."[5] Solomon mentions wisdom, knowledge, and understanding 150 times in Proverbs, an indication of how crucial it is for followers of Christ to plug into God's direction for our lives.

Just a few miles west of Colorado Springs are the foothills of the Rocky Mountains. All the hills look the same, but there's a huge difference between one and all the others. Cheyenne Mountain is hollow! Created as the home of the North American Aerospace Defense Command, buildings under the surface of the mountain house the nerve center for tracking everything flying across the continent.

Satellites transmit sensitive data to huge electronic displays that are monitored constantly by U.S. and Canadian analysts and high-ranking officers. Their job is to detect any possible risks to their nations. The displays provide a God's-eye view of air and space traffic that would be impossible to assemble without the wonders of modern technology.

Through the Holy Spirit, soldiers in the Lord's army have a God's-eye view of what's happening around us. From a vantage point alongside our Commander, we possess a heavenly rather than a worldly perspective.[6] We can see the theater of spiritual operations from above.

We see temptation for what it is: satanic trickery designed to defeat us on our spiritual journey. We understand what's motivating people's words and deeds, discerning what's of God and what isn't. We know instantly what we should say and do, although this doesn't ensure we'll always make the correct choice. All this is possible because God's nerve center within us is constantly collecting and reviewing data, and a senior officer—the Holy Spirit—is there to help us make the decisions required for our action and security.

Supernatural Power to Defeat Evil

In addition to observing and analyzing the situation around us from God's perspective, we can respond to what we see using the power of Christ. Again, the Holy Spirit is the source of this strength. Following Jesus' resurrection, He told His disciples they'd receive power when the Spirit came upon them, and with this power they'd be His witnesses to the remotest part of the Earth.[7]

These faithful followers of Christ did just that. Tradition tells us the disciples preached the gospel in Jerusalem, Judea, Palestine, Assyria, Babylon, Persia, Greece, Turkey, Armenia, Egypt, Ethiopia, and India.

All but one are believed to have died martyrs' deaths as they took the good news of Christ to people across three continents. And the same power displayed by Jesus' initial followers is available to 21st century Christians.

We often hear people today describing their quest for power. In most walks of life—politics, business, entertainment, sports, and many others—the very ambitious try to claw their ways to the top. Many employ honorable methods to obtain their goals, but a few resort to win-at-all-costs tactics to get ahead. I once worked for a colonel who told a group of young officers, "I've done everything possible to become a general, and now I'm so close I can taste it." Unfortunately, his superiors didn't agree. Whether his shortcomings were noble or questionable, his optimism proved to be unwarranted, and he never wore a star.

In the "foolishness" of God's wisdom, we derive spiritual power from an unlikely source: our weaknesses. The Lord made this clear to Apostle Paul, who asked for His help when under attack by a messenger of Satan. God responded, "'My grace is sufficient for you, for power is perfected in weakness.'" The apostle then set out to be content in difficulties of all kinds, "for when I am weak, then I am strong."[8]

When we recognize we're powerless to deal with a challenge and turn it over to the Lord, we discover we can do far more with the power He gives us than we could have done through our own puny, human strength. The power that created the universe is available to us upon request, and absolutely nothing is impossible for God.[9] As Paul tells us, we can do all things through the strength Jesus provides.[10]

Unique Skills to Do Extraordinary Things
When I was a child, a friend introduced me to the wonderful world of tiny army action figures. Unlike the modern version—toys almost as sophisticated as human soldiers—those I played with were dark-green, molded-plastic men wearing pot helmets. Troops measured about two inches tall, and a package contained 25 to 30 figures in around seven poses.

An officer carrying a pistol beckoned his troops to "Follow me!" A soldier in firing position supported a bazooka. One lying on the ground and another kneeling aimed rifles at their foes. A troop manned a machine gun, while still another hurled a hand grenade toward the enemy. The final member of the squad—the radioman—communicated the unit's position and needs to others in the battalion. We played with these soldiers for hours, fighting and winning wars in the jungles of the shrubbery in our front yards.

Each of these toy figures was armed with equipment that allowed him to help the unit achieve its mission. I never purchased a set of plastic soldiers in which every man was carrying a pistol. I never ran across a set in which everyone was an rifleman or a grenade thrower or a radioman. Similarly, individual followers of Christ have been blessed with different skills that complement those of other members of the unit. The Bible calls these the gifts of the Spirit.

The Holy Spirit bestows these special abilities upon all who've received Jesus as Savior.

- Some are blessed with gifts of service, encouragement, giving, leading, or showing mercy.[11]
- Others are armed with wisdom, knowledge, extraordinary faith, the ability to perform miracles, healing power, or the insight to distinguish spirits.[12]
- Some speak messages from God in indiscernible words or syllables, and others interpret these tongues.[13]
- Still others are evangelists, pastors, or teachers.[14]

No follower of Christ has received every spiritual gift, but none has been left without a gift. As we carry out our roles using our spiritual gifts, we all draw closer to the example Jesus set for us, and we help other Christians around us to do the same.

Apostle Paul explains our spiritual gifts are designed so we can serve and build up others in our unit. The goal in a collective sense is identical to the mission each of us is called to as an individual: "We are to grow up in all aspects into Him, who is the head, even Christ."[15] We all must use our spiritual gifts effectively and in harmony if we're to conform to the image of Christ.

One of the greatest challenges we face as Jesus' followers is identifying our gifts. Fortunately, God helps us in this process. First, He makes us aware that all Christians possess spiritual gifts and tells us what the various gifts are. (See Romans 12, I Corinthians 12, and Ephesians 4.)

As we pray that God would show us what gift or gifts He's given us, He'll answer either through direct inspiration or by revealing how He's blessed us as we serve Him in various ministry activities. He may also lead us through comments from other Christians. It may be helpful to tell a follower of Jesus who knows you well that you're eager to discover your spiritual gifts, and ask this trusted person for feedback.

Several Christian ministries have produced inventories—available as booklets or online—to help identify spiritual gifts. Although these questionnaires can't be taken as the final authority in understanding how the Lord has blessed you, the results provide good input for reflection, prayer, and discussion with spiritual mentors.

Armor to Protect Us in Combat

Knowing we have the mind and the power of Christ within us, and having identified our spiritual gifts, we have one more stop at God's armory to pick up some battle gear we'll need as we engage in spiritual warfare. Apostle Paul gives us a good rundown of this equipment.

> Put on the full armor of God, that you may be able to stand firm against the schemes of the devil. ... Take up the full armor of God, that you may be able to resist in the evil day, and having done

everything, to stand firm. Stand firm, therefore, having girded your loins with truth, and having put on the breastplate of righteousness, and having shod your feet with the preparation of the gospel of peace; in addition to all, taking up the shield of faith with which you will be able to extinguish all the flaming missiles of the evil one. And take the helmet of salvation, and the sword of the Spirit, which is the word of God.[16]

Some of this armor is discussed in the Old Testament. Rather than the children of God using the gear, though, it was the Lord Himself. Isaiah tells us God put on righteousness like a breastplate and a helmet of salvation on His head. Today the Lord allows us to employ some of the same armor He uses in the war against evil.[17]

Paul reminds us of the effectiveness of God's equipment. "For the weapons of our warfare are not of the flesh, but divinely powerful for the destruction of fortresses. We are destroying speculations and every lofty thing raised up against the knowledge of God, and we are taking every thought captive to the obedience of Christ."[18] Let's take a look at each of the elements of this powerful armor.

God's truth protects our minds from Satan's attacks. Jesus tells us He is truth,[19] and the Father's word is truth.[20] Just as Jesus used the truth to defeat the father of lies as Satan tempted Him in the wilderness, we must know and employ scripture as our ancient foe seeks to prevent us from conforming to the image of Christ and representing Him among others. The better we know the truth found in God's word, the more likely we'll be to overcome Satan's deceit.

The breastplate of righteousness protects our hearts from Satan's attacks. We're righteous not because we've been able to "clean up our acts" after receiving Jesus as Savior. God looks upon us as righteous because we've placed our faith in His Son.[21] To conform to the image of Christ, we must tap into the power of the Holy Spirit so we can do what is right. Only through a consistent lifestyle as outlined in scripture will we gain an audience when we speak on Jesus' behalf. To paraphrase Paul, we can do all ***right*** things through Christ, Who strengthens us.[22]

The footgear of the preparation of the gospel protects us when Satan tries to keep us from proclaiming God's love. Jesus devoted Himself to helping people draw into a personal relationship with His Father. If we're to conform to His image, we must share the good news of Christ with others. As Paul told the Corinthians, Jesus died for our sins, was buried, and rose again.[23] The apostle's message to the Romans was we can be saved only by confessing Jesus as Lord and believing God raised Him from the dead.[24]

As Peter testified during his trial before Jewish authorities, "'There is salvation in no one else; for there is no other name under heaven that has been given among men, by which we must be saved.'"[25] We take this powerful message into the world knowing it's God's truth.

The shield of faith protects us when Satan's attacks take the form of persecution, temptation, or other adversity. Paul tells us faith comes through hearing, and hearing by the word of Christ.[26] Initially, our faith leads us to receive Christ as Savior. Later, we conform to His image as we step out in faith in every challenge that comes our way. We can trust fully in God regardless of how fiercely the devil tries to defeat us.

The helmet of salvation provides additional protection for our minds when Satan attacks us with seeds of doubt. Our enemy often tries to convince us God is either unconcerned about us or not powerful enough to come to our aid. Satan also wants us to believe we're not good enough to be members of God's family. From the moment we receive Christ and begin to become more like Him, we're assured we'll spend eternity with the Lord.[27] We can be confident that as we take on the challenges of our lives on Earth, we'll be victorious. Although Satan is a powerful enemy, he can't rob us of our place in the kingdom of God.

The sword of the Spirit, which is the word of God, allows us to take the initiative in our battle against Satan. While the other elements of God's armor serve primarily as protection, God's word can be used to defend ourselves as well as to take the offensive. It's living and active, sharper than a sword, and able to judge the thoughts and intentions of the heart.[28]

Despite Satan's attempts to deceive us, we can weigh our thoughts, words, and deeds against the Lord's manual for life to determine whether they're of God or of the devil. If we find our adversary is motivating what we're thinking, saying, or doing, we can quickly tap into God's power and wisdom to get back on track.[29]

Do you see a thread that seems to hold together this suit of spiritual armor? Here's a hint: God's word is truth. Righteousness is our conformity to the standards set out in God's word. The gospel is a very focused portion of God's word. Faith comes by hearing God's word. Salvation is our response to God's word. If you said the thread is God's word, you're correct! As we hear, read, study, meditate on, and memorize the word of God, He'll mold us into the likeness of His Son.

In the early days of my walk with the Lord, I was encouraged to pray each morning as I was "putting on" the armor. I began by saying, "Lord, I now gird my loins with truth," and I continued this pattern until I was fully dressed and ready for battle. This suggests that the prior evening, I carefully removed the armor and propped it up in the corner, ready for the next morning.

This would be fine if spiritual warfare occurred only during our waking hours, but we can be attacked around the clock. Satan doesn't rest in attempting to rob us of joy, sow seeds of doubt, and render us ineffective. Just as he strikes during the day, he also attacks us with worry, discouragement, disillusionment, and a host of other negative thoughts—consciously or subconsciously—as we lay in bed. We need to wear God's armor 24 hours a day. Although this may feel a bit uncomfortable in bed, we need the Lord's strength and protection at all times!

How effective is this armor? A modern chorus reminds us we're invincible when we gird our loins with truth, put on the breastplate of righteousness, cover our feet with the preparation of the gospel, take up the shield of faith, don the helmet of salvation, and grasp the sword of the Spirit.

> In heavenly armor we'll enter the land; the battle belongs to the Lord!
> No weapon that's fashioned against us shall stand; the battle belongs to the Lord!
> And we sing glory, honor, power, and strength to the Lord.
> And we sing glory, honor, power, and strength to the Lord.
>
> When the power of darkness comes in like a flood, the battle belongs to the Lord!
> He's raised up a standard, the power of His blood; the battle belongs to the Lord!
> And we sing glory, honor, power, and strength to the Lord.
> And we sing glory, honor, power, and strength to the Lord.[30]

Character to Take the High Ground

As we gather together our spiritual weapons—the mind of Christ, the power of Christ, the gifts of the Spirit, and the armor of God—we're equipped to engage in battle. Before we enter the fight, though, we must understand the code God will use to judge our actions. Unlike armies that savagely kill beyond strategic necessity, humiliate their captured enemies, and destroy cultural and religious landmarks, we must conduct ourselves according to the high standards the Lord has given us.

During my Academy days, upper-class cadets demanded the doolies correctly repeat material they'd memorized while at the same time undergoing intense physical and mental pressure. This, we were told, would help us to develop the toughness required to fly dangerous combat missions over hostile territory. As the Vietnam conflict dragged on, it seemed at least some of us might one day be placed in such a situation.

One of the items we recited was called *The American Fighting Man's Code of Conduct*. Modified slightly over the years, perhaps because women now serve in battle zones around the globe, the code now includes these provisions:

> *Article I:* I am an American fighting in the forces which guard my country and our way of life. I am prepared to give my life in their defense.
>
> *Article II:* I will never surrender of my own free will. If in command, I will never surrender the members of my command while they still have the means to resist.
>
> *Article III:* If I am captured, I will continue to resist by all means available. I will make every effort to escape and aid others to escape. I will accept neither parole nor special favors from the enemy.
>
> *Article IV:* If I become a prisoner of war, I will keep faith with my fellow prisoners. I will give no information nor take part in any action which might be harmful to my comrades. If I am senior, I will take command. If not, I will obey the lawful orders of those appointed over me and will back them up in every way.
>
> *Article V:* When questioned, should I become a prisoner of war, I am required to give name, rank, service number, and date of birth. I will evade answering further questions to the utmost of my ability. I will make no oral or written statements disloyal to my country and its allies or harmful to their cause.

Article VI: I will never forget that I am an American, fighting for freedom, responsible for my actions, and dedicated to the principles which made my country free. I will trust in my God and the United States of America.[31]

As troops serving in combat adhere to a code of conduct, Christians should live within certain guidelines as we engage in spiritual warfare. If we try to accomplish our mission in unethical or unprofessional ways, we'd be nothing more than mercenaries. The end would justify the means, no matter how disgusting God might find our actions. We'd hardly conform to the image of Christ.

Fortunately, God has provided us a code of conduct and also the means to comply with it. Not only does the Holy Spirit enable us to tap into the mind and the power of Christ, He also allows us to exhibit the character of Christ. Paul's letter to the Galatians explains how this is possible.

Before we receive Christ as Savior, we're motivated to fulfill our own desires. We seek immediate gratification, physically and emotionally. Apostle Paul says these worldly passions consume us and lead to immorality, impurity, sensuality, idolatry, sorcery, strife, jealousy, anger, disputes, dissension, envy, drunkenness, and carousing.[32]

These traits are common to what Paul calls the old self—what we were before becoming Christians. He encouraged the Ephesians to lay aside this former conduct and to put on the new self, which in the likeness of God has been created in righteousness and holiness.[33] This new self is to be marked by nine qualities that reveal a code of conduct dramatically different from our previous lifestyle. Paul says those who belong to Christ will bear the fruit of the Spirit: love, joy, peace, patience, kindness, goodness, faithfulness, gentleness, and self-control.[34] These traits are identical to the character displayed by Christ during His time on Earth.

We see instructions on these qualities dotted throughout the New Testament. We're told to:

- ***Love*** one another as Jesus loves us.[35]
- Find ***joy*** even in times of trial.[36]
- Pursue ***peace***.[37]
- Move forward with ***patience*** in our walk with Christ.[38]
- Put on a heart of ***kindness***.[39]
- Act with moral excellence, a synonym of ***goodness***.[40]
- Walk (or live) by ***faith***.[41]
- Pursue ***gentleness***.[42]
- Temper our knowledge by ***self-control***.[43]

Practicing these traits isn't just difficult; it's impossible apart from the supernatural work of God's Holy Spirit, Who produces the character of Christ in us. In essence, we're able to comply with these instructions by allowing the Spirit to ***be*** these qualities in us. In other words, we don't have to try our hardest to love others, to be filled with joy, to be at peace, and so on. The Holy Spirit will be love, joy, peace, and these other qualities within us as we permit Him to take control, at the same time yielding our human desire to do it all ourselves.

How does this work in practice? Like so many other aspects of our Christian experience, we must pray passionately that the fruit of the Spirit will develop in us and be evident in all our relationships with others. Just as apples, oranges, and bananas don't emerge in their final forms instantly, the fruit of the Spirit may develop slowly. As we allow the Spirit to be our love, our joy, our peace, and the other elements of spiritual fruit, these traits will become more consistent in our lives. Our conduct will reflect the character of Christ.

In addition to these nine qualities, we must allow God to fashion one more characteristic within us: humility. Apostle Paul instructs us to be humble, regarding others more important than ourselves and looking out for their interests, not just our own.[44] He then suggests Jesus is the perfect example for us.

Despite the facts that Christ is God, that He created the world and everything in it, and that He now rules the universe, Jesus lived His earthly life as a humble servant. Paul encourages us with these words:

> Have this attitude in yourselves which was also in Christ Jesus, Who, although He existed in the form of God, did not regard equality with God a thing to be grasped, but emptied Himself, taking the form of a bond-servant, and being made in the likeness of men. And being found in appearance as a man, He humbled Himself by becoming obedient to the point of death, even death on a cross.[45]

Because humility is relatively rare, we instantly recognize people who demonstrate it. Mother Teresa was revered for her humanitarian service to the poorest of the poor, but she downplayed the admiration. "It's [God's] work. I'm like a little pencil in His hand. That's all." She added, "I think God wants to show His greatness by using [our] nothingness."[46]

Napoleon Bonaparte isn't someone we immediately think of as a humble person. Despite his prominence as an outstanding military and political leader, he acknowledged he wasn't the greatest man who'd lived on this planet. Napoleon concluded the most notable person ever was Christ. "I marvel that whereas the ambitious dreams of myself, Caesar, and Alexander should have vanished into thin air, a Judean peasant—Jesus—should be able to stretch His hands across the centuries and control the destinies of men and nations," said the emperor.[47]

Mother Teresa and Napoleon, and many others who've been viewed with great respect through the centuries, recognized their achievements weren't to be measured by comparison to mere mortals. They set the standard for self-assessment not by what those around them did but by how their lives stacked up when compared to the life of Christ. Warriors in God's army must adopt this same humble attitude as we carry out our duties. In the words of Prophet Micah, the Lord requires that we do justice, love kindness, and walk humbly with our God.[48]

Jesus wanted His disciples to understand the need for humility as He rebuked them when James and John asked to be elevated above the other 10 in heaven. "'Whoever wishes to become great among you shall be your servant; and whoever wishes to be first among you shall be slave of all. For even the Son of Man did not come to be served, but to serve, and to give His life a ransom for many.'"[49]

Much like the fruit of the Spirit, humility isn't something we can cultivate within ourselves. We must allow God to form this quality in us, and He does this in the same way as with the other character qualities of Christ. As we permit the Holy Spirit to destroy the pride, arrogance, and self-centeredness we've developed over the years, He'll replace these negative traits with a deep humility. He'll channel our thoughts so that rather than comparing ourselves to others and discovering aspects in which we're superior, we'll compare ourselves with Christ and see we can never approach His perfection. It becomes a bit easier to consider others more important than ourselves when we realize we fall far short of the example Jesus set for us.

Armed with the mind and power of Christ, gifts of the Spirit, and armor of God—and wielding them with the character of Christ—we step into conflict. All God's warriors are called to engage in a lifelong battle to become more like Christ and to help others do the same. We take on the forces of evil with the certainty that the Lord enables His army to fight and win.

Lessons Learned

- Among the weapons the Holy Spirit provides to warriors in God's army is the mind of Christ—the ability to see everything around us from the Father's perspective.
- We also are blessed with the power of Christ, supernatural strength required to accomplish all God asks us to do.
- The gifts of the Spirit are unique and extraordinary skills, and God gives one or more to each Christian. Using these gifts as we work with others in our unit, we're capable of winning the battles we fight with Satan and his forces.
- God's armor protects us when our adversary attacks and also allows us to take the initiative in sharing the good news of Christ with others.
- The Holy Spirit also develops the character of Christ—the fruit of the Spirit—within us so our service in accomplishing the orders God has given us is honorable and above reproach.
- In addition to the Spirit's fruit, the code of conduct for members of God's army requires us to serve with the humility of Christ as we carry out our duties.

Unit Analysis

To download Unit Analysis and Personal Battle Plan material, please go to www.forwardintobattle.com.

As we learn to employ the weapons at our disposal—the mind of Christ, the power of Christ, the gifts of the Spirit, and the armor of God—with the character of Christ, we'll sense Jesus working through us to defeat the forces of evil. As He enables us to conform to His image, He'll also help us to assist others to become like Him. We know Christ has won the ultimate battle over Satan through His death on the cross and glorious resurrection. We know, too, He's coming again, and His victory will be visible for all to see. Until His return, though, He's directed us to overwhelm the forces of darkness that seek to destroy His reputation and lead people into an eternity apart from God. Sounds like Mission: Impossible, but we can do all things through Christ, Who strengthens us!

1. Take a look at James 1:5. Think about a challenge in which you tried valiantly—but unsuccessfully—to determine the best course of action. Share about the situation and how your human wisdom was insufficient to resolve it. Now tell how you were able to overcome your problem as you prayed for God's wisdom and direction.
2. Read I Corinthians 1:18-25. In your time as a follower of Christ, what spiritual truths has God revealed to you that people who aren't Christians would consider foolish? What conventional wisdom is nonsense when viewed from a spiritual perspective?
3. Discuss the methods you've seen people use to become more powerful in their jobs. How do people who've obtained power in worldly pursuits use it? According to Psalm 62:11, what's the real source of power? Read Acts 1:8. How have you tapped into the Holy Spirit's power to live a life that is pleasing to God? How has the Spirit strengthened you in your quest to become like Christ and to share His love with others?
4. The gifts of the Spirit mentioned in Romans 12, I Corinthians 12, and Ephesians 4 are listed following the Personal Battle Plan. Review the definitions, and share among group members which gifts you've observed in one another.
5. According to Ephesians 4:12-16, why has God bestowed spiritual gifts on His children? How should we use these attributes?
6. How do the following weapons from Ephesians 6:10-17 enable you to carry out the mission God has given you? What do verses 18-20 reveal about the importance of prayer as we engage in our spiritual responsibilities?

    a. Truth:
    b. Righteousness:
    c. Preparation of the gospel:
    d. Faith:
    e. Salvation:
    f. Word of God:

7. The nine qualities outlined in Galatians 5:22-23 are identical to many of the character traits of Christ. We can take comfort in knowing it's not up to us to produce these qualities in ourselves through hard work or human wisdom. The Holy Spirit produces these elements of fruit in us. What's our responsibility if we're to see them grow and flourish?

8. How is the humility of Christ revealed in Philippians 2:1-11? How can we demonstrate the same humility in our Christian walks?

9. In Luke 10, we read that Jesus sent out 70 followers to minister in His name. When they returned following a fruitful mission, He rejoiced at their accomplishments. Read verses 17-20. What encouragement do you feel as you see how the Lord used these faithful warriors?

Prayer Points

- Praise our wise and all-powerful God that He's provided us the wisdom and the power of Christ through the Holy Spirit Who dwells within us
- Thank God for blessing every follower of His Son with at least one spiritual gift that we may use in His service and for the protection we receive through His armor
- Ask God to reveal the spiritual gift or gifts He's given you and for the strength to use it or them to touch the lives of family, friends, business associates, neighbors, and others
- Commit to allowing the Holy Spirit to produce in you the character traits Jesus exhibited during His days on Earth

Personal Battle Plan

1. In order for us to grasp what's happening around us with the mind of Christ, we must eliminate from our thinking everything that is not of God. **List the thoughts that run through your mind regularly that are not pleasing to the Lord.** Confess these distractions, and ask God to help you to "take every thought captive to the obedience of Christ." (II Corinthians 10:5) As you move forward in your walk with the Lord, be aware of evil thoughts Satan puts into your mind, confess them immediately, and thank God for giving you the ability to rid your mind of unworthy thinking.
2. Philippians 4:8 instructs us to let our minds dwell on all that is true, honorable, right, pure, lovely, good, excellent, and praiseworthy. **Jot down a few spiritual elements that fit into this description** (i.e.: God's love, compassion, forgiveness, faithfulness, strength; our salvation and eternal life in Christ). Ask God to help you recall these blessings immediately when Satan throws evil distractions at you, and ponder them often throughout the day even when our adversary is not on the attack.
3. Consider the major challenges you've faced over the past several months. **Honestly assess the point at which you turned to God for help.** You'll probably discover you often requested His assistance only after you'd failed repeatedly to resolve these situations relying on your own strength and common sense. Praise God that His power is available to you whenever you need it, and begin to tap into it as soon as a problem develops—not after it's become a disaster.
4. Review the definitions of the gifts of the Spirit on the following pages. **Prayerfully determine which of these gifts you believe God has imparted to you and list them.** Arrange to meet with a Christian you respect, inform him or her of your assessment, and ask for feedback on your analysis. Ask your trusted friend to join you in praying

that God will continue to help you appreciate the gifts He's blessed you with and that He'll help you to use them to His glory.
5. **Describe in practical terms how you will use God's armor to defeat Satan's attacks** in each of the following areas. For instance, when he seeks to deceive you, you can turn to God's truth as revealed in scripture to dispel any false ideas.
   a. God's truth to protect your mind:
   b. The breastplate of righteousness to help you not to do wrong:
   c. The footgear of the gospel to help you in proclaiming the good news:
   d. The shield of faith to carry you through hard times as you fully trust in God's help:
   e. The helmet of salvation to defeat the seeds of doubt Satan sows:
6. The sword of the Spirit—the word of God—can be used as an offensive weapon. In other words, we can take the initiative to employ scripture in helping others draw nearer to the Lord. God regularly brings us into contact with people who have physical, emotional, and spiritual needs. Unfortunately, we often try to help them based on our own home remedies, or we fail to pick up on their concerns. Think back over the past month and jot down the names of people who've mentioned they've fallen on tough times. **Prayerfully commit to seeking them out and sharing God's love and His word with them**. As they see your concern and come to trust you, your support may well lead to an opportunity to share the gospel with them. In the future, ask God to enable you to recognize people needing help He brings your way, and tap into His power and wisdom to come to their aid on the spot.
7. The fruit of the Spirit isn't produced by our hard work. It grows in us as we allow the Father to conform us to the image of His Son and as we turn ourselves over to His care. **Assess how well your words and deeds reflect these character traits of Christ** in your

daily relationships. If you determine others seldom witness some of these qualities in you, ask God to allow the Spirit to cultivate His fruit in you.

	Never Noticeable	Sometimes Seen	Often On View	Constantly Conspicuous

- a. Love
- b. Joy
- c. Peace
- d. Patience
- e. Kindness
- f. Goodness
- g. Faithfulness
- h. Gentleness
- i. Self-control

8. **Prepare for the next session** by assessing how passionate you are in carrying out your duties for the Lord. Are you laboring in earnest in the midst of the violent spiritual war that surrounds us?

Spiritual Gifts[50]

Romans 12

- **Service**: ability to identify the unmet needs involved in a task related to God's work and to use available resources to meet those needs and help accomplish the desired results (v. 7)
- **Exhortation**: ability to minister words of comfort, consolation, encouragement, and counsel to other Christians so they feel helped and healed (v. 8)
- **Generosity** (giving): ability to contribute material resources to the work of the Lord abundantly and cheerfully (v. 8)
- **Leadership**: ability to set goals in accordance with God's purpose for the future and to communicate these goals to others so they voluntarily work together to accomplish the goals for the glory of God (v. 8)
- **Mercy**: ability to feel genuine understanding and compassion for others (Christians and non-Christians) who suffer distressing physical, mental, or emotional problems, and to cheerfully carry out deeds that reflect Christ's love and ease the suffering (v. 8)

I Corinthians 12

- **Wisdom**: ability to apply spiritual truth to an issue in a specifically relevant fashion and to make proper choices in difficult situations (v. 8)
- **Knowledge**: ability to discover, accumulate, analyze, and clarify information and ideas that are important in the well-being of God's people (v. 8)
- **Faith**: ability to discern with extraordinary confidence the will and purposes of God for His work and to act on this knowledge (v. 9)

- **Healing**: ability to serve as human intermediaries God uses to heal other people's physical or emotional needs (vv. 9, 28)
- **Miracles**: ability to serve as human intermediaries God uses to perform powerful acts that are seen by observers to have altered the ordinary course of nature (vv. 10, 28)
- **Discerning of spirits**: ability to know with assurance whether certain behavior said to be of God is in reality divine, human, or satanic (v. 10)
- **Tongues**: ability to speak a divinely anointed message in a language one has never learned but that's known to hearers (vv. 10, 28)
- **Interpretation of tongues**: ability to make known the message of one who speaks in tongues (vv. 10, 30)
- **Helps**: ability to invest one's talents in the life and ministry of other Christians, often in very practical ways, thus enabling them to increase the effectiveness of their own spiritual gifts (v. 28)
- **Administration**: ability to understand clearly the immediate and long-range goals of a particular group of Christians and to develop and execute effective plans to accomplish those goals (v. 28)

Ephesians 4

- **Apostle**: ability to assume and exercise general leadership over a number of churches with an extraordinary authority in spiritual matters that is spontaneously recognized and appreciated by those churches; this isn't the same as the apostles who established the early church (v. 11; I Corinthians 12:28)
- **Prophet**: ability to proclaim the word of God with divine anointing, which brings conviction to the hearers so they recognize it's truly the word of God and they must do something about it (v. 11; Romans 12:6; I Corinthians 12:10, 28)

- **Evangelist**: ability to share the gospel with people who aren't Christians so they become followers of Jesus, to a degree much greater than what's expected of the average follower of Christ (v. 11)
- **Pastor**: ability to take long-term, personal responsibility for the spiritual welfare of a group of Christians, moving them to a deeper spiritual connection and maturity with Christ (v. 11)
- **Teacher**: ability to communicate information relevant to the health and ministry of the church and its members in a clear and concise way so they will learn (v. 11; Romans 12:7; I Corinthians 12:28)

Other Passages

- **Celibacy**: ability to remain unmarried and not suffer undue sexual temptations (I Corinthians 7:7)
- **Voluntary poverty**: ability to lay aside material comfort and luxury and adopt a personal lifestyle equivalent to those living at the poverty level in order to serve God more effectively (I Corinthians 13:3)
- **Martyrdom**: ability to choose to suffer or die rather than give up one's faith (I Corinthians 13:3)
- **Hospitality**: ability to provide an open house and a warm welcome to those in need of food and lodging (I Peter 4:9-11)
- **Missionary**: ability to minister through spiritual gifts in a second culture (Romans 10:15; Ephesians 3:1-9)
- **Intercession**: ability to pray for extended periods on a regular basis and see frequent and specific answers to prayer, to a degree much greater than what is expected of the average follower of Christ (James 5:16)

CHAPTER 8

Fighting and Winning

It is not the critic who counts; not the man who points out how the strong man stumbles, or where the doer of deeds could have done them better. The credit belongs to the man who is actually in the arena, whose face is marred by dust and sweat and blood; who strives valiantly; who errs, who comes short again and again, because there is no effort without error and shortcoming; but who does actually strive to do the deeds; who knows the great enthusiasms, the great devotions; who spends himself in a worthy cause; who at the best knows in the end the triumph of high achievement, and who at the worst, if he fails, at least fails while daring greatly, so that his place shall never be with those cold and timid souls who neither know victory nor defeat.

Teddy Roosevelt[1]

MY ACADEMY GRADUATION ceremony is a total blur. I remember the morning in early June was cloudless and sunny. I also recall the Air Force Thunderbirds roaring overhead as the event ended—a tradition that delighted the cadets, family members, and friends who packed the football stadium. Within a couple of years, I'd forgotten who the keynote speaker had been, and I couldn't recall the wisdom he shared with the class of 1972.

Back at the dormitory after the ceremony, 750 Corvettes, Camaros, Firebirds, and other sporty cars were lined up as if awaiting the start of the Indianapolis 500. Each was packed with everything its owner had accumulated during his residence at the Academy.

Many of the new lieutenants were headed to Arizona, Alabama, Mississippi, or Texas to begin a challenging year of training that would lead to their pilots' wings. Others would drive to California, where they'd start the program through which they'd become navigators in bombers, transports, and refuelers. Still others were bound for bases throughout the U.S. and around the world to serve as support officers.

A few of the lucky graduates—I was one of them—had a couple of months of leave before reporting to our initial assignments. Regardless of our final destinations, all of us departed the Academy with several copies of our assignment orders. These documents sent us into active duty in the service of our nation. We were entering the operational world we'd dreamed about for the past 1,447 days.

Not all those commissioned for service in God's army have responded with the enthusiasm of these second lieutenants. Some have received their orders with excitement and taken action immediately. Others have reflected on their limitations rather than God's strength and have bartered with the Lord in an effort to get out of the assignment.

Noah: Responsiveness

God's orders for Noah came with an explanation of why He'd decided to call this righteous man into action. "'The end of all flesh has come before Me; for the earth is filled with violence because of them; and behold, I am about to destroy them with the earth.'" This certainly wasn't a happy scene. The Lord then issued Noah's orders: He was to build an ark. History's first navy was about to be launched.

Having never built an ark, Noah was in the dark as to how to proceed, so God gave him very specific instructions. He also told Noah what to do when the ark was completed. He was to load two of every kind of living thing onto the ship. That sounds like a pretty tall order, but Noah didn't hesitate. "According to all that God commanded him, so he did." Noah reacted to the Lord's orders with responsiveness. Prior to, during, and following God's sending rain upon the planet, He continued to make requests of Noah, and he continued to obey His commands. And all this occurred when Admiral Noah was 600 years old![2]

Abram: Resolve

The Lord issued Abram's orders when he was considerably younger—75 years old. In a very matter-of-fact three verses, we see God directing Abram to go forth from his country and his family to a land He would show him. The Lord added some incentive. He said He'd make Abram's descendants a great nation, and He'd bless all the families of the Earth through him. Abram's reaction: With great resolve, he went forth just as the Lord had spoken to him.[3]

Abram must have been tempted to stay in Haran. His father had moved the family all the way from Ur to its new home 600 miles up the Euphrates River. But when God called Abram to head to Canaan, he obeyed immediately. Abram's great resolve in carrying out God's permanent-change-of-station orders and further commands was rewarded in the inheritance the Lord had promised: His spiritual descendants have become as innumerable as the stars in heaven.[4]

Moses: Reluctance

Moses was reluctant when he received God's orders. The Lord directed him to confront the most powerful ruler of the day—the mighty Pharaoh—and announce that a couple million Hebrew slaves would soon depart Egypt. The excuses began immediately. "'Who am I, that I should go to Pharaoh, and that I should bring the sons of Israel out of Egypt?'"

What do I tell the Israelites if they ask me Your name? What if they don't believe me? I'm not eloquent. I'm not very good at public speaking. Can't you find someone else to take this message to Pharaoh? Though the Lord was angry at Moses, He gave him power, issued several more orders, and sent him on his way.[5]

Probably still grumbling under his breath, Moses set out and, probably much to his own surprise, accomplished all the Lord had ordered him to do. In the process, God stripped Moses of his fear and molded him into a prophet unlike any other, a man "whom the LORD knew face to face, for all the signs and wonders which the LORD sent him to perform in the land of Egypt against Pharaoh, all his servants, and all his land, and for all the mighty power and for all the great terror which Moses performed in the sight of all Israel."[6]

Joshua: Relentlessness

As Moses handed over leadership to Joshua, the Lord told the general what would be required of him. His orders were to cross the Jordan River and to occupy the land with which God would bless the Israelites. The Lord promised to give this vast territory into Joshua's hands, encouraging him to be strong and courageous because He'd be with His people and would not fail them.[7]

Following this pep talk, Joshua began a relentless pursuit of what the Lord had ordered him to do. Courageously, he led the Israelites through great military battles to the Promised Land, where Joshua and his people founded their nation in the region God carved out. The leader's relentlessness was evident right up to his final address to the Israelites, when he forcefully proclaimed, "'Choose for yourselves today whom you will serve: whether the gods which your fathers served which were beyond the River, or the gods of the Amorites in whose land you are living; but as for me and my house, we will serve the LORD.'"[8]

Isaiah: Readiness

After a tour of the splendor of heaven—including a glimpse of the Lord seated on His throne—Isaiah couldn't wait to receive his orders. In fact, in the midst of his heavenly vision, he heard God ask whom He could send on a special mission, and Isaiah responded in enthusiastic readiness, "'Here I am. Send me!'"[9] His excitement was much like a substitute sitting on the bench longing to play in the championship game. The player's subconscious pleas grow more passionate as the game progresses: "Put me in, coach; put me in!"

Athletes waiting to enter a game know exactly what to expect. They've practiced their roles and executed them in previous contests. Isaiah, however, had no idea what the Lord wanted. Only after the prophet expressed his readiness did God give him his orders: Isaiah was to tell the disobedient children of Israel they were in for some serious punishment. Fortunately, he was given further orders to make a much more positive announcement. God told him to inform King Ahaz of the coming of Christ.[10]

Jesus' Disciples: Reverence

Jesus issued several orders for His disciples during His few years with them. For Simon and Andrew, and possibly for James and John, the initial instructions were very simple: "'Follow Me, and I will make you fishers of men.'"[11] Jesus told the fishermen their first duty was to attend basic training, observing His ministry and absorbing His teaching. Only then would they be ready to "fish" for others. Christ chose 12 men to be with Him so He could prepare them to go out to preach and to cast out demons.[12]

Simon, Andrew, James, and John immediately left behind the tools of their trade and followed Jesus. Philip followed Christ without delay, and he recruited Nathanael to join the group. At first skeptical, a brief conversation with Jesus quickly convinced Nathanael that He was worthy of being followed. In reverence, Nathanael verbalized what the others must have been thinking: "'You are the Son of God; You are the King of Israel.'"[13]

Following their initial boot camp (or was it sandal camp?), Christ issued new orders. The disciples were to go to the lost sheep of Israel preaching, healing the sick, raising the dead, cleansing lepers, and casting out demons.

Aware that this might have seemed an impossible challenge to the dozen mere mortals, Jesus explained the true source of their ability to accomplish His orders. He told them not to be anxious about what they'd say because God's Holy Spirit would speak through them. Recognizing they'd been dispatched with the authority of the Son of God and armed with weapons from the arsenal of the Holy Spirit, the disciples traveled to the surrounding villages, preaching the gospel, casting out demons, and healing everywhere.[14]

Eleven of the disciples met Jesus on the Mount of Olives to receive His final set of orders after He'd been crucified, buried, and raised from the dead. Still fearful—they'd abandoned Him in the Garden of Gethsemane when armed men arrived to arrest Jesus—they regained courage when Christ called on His authority as the Son of God to announce their orders: "'Go therefore and make disciples of all nations, baptizing them in the name of the Father and the Son and the Holy Spirit, teaching them to observe all that I commanded you; and lo, I am with you always, even to the end of the age.'"[15]

With great reverence, knowing they wouldn't see Jesus again until they arrived in heaven, the disciples did go, did make disciples, did baptize, and did teach. Tradition tells us Andrew went to Scythia (the region of modern-day Iran, Armenia, and Azerbaijan), Greece, and Asia Minor (Turkey). Nathanael (also known as Bartholomew) was a missionary in Armenia. James, the brother of John, stayed closer to home, preaching in Jerusalem and Judea. James, the son of Alphaeus, served in Palestine and Egypt. John—the only disciple to escape a martyr's death—preached in Asia Minor and was exiled to the Isle of Patmos.

Jude, or Thaddaeus, ministered in Assyria and Persia. Matthew followed the Lord's call to Ethiopia. Peter ventured as far as Babylon. Philip is said to have served in Phrygia—a large province in what is now Turkey. Although we're not sure where Simon the Zealot traveled in his ministry, he's believed to have died a martyr. Finally, Thomas, after spending time in Persia, was a missionary to India.

Rich, Young Ruler: Regret and Rejection

Jesus once was approached by a rich, young ruler. Having assured Christ he'd consistently obeyed the Lord's commandments, the man asked Him for his orders. "'Go and sell your possessions and give to the poor, and you shall have treasure in heaven; and come, follow Me.'" Because the man's wealth was his consuming passion, he met Jesus' invitation with regret and, ultimately, rejected the offer.[16]

Imagine that! Jesus' invitation to this young ruler was identical to His words to Simon, Andrew, Philip, and Matthew: "Follow Me." Although these four and many others had walked away immediately from all they possessed to become a part of the Lord's army, this prospective soldier turned his back on the opportunity of a lifetime—the opportunity of an eternal lifetime!

Sadly, this scene has been repeated millions of times since then. When faced with sacrificing the fleeting pleasures of the world to enjoy God's bountiful riches for eternity, many turn down Jesus' orders to receive Him, follow Him, and serve Him. Choosing instead the instant satisfaction offered by enemy commander Satan, these people forfeit joy that will last forever and often experience a less-than-fulfilling existence throughout their days on Earth.

Saul: Restlessness

Saul—who was later known as Paul—was very close to making the same mistake as the rich, young ruler. He delighted in his brutal persecution of new

Christians. When Jesus confronted Saul on the road to Damascus, His initial orders were quite simple. Saul's speechless companions were to lead their sightless leader into the city, where he'd be given further instructions. Saul must have been restless; nothing happened for three days. Finally, Ananias arrived at the house where Saul was staying and helped him to regain his sight.

The new apostle spent several days with followers of Christ in the city. He then received orders from the Lord: Saul was to tell Gentiles, kings, and the sons of Israel about Jesus, even though he'd suffer a great deal for the sake of Christ. Saul's restlessness soon disappeared as he was baptized and immediately began preaching in Damascus.[17] He went on to minister throughout the Mediterranean and wrote 13 of the 27 books of the New Testament.

Ananias: Resistance and Reservation

God's man in Damascus, Ananias, exhibited quite another reaction when he received directions from the Lord. God came to him in a vision and issued some startling orders. He gave Ananias the precise grid coordinates where he'd find the despised Saul, whose reputation for persecuting the followers of Christ was well known throughout the Christian community.

Ananias may have thought the Lord wanted him to do some spiritual espionage. Perhaps his mission would be to determine Saul's plans so he could warn those on the evil man's hit list. Maybe God would call Ananias to "eliminate" Saul, to become an assassin for the Lord. Actually, God sent Ananias to restore Saul's sight.

With great boldness, Ananias resisted God's orders. His reservation was based on intelligence that Saul had done significant harm to Christians in Jerusalem, and he was planning equally cruel acts in Damascus. God didn't react in anger. He explained the importance of Ananias' task for furthering His kingdom, and the faithful servant immediately set out to accomplish his duties.[18] Despite Ananias' concerns, God used him to help launch the ministry of another who was to have a huge impact on followers of Christ for all time.

Heroes of Faith: Resilience

Those whose names are recorded in the Hall of Faith in Hebrews 11 also were true to God's orders. While their tasks varied, all were called to represent the Lord in a fallen world, to serve as ambassadors for good among those who delighted in evil, and to help others draw closer to God.

Through great adversity, these mighty men and women displayed tremendous resilience as they conquered kingdoms, performed righteous acts, sparred with lions, quenched the power of fire, escaped by the edge of the sword, and put foreign armies to flight. No task was too hard, no adversary too threatening that they compromised the role God had called them to perform. Through poverty, torture, mocking, scourging, stoning, and imprisonment, these valiant soldiers were made strong despite their own weaknesses. They kept the faith. They fulfilled their orders.

All God's Warriors: Reliance on the Lord

What single trait is apparent among all those who accepted God's orders? While individual reactions varied, all carried out their duties with absolute reliance upon God for strength, wisdom, and endurance. These warriors relied on the Lord:

- To overcome initial fears.
- To harness and focus their early eagerness.
- When they seemed to have their enemies on the run.
- For the will to carry on when it appeared their adversaries were about to overwhelm them.
- When He told them to wait quietly until He was ready to reveal their next steps.

These faithful servants acknowledged God was almighty, all wise, and ever present, and He rewarded their faith in performing the tasks He'd assigned them.

And what orders has Christ issued to His followers in the 21st century? Our role is identical to what Jesus sent His disciples to do after His resurrection. As we conform to the image of God's Son, we're to make disciples among those around us. We're to build up the faith of soldiers in God's army while encouraging the forces of Satan to desert and pledge their allegiance to Christ.

To accomplish these orders, we must maintain a continual state of readiness as we engage in both defensive and offensive operations. Most instruction on spiritual warfare focuses on how to react to Satan's attacks. We've seen earlier he desires first to bar entry into God's kingdom for those who don't yet know Christ as Savior. When unsuccessful, Satan then directs his forces to launch a full assault to keep Christians from conforming to the image of God's Son.

Defending Ourselves When Satan Attacks

During my days at the Academy, preparation for survival as prisoners of war was one of our most realistic training programs. Over several days in a mock POW camp, we learned how to resist our "captors." The training also helped us understand values, strengths, and emotions crucial in the development of the character we needed to make it through tough times ourselves and to lead our subordinates during significant challenges.

Before we were captured, we were given details of our missions flying over hostile territory. Camp guards employed various tactics to get prisoners to provide classified information concerning our operations and to publicly discredit the "illegal and immoral operations" of U.S. forces in their sovereign nation. We were allowed little sleep, provided little food, and roughed up as much as permitted in a training environment.

Interrogations ranged from loud demands for information with physical punishment or the withholding of food for those who failed to cooperate to gentle pleas that often included lies about details other captives had provided. The reward for those who acted dishonorably was instant gratification: food and rest. If the guards were unable to pry any information from us, they ushered us to wooden boxes just large enough for a prisoner to sit knees to chin. Our enemies expected several hours of solitary confinement would produce the traitorous words and deeds they desired.

Warriors in God's army constantly are engaged in defensive operations, battling the attacks of Satan and his evil forces. We're often enticed to enjoy physical, sensual, and emotional satisfaction that is totally outside the boundaries God has set for us. The father of lies tries to convince us—often successfully—that we'll feel great if we lay aside our morality and have a little fun. "After all," he reasons, "who's really going to be hurt by such a tiny lapse?"

If the subtle approach fails, Satan pulls out the big guns. The loss of a job. The death of a loved one. A serious illness that requires an extended hospital stay. A spouse's adulterous affair. A rebellious teenager. The list goes on and on. How can we survive these attacks and defeat the devil soundly when he launches an offensive? Here are a few ideas to get you started down the road to victory when Satan attacks.

Knowing the Devil's Plans

First, we must know Satan's nature and tactics before he unleashes his assaults on us. As we saw in Chapter 6, the devil's schemes aren't a big secret. We shouldn't be surprised by his devious operations. As an angel, he wanted to elevate himself above God, and now he tries to convince us to place ourselves above the Lord. After being banished to Earth thousands of years ago, Satan has used the same methods to beat down mankind. To defeat his attacks, we must look for the warning signs that accompany them. He'll:

- ***Disguise*** himself as a member of our unit, perhaps even our Commander, as he tries to lead us astray.
- Tempt us to ***doubt*** the Lord's love for us or to ***disengage*** from other warriors in God's army.
- ***Distract*** our attention away from our mission and orders.
- ***Disorient*** us so we head out smartly, but along a path God hasn't chosen for us.
- ***Destabilize*** our lives to the point of discouragement.
- ***Deceive*** us into thinking his ways are God's ways.
- ***Discredit*** us in the eyes of those who are watching when we recognize the devil's evil plans and defeat them.
- Try to ***disarm*** us so we'll fail to accomplish the divine orders we've received.

Knowing God's Word

Simply knowing what to expect won't guarantee our defensive operations will be successful. We also must know God's word and be fully confident in His promises. Some of us learn to recite scripture, but not all of us let its truth guide our thoughts and actions. Rather than gaining direction and encouragement from God's word, we raise the white flag of surrender immediately when Satan and his evil henchmen open fire at us. This rapid retreat is hardly what we'd expect from a human army; it should be no less an alternative for warriors in God's army.

Here's how we can use scripture to defeat the devil's wicked tactics.

- If it seems Satan is approaching ***disguised*** in the uniform of God's forces, we can be confident Jesus is the good Commander; He knows His soldiers, and we know Him.[19] If we love and obey our Leader, He'll disclose Himself to us.[20]
- When our adversary sows seeds of ***doubt*** about God's love, we can be assured nothing can separate us from the unlimited love of our heavenly Father.[21]

- If we're tempted to ***disengage*** from others in our unit, we can recall the strength we gain from one another and from Christ. Jesus promised, "'Where two or three have gathered together in My name, there I am in their midst.'"[22]
- As Satan attempts to ***distract*** us from our focus on Christ, we can be encouraged by scripture's counsel that we're to fix our eyes on Jesus.[23]
- When the enemy ***disorients*** us, we can trust God's word will light the path we should take.[24]
- If the devil tries to flood our minds with worries to ***destabilize*** and discourage us, we know we're to be anxious for nothing because God will supply all our needs.[25]
- Satan's efforts to ***deceive*** us are futile when we recall we have access to God's perspective.[26]
- When the devil ***discredits*** us and those around us fail to acknowledge what God has done in and through us, we can experience peace in knowing we work for Him and not other men and women. "It is the Lord Christ Whom [we] serve."[27]
- As Satan seeks to ***disarm*** us, we're confident because we're entitled to draw from a constantly stocked divine armory.[28]

Despite our enemy's fierce attacks, we can emerge victorious by recognizing his tactics and resisting them through faith and the power of God's word.[29] Sure, he might sneak up and throw us to the ground initially, but we must get up immediately, stand firm, and use God's word to launch a counterattack that will defeat our wicked adversary. After all, the precedent for this was set when our Commander defeated the devil's temptations after fasting 40 days in the wilderness.[30]

Getting Help from the Spirit and Our Fellow Soldiers

To be successful in battle, we must rely on the power of the Holy Spirit to defeat the attacks of our enemy. Paul's encouragement that "I can do all things through Him Who strengthens me"[31] reminds us the Holy Spirit provides overwhelming power to accomplish the spiritual duties we've been assigned. Apostle John reminds us we can overcome the evil spirits around us because "greater is He Who is in you than he who is in the world."[32] The Spirit's presence in the hearts of Jesus' followers should give us enormous courage as we battle forces of evil.

We can also face the attacks that come our way by maintaining accountability relationships with others in our unit. God calls us to "stimulate one another to love and good deeds."[33] As we pray for and encourage those serving alongside us, we fight not as lone rangers, but as a team of warriors.

In reinforcing the importance of building up one another, King Solomon explains two are better than one because they have a good return for their labor. If one falls, the other will lift up his companion. One person alone can be easily overpowered, but two can resist an attack. "A cord of three strands is not quickly torn apart."[34]

First, then, we are to be prepared when the enemy attacks. Second, we must know, trust, and immediately employ God's truth when we're ambushed. Next, we must resist the urge to give in without a fight, tapping into the power of the Holy Spirit. Additionally, we must support those in our unit as they support us. As we defend ourselves in these ways, we can seize the initiative in taking the battle to our evil adversary.

Taking the Offensive

I once heard a pastor explain our offensive operations. He suggested our primary duty is "to transform atheists into missionaries." If these are our orders, ***we must become missionaries*** ourselves. You might think this involves traveling to a far-off land to aid poor, starving, ignorant folks to become Christians. This is the picture painted by a missionary wife serving near Dar es Salaam, East Africa in July 1935.

In a letter to my grandmother in California, Anna Bigelow described her husband's ministry.

> Mr. Bigelow returned last week from a visit to one of our little groups. Baptized 7 while about 10 took a stand. They need much prayer that they may stand true in their many tests and temptations. At present we are considering having a small songbook printed. It has been a need for some time. … What we would like is a car with tent for services, for living, and just travel from place to place. Preach, have plenty of scriptures, [and] put out simple tracts and messages on the way of salvation to give to all.
>
> There are very few missionaries who are interested or care to work with these half-civilized natives. My husband has just left on his bicycle, having sent his bed and a little food ahead where he will sleep tonight. He will then arrive tomorrow. About half the way is climbing, which means pushing his bike [through the jungle].

The dictionary defines a missionary as a messenger or representative sent out with authority to perform a special service. For example, a religious organization may send out someone to preach, teach, and convert others. The missionary's goal is to accomplish the unique purpose for which he or she is destined.

While we may have heard of missionaries who've traveled to distant countries, this isn't a requirement. God's soldiers can be missionaries where we are—with family and friends, in our neighborhoods, at work. Some of the Lord's forces spend years praying God will call them into ministry on foreign shores and, in the meantime, do nothing where they are. As a wise Christian said, we need to press on in our service where we are because we can't serve the Lord where we aren't.

Paul's missionary service provides a good example for us. As a handful of Christians ministered, prayed, and fasted in Antioch, the Holy Spirit announced He had a mission for Paul and Barnabas. After more praying and fasting, they set out under the leading of the Spirit to proclaim the word of God throughout the region.[35] What we often miss is that Simeon, Lucius, and Manaen remained in Antioch carrying out their duties as prophets and teachers.

Now for the $64,000 question: Who were the missionaries? Answer: All five! Two took their mission on the road (actually, the sea), while three carried out their mission among people where they resided. Today, some of God's warriors receive orders to minister abroad, and others receive orders to serve Him at home.

In addition to ministering as missionaries in offensive operations, **we're also Christ's ambassadors.** In an earthly sense, those who serve in this capacity represent their national leaders in other countries. Ambassadors present the positions of their governments to the political leaders and the citizens in the lands where they're posted. In addition, ambassadors ensure citizens of their host nations are aware of rules on immigration to the countries they represent, assisting them to complete all necessary entry requirements. These officials also care for the safety and needs of residents of their nations who visit the countries where they serve.

As followers of the King of kings, we're citizens of heaven serving as ambassadors to those who exist outside His kingdom. In what we say and do, we represent God in our dealings with other people. The Lord has given us His word to share among those who don't know Him so they can understand and comply with the entry requirements for heaven. We also assist Christians—our fellow citizens of heaven now residing on Earth—in conforming to His image.

Apostle Paul recognized our role as representatives of God when he explained, "We are ambassadors for Christ, as though God were entreating through us; we beg you on behalf of Christ, be reconciled to God."[36] The apostle also understood an ambassador didn't need freedom of movement to serve effectively. As Paul sat bound to a guard in Rome, he wrote, "I am an ambassador in chains," and he asked for prayer that he'd proclaim boldly the gospel of Jesus Christ.[37]

Winning Our Spiritual Battles
Members of the armed forces know there's no room in combat for prima donnas or for soldiers who want to ad lib. The hallmark of a successful military unit is unity. All team members must perform their roles to perfection, working from the plan handed down by the commander. The battle will be lost if the soldiers fail to adhere to the strategy developed by leaders who have a much better grasp of the situation and objectives than what they possess in the trenches.

During combat, soldiers aim to win. In facing our powerful foe, Christians must engage our adversary in a manner that ensures success. We know the ultimate victory already has been won. Jesus has defeated Satan once and for all. Because Christ has emerged victorious, His followers are guaranteed they'll spend eternity with Father, Son, and Holy Spirit.

This doesn't mean our day-to-day battles will always go our way. As long as Satan is allowed to reign over the fallen world, it won't be easy to conform to the image of Christ and help others to develop a relationship with Him. Therefore, God has handed down a simple strategy for our spiritual warfare. The devil will never cease to target us for his evil schemes, but we can defeat him in every skirmish by allowing the Lord to fight with us rather than taking on Satan on our own.

The Old Testament is packed with pre-battle pep talks and after-action reports that reinforce this truth. God Himself instructed warriors in the Jewish army, "'When you go out to battle against your enemies and see horses and chariots and people more numerous than you, do not be afraid of them; for the LORD your God, Who brought you up from the land of

Egypt, is with you. ... Do not be fainthearted. Do not be afraid, or panic, or tremble before them, for the LORD your God is the One Who goes with you, to fight for you against your enemies, to save you.'"[38] The Lord assured the Israelites that He'd walk in the midst of their camp to deliver them and to defeat their enemies.[39]

This was true as Joshua and his army entered the land God had promised them. On some occasions, prior to the Israelites' conquests of Jericho and Ai for example, God guaranteed victory.[40] When God's people marched through Canaan, the Lord fought for Israel.[41] As God's present-day warriors engage in the battles of this life, we gain strength from Joshua's farewell address: "'Cling to the Lord your God, as you have done to this day. ... for the Lord your God is He Who fights for you, just as He promised you.'"[42]

As Gideon and his army of 32,000 men prepared to fight the Midianites—a force more than four times larger than the Israelites—God appeared to the Jewish commander and instructed him to trim the size of his army. The Lord's reason: "'The people who are with you are too many for Me to give Midian into their hands, lest Israel become boastful, saying, "My own power has delivered me."'"

Gideon followed God's direction, cutting his force to 300 to take on the opposing 135,000. Although God promised Gideon his soldiers would be victorious, the Jews then were outnumbered by a ratio of 450 to 1! If an army tried to fight against these odds today, the second wave of its forces would be composed entirely of hearse drivers, chaplains, and gravediggers. But God had promised victory, and He delivered. Only 15,000 Midianite soldiers survived. By tapping into the Lord's strength, the vastly outnumbered Jewish army defeated its numerically superior foe. (See Judges 7.)

In a one-on-one fight with the giant Goliath, David realized he could be victorious over the Philistine. "'The LORD does not deliver by sword or by spear,'" the teenager shouted, "'for the battle is the LORD'S and He will give you into our hands."[43] Years later, through David's experiences and his thorough knowledge of God's deliverance of the nation of Israel, the king exalted the Lord in many of the songs and poems he wrote:

- "Some boast in chariots, and some in horses; but we will boast in the name of the LORD, our God."[44]
- "The LORD will swallow up [your enemies] in His wrath, and fire will devour them. ... Though they intended evil against Thee, and devised a plot, they will not succeed. ... Be Thou exalted, O LORD, in Thy strength; we will sing and praise Thy power."[45]
- "O give us help against the adversary, for deliverance by man is in vain. Through God we shall do valiantly, and it is He Who will tread down our adversaries."[46]

The Lord sent forces to protect Elisha and his servant from the Arameans. Although a huge army of soldiers, horses, and chariots surrounded the prophet, they were no match for the heavenly horses and chariots of fire God had arrayed against them.[47]

When righteous King Asa ruled Judah, he assembled an army of 300,000 men from his people and an additional 280,000 from the tribe of Benjamin. These valiant warriors were well armed with bows, spears, and shields. With a force of one million men and 300 chariots, Zerah from Ethiopia determined he could defeat Asa's army. The king, though, called out to God, "'LORD, there is no one besides Thee to help in the battle between the powerful and those who have no strength; so help us, O LORD our God, for we trust in Thee, and in Thy name have come against this multitude. O LORD, Thou art our God; let no man prevail against Thee.'" God answered by routing the Ethiopians.[48]

Asa's son and heir to the throne, Jehoshaphat, faced a similar challenge. When warriors from among the sons of Moab and Ammon attacked Judah's army, Jahaziel told the king not to fear as the battle was the LORD's. The prophet's instructions worried the Jewish commanders. Jehoshaphat, his military leaders, and their troops were to assemble across the battlefield from the opposition and ... do nothing! The king rallied his soldiers to put their trust in the Lord. As the forces of Judah sang praises to God and watched in amazement, the Lord crushed their foes, ultimately causing them to destroy one another. (See II Chronicles 20.)

Victory for God's Warriors Today
In Old Testament times, God brought victory to His people in physical battles when they trusted Him. Today He enables us to emerge victorious in spiritual battles when, by faith, we allow Him to fight alongside and for us. Paul recognized this, as we see in several of his letters to the early followers of Christ.

The apostle reminded the Corinthian church that God always leads us in His triumph through Christ.[49] Paul encourages God's warriors not to allow adversity to rob us of the victory we have in Jesus. "We are afflicted in every way, but not crushed; perplexed, but not despairing; persecuted, but not forsaken; struck down, but not destroyed." Even during Satan's attacks, the apostle tells us, we can accomplish our mission of being conformed to the image of God's Son: "... the life of Jesus also may be manifested in our body."[50]

Paul wrote this with confidence. He knew soldiers in God's army wielded not fleshly but divinely powerful weapons. As we tap into the might of the Holy Spirit to obey the directions of our Commander, we're able to defeat any force that attempts to destroy our relationship with God.[51]

Soldiers in God's army can join the apostle in rejoicing about the outcome of individual spiritual battles as well as the great war between good and evil. "Thanks be to God," Paul exulted, "Who gives us the victory in our Lord Jesus Christ. Therefore, my beloved brethren, be steadfast, immovable, always abounding in the work of the Lord, knowing that your toil is not in vain in the Lord."[52]

In addition to his reassurance for the church at Corinth, the apostle encouraged the Ephesians to "be strong in the Lord, and in the strength of His might." By employing God's armor, His warriors are able to stand firm against every scheme of our devious adversary.[53]

When we follow Paul's advice, we can be sure Satan won't defeat us. As the apostle reminded the Corinthians, we can be victorious over every temptation the devil lays before us because "God is faithful, Who will not allow you to be tempted beyond what you are able, but with the temptation will provide the way of escape also, that you may be able to endure it."[54]

Paul isn't the only New Testament author who spurs members of God's army to victory. The writer to the Hebrews reminds us that through Jesus' death, He has disarmed Satan.[55] As long as the Lord's soldiers engage the enemy through the strength Christ provides, we can defeat our evil foe. James reinforces this when he urges us to "submit ... to God. Resist the devil and he will flee from you."[56]

Martin Luther, one of the preeminent Protestant reformers, understood our need to tap into God's strength to emerge victorious in our daily battles. Nearly five centuries ago, in 1529, Luther wrote the classic hymn "A Mighty Fortress Is Our God." Its words provide great counsel as we seek to conform to the image of Christ through the strength we can derive only from Him.

> A mighty fortress is our God, a bulwark never failing;
> Our helper He, amid the flood, of mortal ills prevailing:
> For still our ancient foe doth seek to work us woe;
> His craft and pow'r are great, and, armed with cruel hate, on earth is not his equal.

Did we in our own strength confide, our striving would be losing;
Were not the right Man on our side, the Man of God's own choosing:
Dost ask who that might be? Christ Jesus, it is He;
Lord Sabaoth, His name, from age to age the same, and He must win the battle.

And tho this world, with devils filled, should threaten to undo us,
We will not fear, for God hath willed His truth to triumph thro' us:
The Prince of Darkness grim, we tremble not for him;
His rage we can endure, for lo, his doom is sure, ...[57]

Apostle Paul reminds us, "I can do all things through [Christ] who strengthens me."[58] As we engage in spiritual warfare, we can draw great encouragement in knowing we can conform to the image of Christ through the power He gives us to do all things!

God's warriors must tap into the Holy Spirit's power to defend ourselves from Satan's attacks as we carry out our orders to share the gospel with others—at home or around the world as the Lord specifies. As we serve faithfully as Christ's missionaries and ambassadors through the years, the Lord calls some of us to promotion. The attributes He's blessed us with and the experiences He's seen us through enable us to lead other soldiers in His army.

Lessons Learned

- While carrying out our mission of conforming to the image of God's Son, we receive orders to share the good news of Christ with others.
- We must accomplish these duties with the responsiveness, resolve, relentlessness, readiness, reverence, resilience, and reliance demonstrated by God's soldiers of old.

- At the same time, we must guard against the reluctance, regret, rejection, restlessness, resistance, and reservation with which God's orders were met by others He chose for significant responsibility.
- It's inevitable that Satan will attack us. Our defensive operations include being prepared for his wicked tactics, using God's word to defeat these assaults, relying on the power of the Holy Spirit, and gaining strength from the other warriors in our unit.
- We also must launch offensive operations to share the gospel as missionaries and ambassadors.
- As Christian warriors employ God's power when we engage in combat with Satan and his forces of evil, we know the Lord is fighting alongside us, and victory is assured.

Unit Analysis
To download Unit Analysis and Personal Battle Plan material, please go to www.forwardintobattle.com.

As followers of Christ, we all have the same mission: to conform to His image. In the process of becoming more like Jesus, we're all commissioned into His service as citizens of heaven and aliens residing on planet Earth for a limited time. Identical mission and commission, however, don't equate to identical orders. As we see through the lives of the children of God in the Old Testament and the disciples of Christ in the New Testament, the Lord issues a variety of orders to those in his earthly army. As we perform our duties, the challenge is to respond in the positive way we see in many of the saints of old. We must take care not to reject the opportunity the Lord gives us to touch the lives of others in His name. When we seek to accomplish God's orders, Satan will do all he can to prevent us from being fruitful, so we have to be prepared to defend ourselves against his assaults. As we tap into the Lord's strength, we'll be victorious in our efforts to take the message of Christ to those God places in our paths.

1. When you've received orders on the job or in ministry, especially when you've been asked to do something you prefer not to do, how have you responded? How did you get beyond your initial frustration, disappointment, or fear to execute your orders with excellence?
2. Noah was ***responsive*** to God's orders. (Genesis 6:5-22) He got to work on the ark as soon as the Lord told him what to do. Isaiah was excited about doing what God wanted, pledging his ***readiness*** even before the Lord explained his task. (Isaiah 6:1-13) How can we prepare ourselves in advance so we're responsive and ready when God provides us a new set of orders?
3. Abram set out on what was a very frightening challenge—moving to a faraway land—with great ***resolve***. (Genesis 12:1-4) Joshua was ***relentless*** in leading the Israelites into battle as God had directed. (Deuteronomy 34:9-12, Joshua 1:1-18) Gideon, Samson, David, and the other heroes of Hebrews 11 displayed tremendous ***resilience*** in the face of great adversity. (Hebrews 11:32-40) Where did they get the courage to engage in spiritual battles that led all of them into danger and many to martyrdom? How can you be courageous today as you carry out the orders God has issued you?
4. Nathanael demonstrated exceptional recognition and ***reverence*** when introduced to Jesus. He recognized Christ as the long-awaited Messiah, and he revered Him as the Son of God. (John 1:45-51) Even in our most devoted service, we sometimes allow the activity to obscure the glory of the One we serve. How can we ensure our highest priority remains acknowledging the majesty of Christ as we minister in His name?
5. Moses was ***reluctant*** to take on the monumental task God asked him to perform. (Exodus 3:1-14, 4:1-13) Following their encounter on the

road to Damascus, Saul was **restless** as he awaited Christ's further instructions. Ananias was **resistant** when he felt God directing him to do something that made very little sense. (Acts 9:1-20) How can we cope with uneasiness when the Lord gives us orders that seem impossible or confusing and when He seems to be withholding His direction when we're eager to take the next step?

6. The rich, young ruler missed out on a wonderful opportunity to follow Christ in His ministry because his **regret** at hearing what would be required led him to **reject** Jesus' offer. This may have resulted in his not obtaining the eternal life he was seeking. (Matthew 19:16-26) Oswald Chambers, in *My Utmost for His Highest*, warns that we sometimes allow good things we're doing in our Christian service to get in the way of the best the Lord has for us. How have you turned away from what God called you to do because you were comfortable in what you already were doing? How can you be prepared to step out in faith to a higher calling, even if it takes you outside your comfort zone?

7. In carrying out our orders to help others draw closer to Christ, we'll have to defend ourselves against Satan's assaults. Read the following verses. Do you believe these truths of scripture? How does Satan try to lessen the impact of these passages in the lives of Christians by subtly changing a few words (*"Only a few* temptations ..." and "I can do *some* things ...")? What do these examples tell us about the importance of God's word in our defensive operations? How would complete confidence in these verses enable you to accomplish your orders?
   a. I Corinthians 10:13
   b. Philippians 4:13

8. Have you ever thought of yourself as a missionary or ambassador? You don't have to travel to a remote spot halfway around the globe to fulfill these duties. You can represent Christ in your everyday relationships right where you currently reside. How can you be more open about sharing the love of God and the gospel message with others?

9. As we take part in both defensive and offensive operations, all the responsiveness, readiness, resolve, and reverence we can muster from deep within ourselves is nowhere near what we need to accomplish the tasks God sets out for us. According to John 15:5, how can we assure victory in our day-to-day spiritual battles? The key to being fruitful is ***reliance*** on God's Holy Spirit. How has the Spirit helped you in your walk with the Lord? What practical steps can we take to ensure the Holy Spirit is at work within us?

Prayer Points

- Praise the Lord that He is all-powerful and that He gives us the strength to conduct defensive and offensive operations in our spiritual battles
- Thank God for issuing a unique set of orders for each of the followers of His Son
- Ask God to help you to be responsive to His call, ready to perform your duties, resolved to go to whatever lengths He requires, relentless in taking the battle to the enemy, and resilient in the face of seemingly insurmountable odds stacked against you
- Commit to relying on the Holy Spirit to carry you through to victory while revering Jesus as God's Own dear Son, Who died on the cross to secure a place in the kingdom of heaven for you

Personal Battle Plan

1. **Assess your readiness to respond to God's call on your life**. Is your readiness conditional: "Lord, I'll do anything You require, but please don't ask me to ...."? Is your readiness half-hearted: "I'll do what God wants, but I'd really rather be ...."? Is your readiness based on confidence in your own wisdom and strength or what the Lord

can do in and through you? Ask the Lord to help you to be ready to serve Him unconditionally and enthusiastically, even before He tells you what He expects.

2. When you receive your orders and carry out your tasks, you have a choice of how you'll respond to the challenges that emerge along the way. **Evaluate your typical response to God's call** by placing an "X" on each of the lines below.

Move out smartly_____Tend to drag
when I get my orders   my feet in anxiety and
                                             uncertainty

Resolve to allow nothing _____Expect to be knocked off
to slow me down   course early and often

Relentless in pursuit _____Hold back a little to
of what God requires   ensure I'm safe and rested

Bounce back decisively _____Head for the field hospital
amidst various setbacks   after the first flesh wound

3. Based on the answers to question 2, **determine areas in which you need to improve**. List what you can do to become more responsive, resolved, relentless, and resilient as you serve the Lord, and pray for His strength as you seek to make progress in these areas.
4. Is your worship confined to an hour each Sunday morning, or do you see opportunities in the midst of your Christian service to revere the God of the universe, His Son our Savior, and the Holy Spirit Who lives within us? **List activities other than formal worship in which you can pause and praise the Lord** as you carry out your orders.

5. Think back over the past year. **Jot down specific situations in which you responded in a negative way to God's call**. Perhaps you were reticent, wrestling with God over what you thought was a wiser course than the one He seemed to have in mind. Maybe you felt regret over what you perceived you'd have to give up to fully follow His orders. You may even have rejected His desires because they seemed well beyond your comfort zone. If you haven't already done so, confess these rebellious reactions, and ask God to help you to overcome this type of response in the future.

6. In defending ourselves against Satan's assaults and carrying out our orders to tell others about Christ, we must consistently tap into God's power to do what He requires of us. **List the spiritual duties in which you're currently engaged**. Compare how much you're relying on God's Holy Spirit to accomplish these tasks to how much you're relying on your own strength, wisdom, experiences, position, etc. to get the job done. Pray for God's help in relying primarily on the empowerment of the Spirit, putting what you bring to the battle in the proper perspective.

7. **Prepare for the next session** by listing the most important character traits of the best leaders you've served.

Leading a Unit: Assumption of Command

NEARLY A DOZEN volumes on the art of leadership reside in my bookcase. *Be a Leader People Follow. Taking Charge. The Heart of Godly Leadership. Leadership Lessons of Jesus.* These and several other books should provide great leading on leading. You'd think the authors would begin with a definition of leadership, but they don't. A few briefly explain what leadership is, but most launch directly into suggestions for what a leader should do. The assumption seems to be that leadership is a well-understood concept, and if we simply put their advice into practice, we'll be transformed into gifted leaders.

Unfortunately, it's not that simple!

Let's take a quick look at what a leader is before we seek to understand how to lead others on their spiritual journeys. In the absence of descriptions of leaders in the various books I've read, we turn first to a few dictionary definitions.

- *leader* (noun): a person or thing that leads; directing, commanding, or guiding head
- *lead* (verb): show the way to or direct the course of by going before or along with; guide or direct by persuasion or influence to a course of action or thought

Based on these definitions, we can describe a leader as a person who guides others, showing them the way both by example and by directing or commanding. This guidance—whether by demonstration, instruction, or persuasion—causes those being led to take the actions or adopt the thoughts set out by the leader. Both the leader and the led move in harmony to achieve the group's objectives.

As His ministry on Earth was about to end, Jesus made an interesting comment as He talked with His disciples. "'Truly, truly, I say to you, he who believes in Me, the works that I do shall he do also; and greater works than these shall he do; because I go to the Father.'"[1] Because it's challenging, we often jump from the previous verse to the one immediately following these difficult words.

While this encouragement of Jesus may be puzzling, we can draw a few conclusions from it. Our Commander wasn't suggesting His followers through the centuries would surpass some of His most astonishing achievements. In nearly five decades as a follower of Christ, I've never turned water into wine or observed anyone else accomplish this feat. No one I know has walked on water or raised someone who'd been dead four days.

In this passage, Jesus isn't saying His disciples and their successors would perform one breathtaking miracle after another. What He was driving at was that the combined impact of His followers would be greater over the centuries than what He achieved during His three years of ministry. For this to be true, Jesus' disciples—and countless other Christians through the ages—would have to take on the roles Christ performed during His days on Earth. One of these is leading other believers.

Jesus selected disciples to be with Him, men He'd eventually send out to preach and to cast out demons.[2] Do you see how Jesus' leadership fits the definition we came up with? He guided His disciples, showing them the way both by example and by instruction. This guidance caused Peter, James, John, and their colleagues to take the actions and to adopt the thoughts Christ taught. Jesus and His disciples moved in harmony to achieve the Father's objectives.

The disciples' initial training was to watch and listen to Jesus. When He determined they were ready, He sent them on their first field training exercise with the task of preaching and healing.[3] Their success in this test, coupled with further observation and instruction at the feet of the Master, led to Jesus commissioning the disciples to lead others following His death. Their "greater works" came not just in the miracles they performed through the power He'd given them, but also in identifying and preparing others who'd take on the Father's mission after the first generation of Christians was gone. For some of us, the greater works God desires to do through us include leading others in their service as God's warriors.

One of the lessons the disciples learned as they observed Jesus was that leaders must possess a high degree of humility. Christ demonstrated this as He washed His followers' feet just prior to His arrest. Apostle John tells us Jesus laid aside His garments, but He also laid aside His position of authority to minister to the disciples in a very practical way. When He completed this act of kindness, Christ encouraged those who would lead the church with these words: "'You call Me Teacher and Lord; and you are right, for so I am. If I then, the Lord and the Teacher, washed your feet, you also ought to wash one another's feet. For I gave you an example that you also should do as I did to you.'"[4]

As we become leaders, we can draw on what we've learned while following Jesus. All we've picked up in Bible studies, Sunday school lessons, and sermons combined with all we've experienced as we've ministered in His name provide the foundation for helping others to labor and, eventually, to lead. As we faithfully build the disciples God gives us, He'll use us—and them—to reach more and more people with the good news of His Son. The impact of our leadership will be felt by successive generations beyond anything we can imagine today.

Forward into Battle

A quick example. On April 21, 1855, Edward Kimball, who taught Sunday school at the Mount Vernon Congregational Church in Boston, walked into Holton's Shoe Store to visit a boy in his class. He found Dwight L. Moody in the back of the store wrapping shoes. Kimball shared the gospel, emphasizing God's love for him, and the student received Christ as his Savior.

Moody became one of the world's greatest evangelists. After one of his meetings in Chicago in the late 1870s, his personal counseling helped J. Wilbur Chapman, a student at Lake Forest College, to receive assurance of his salvation. He, too, went on to become an effective evangelist. A volunteer named Billy Sunday—a former major-league baseball player—helped organize Chapman's crusades. Sunday eventually took over the ministry, and thousands came to Christ through his dynamic preaching.

Inspired by a 1924 Billy Sunday crusade in Charlotte, North Carolina, a group of Christians set up a men's fellowship group. When evangelist Mordecai Ham held revival meetings at the club in 1934, a 16-year-old named Billy Graham received Christ as his Savior. In ministry that spanned more than half a century, Graham shared the gospel with more people than any other person in history—around 215 million in 185 countries and territories around the world. This incredible legacy—that started because a Sunday school teacher obeyed God's call to visit a young man at a local shoe store—spanned 150 years. And it continues through the collective influence of all those who have served God as a result of the ministry of Billy Graham![5]

As we determine how to lead our fellow Christians, we can pick up some valuable lessons from scripture. **We can learn from those who have gone before us** many of the character traits we'll need to employ. Based on these models, we can set a course for the actions we should take to **get the most from our troops**.

CHAPTER 9

Learning from Those Who Have Gone Before Us

Leadership is a potent combination of strategy and character. But if you must be without one, be without the strategy.

General Norman Schwarzkopf[1]

THROUGH OUR EXPERIENCES in God's army over the years, we develop the knowledge and ability to lead others. As we conform to the image of His Son, the Lord allows us to help other warriors to become more like Christ.

We may lead small platoons, such as our families. The Lord may put us in charge of huge divisions—a church or a national or international ministry. Regardless of the number of followers or the scope of operations, God expects us to lead with excellence, and He provides some outstanding models whose words and actions can help us to become effective leaders.

A number of people have provided excellent examples of leadership throughout my life. In my youth, my father was my primary model. I watched the way he barbecued and asked if he'd let me have a try. I observed his firewood-chopping technique during our annual vacations to the mountains and followed his style—under his close supervision. Whatever my father did, I kept an eye on him and wanted to do the same.

Perhaps his greatest impact on me came when he coached my Little League baseball team. As a 12-year-old, I was totally focused on myself. Arrogance gave way to curiosity one day when my father told the family he was going to drive Luis and Frank to G&L Sports on Blackstone Avenue to buy some baseball shoes for them. They were sons of migrant workers who spent their summers as farmhands in the fertile Central Valley of California.

When Luis and Frank arrived for our first game, their faces beamed with pride as they walked onto the field wearing their new baseball shoes. No one knew where the shoes had come from; my father said nothing, and the boys kept the secret. His generosity was a great lesson for me, and it helped me develop a concern for the less fortunate.

Other leaders emerged as my life continued: the basketball coach who believed in me despite my never having played the game before, the senior cadet at the Air Force Academy who led me to Christ, the Fellowship of Christian Athletes sponsor who encouraged me as I grew closer to the Lord, the Air Force colonel who'd been a Rhodes Scholar. These people attracted my attention by the strong character they displayed, and I tried to model my efforts in leading others on what I'd observed in them.

During my 33 years in the armed forces, I witnessed many leaders whose character was beyond reproach. One had the vision to see that a time-consuming project would have great benefit for the Air Force over the long term, and he pursued the idea despite challenges from other senior leaders in the Pentagon. Another general persevered in his duties after his four-star boss publicly—and unfairly—criticized him. A third senior officer had the courage to confront a top general concerning a decision that, while it would raise funds for recreational programs, had the potential to cause financial hardship for many families on the base.

An admiral demonstrated his wisdom as he oversaw the planning of a complex military operation in a very politically charged environment. On more than one occasion, I observed the obedience of a senior leader who, during planning sessions, offered alternatives to his commander's proposals but followed orders to the letter when the boss didn't change his mind.

Several top officers made themselves available to take on positions they'd have preferred to avoid when told the assignments were in the best interest of the armed forces. One stepped out in faith that God would provide for his future when he was removed from his leadership role because his boss wanted to fill the position with someone else as a favor to a higher-ranking officer.

Of course, I learned a great deal about character from other leaders who were lacking in this area. Among them was a commander who didn't have the courage to make hard decisions and who displayed a lack of integrity by instructing that funds be used for his change of command that weren't authorized for this purpose. Other leaders also were short on integrity, withholding their legitimate concerns about projects to earn points with more senior officers who approved of the plans. Still others lacked humility, taking credit for their subordinates' ideas and looking down on those of lower ranks.

Character Traits of God's Leaders

In addition to picking up pointers by watching excellent leaders who God puts in our paths—and avoiding the practices of those whose performance is lacking—we also learn a great deal about leadership through reviewing the influential people whose stories we read in scripture. Before we look at a few examples, though, a warning is in order.

We often consider the outstanding leaders in biblical days to have been superhuman, blessed by God with genes vastly superior to those of mere mortals. We see the Lord somehow reaching down from His throne on high and gently managing the thoughts and deeds of those He placed in positions of responsibility—thinking for, speaking for, and moving these humans almost as a young boy plays with his plastic soldiers. This isn't the case. As a wise Sunday school teacher once informed his class, the Bible is full of tales of ordinary people doing extraordinary things.

"Wait a minute!" you protest. "Are you trying to tell me that Moses, Joshua, Solomon, and Daniel were just average men who somehow became great leaders?" Absolutely! These and other superb leaders were made of identical percentages of flesh, blood, and bone as everyone else. There's nothing in scripture to suggest they were born brilliant, and we see evidence that many of them didn't approach their assigned tasks with great confidence. Some displayed weaknesses that could only be described as criminal.

These men weren't born with superhuman power and noble character. God's usual practice was to select people who loved Him, make His wisdom and strength available to them, and tell them what He wanted them to do. As they followed His direction and made use of the attributes He provided, they completed the tasks He assigned them. Let's take a look at a few examples.

Joseph: A Visionary Leader

In Genesis we read about Joseph, a leader of great vision. When he was around 17 years old, Joseph predicted his rise to power. His announcement inspired jealousy and hatred among his brothers. Some concluded the only way to rid themselves of Joseph's arrogance—and his favor with Dad—was to kill him, but they chose instead to sell him to a band of Ishmaelite slave traders for 20 shekels of silver.

After serving as a devoted slave in the house of the captain of Pharaoh's bodyguard, Joseph was thrown into prison based on a false accusation by his master's wife. Following several years as a model prisoner, he was called into service by Pharaoh, who soon elevated Joseph—at the ripe old age of 30—to the second-highest position in the country. Why? Because Joseph discerned a famine was headed Egypt's way, and he devised a plan to gather and store food to preserve the nation over the seven years the land would fail to produce crops. (See Genesis 37-47.)

The Lord blessed Joseph with the ability to look ahead and determine the best course of action for himself and others. As we lead, we can tap into God's vision, trusting Him to reveal the paths He'd have us take. When we do, we must remember the advice of Jesus' brother James: "Come now, you who say, 'Today or tomorrow, we shall go to such and such a city, and spend a year there and engage in business and make a profit.' Yet you do not know what your life will be like tomorrow. You are just a vapor that appears for a little while and then vanishes away. Instead, you ought to say, 'If the Lord wills, we shall live and also do this or that.'"[2]

The vision we seek as leaders must not be a product of our own human thoughts or desires; it must be inspired by God. Jesus tells us the Holy Spirit will help us to anticipate what's coming.[3]

Joshua: A Courageous Leader

When God commissioned Joshua to succeed Moses, He encouraged him with these words: "'Be strong and courageous, for you shall bring the sons of Israel into the land which I swore to them, and I will be with you.'"[4] Following Moses' death, the Lord again provided a pep talk for the new leader. Three times God directed Joshua to be strong and courageous in accomplishing the duties He'd assigned.[5] The general listened, and he tackled every responsibility with godly courage. Joshua's example encouraged the Israelites to believe defeat wasn't an option.

Armed with supernatural courage, Joshua and his troops conquered a significant tract of real estate. Their push to the Promised Land included great highlights, such as a miraculous crossing of the Jordan River, a dramatic victory at Jericho, and crushing military triumphs all along the route the Lord directed. Their conquest complete, the 12 tribes of Israel settled in Canaan. The adventure also included a few lowlights, such as an unexpected defeat at Ai brought about when a single Jewish soldier disobeyed and an unwise alliance with the Gibeonites that was made because the Israelites failed to seek God's counsel.

What enabled Joshua to lead the Israelites to victory? Was it simply God's instruction to be strong and courageous? The general obviously desired to do as the Lord commanded, but what gave him the strength to awaken each morning, grab his sword, and step out in front of his troops was the promise that went along with the instruction: "I will be with you."

God made this commitment in conversations recorded in Deuteronomy 31 and Joshua 1. The Lord declared He'd give Joshua possession of the vast territory He'd promised Moses, and He added no man would be able to stand against him. In spiritual combat, God calls us to lead with courage, assured He'll be with us and will grant us victory as we rely on His strength and follow His direction.[6]

Nehemiah: A Leader Who Persevered

Courage in the face of powerful enemies is made somewhat easier by the thought that individual skirmishes generally are over in a relatively limited time. Prolonged battles are much more difficult to endure. In these longer challenges, perseverance is crucial. Nehemiah and his colleagues demonstrated this quality in rebuilding Jerusalem's wall.

Prior to becoming leader of the reconstruction team, Nehemiah was a wine steward in the court of Artaxerxes, the king of Persia. A Jew living in captivity in Babylon, Nehemiah served the king's beverage and ensured it wasn't tainted. That this humble servant rose to the exalted position of governor of Jerusalem illustrates how God uses ordinary people to do extraordinary things.

When reports on the condition of Jerusalem reached Artaxerxes' palace, Nehemiah was moved to tears. The wall surrounding the Jewish capital had been broken down and its gates burned. After fasting and praying, Nehemiah appeared sad as he served the king. Artaxerxes asked what was worrying his servant. Explaining that Jerusalem had been devastated, the lowly cupbearer requested permission to return to Judah to rebuild the city. The ruler agreed and sent Nehemiah on his way with official documents to pass safely from Babylon to Jerusalem.

As Nehemiah's team began to repair the city wall, a trio of detractors mocked them and then assembled a force to attack the builders as they worked. Nehemiah called on the Lord for protection, and team members alternated between construction work and standing guard for others who were rebuilding. Fifty-two days after work began, the wall was completed. Through Nehemiah's perseverance, the Lord blessed the project. (See Nehemiah 1-6.)

Our mission of conforming to the image of Christ—and leading others to do the same—has been referred to as a marathon, not a sprint. The moment we receive Christ as Savior, the race begins. In order to reach the finish line, we must persevere through all the challenges Satan hurls at us. As Nehemiah demonstrated, our perseverance must be accompanied by regular and sincere prayer.

Solomon: A Wise Leader

Among several traits of a godly leader King Solomon exhibited, the most significant was wisdom. When he assumed the throne, God appeared to him in a dream and asked what Solomon wanted the Lord to give him. The king might have thought first about wealth or prestige. He could have asked for several more wishes to be used after his first request. Instead, he prayerfully considered the enormous responsibility he'd inherited and made a simple petition. He asked God to bless him with an understanding heart to judge the people of Israel and to discern between good and evil. The Lord was so pleased He gave Solomon a wise and discerning heart; no one before or after the king has possessed such wisdom. God also added two blessings Solomon didn't request: riches and honor.[7]

The first example of the wisdom God bestowed on Solomon was his judgment in the case of two prostitutes, each claiming to be the mother of the same baby. The king ordered the child be cut in half, with each woman receiving a portion. The rightful mother offered to give up her claim so the child would live; the impostor insisted the boy be divided. Solomon, recognizing the love of the true mother, awarded the child to her.[8] The ruler's wisdom was exhibited in the building of God's temple and his own palace. It was also evident in his teaching on a variety of diverse topics.

Sadly, this great wisdom wasn't enough to keep the king on the path of righteousness all his days. His 700 wives and 300 concubines led him to disobey God's commands—not surprising considering the challenge of meeting the needs of just one spouse and a couple of children while giving the Lord His due! Solomon's lesson for Christian leaders is that we must obtain wisdom from the Lord. (See I Corinthians 1-2.) We must use it with gratitude and in constant consultation with Him, and we must be wary of people and circumstances that might distract us from His direction. As the wise king learned, God's blessing may be stripped away if we don't follow His leading.

Daniel: A Leader of Integrity

In most textbooks on leadership, one of the early chapters deals with integrity. Many suggest this is the most crucial quality for those who guide others. King David recognized its importance, acknowledging his integrity had produced God's favor.[9]

During my days in the Air Force, top officials followed the example of corporate America and designated three core values: integrity first, service before self, and excellence in all we do. Whether we're serving our bosses, our nation, or our Lord, integrity must be the foundation of our actions. While we might achieve our goals acting without honor, we'll justify using any means—regardless how unethical—to come out on top.

When King Nebuchadnezzar conquered Israel, he selected several intelligent, young Jews to be educated in Babylon's traditions and then to serve in his court. Daniel saw the academy's dietary rules conflicted with

Jewish law, and he approached the commander, asking for permission to consume only vegetables and water. Following a 10-day test, Daniel was healthier than those who'd dined on the king's choice food and wine, so he was allowed to continue with his special menu. Later, when Daniel interpreted the king's troubling dream, Nebuchadnezzar appointed him "ruler over the whole province of Babylon and chief prefect over all the wise men of Babylon."[10]

Daniel's integrity—and faith—were tested when Darius became king. He reorganized the nation's government, appointing 120 governors to rule the land. Daniel was appointed one of three commissioners to oversee these officials. When Darius was about to elevate Daniel to a position over all the other leaders, they plotted to prevent the king from following through on his plan. They convinced Darius to set up a statute prohibiting worship of anyone but the king. Daniel again remained true to his faith, praying to the God of Israel three times a day in full view of anyone who passed his home.

Despite his high regard for Daniel, the king had his servant cast into a den of lions, as the royal decree required. In response to Daniel's integrity, God delivered him from harm. Darius was delighted and satisfied the hungry lions by feeding them Daniel's accusers and their families. The king also exalted the Lord, called on his kingdom to tremble before God, and set Daniel on a road to success during his reign as well as the rule of the next king. (See Daniel 6.)

Vision. Courage. Perseverance. Wisdom. Integrity. These traits are common in both secular and spiritual leadership. In addition, a Christian leader must possess several characteristics seldom discussed in leadership manuals.

Moses: A Humble Leader

Our worldly view of leadership often focuses on strength, decisiveness, and authority. A leader, we're told, is a person with charisma who builds confidence and respect among those being led. While this is true to an extent, it places the emphasis on human abilities. If we start to believe the qualities we need come only from within, we're setting ourselves up to be very proud when a bit of success comes our way. As Solomon warns, "Pride goes before destruction, and a haughty spirit before stumbling."[11]

As Christian leaders, our goal is to combine traditional leadership traits with a sense of humility produced and nourished by the Lord. Humility isn't thinking you have no value. It's simply recognizing that whatever you do well is a blessing from God. It's a matter of acknowledging—prayerfully and publicly—that He alone is the source of all you are and do.

Moses had an excellent grasp of this truth. The prophet displayed great reluctance when God called him to stand up to the powerful Pharaoh. This response was built on much more than sheer terror at what the Lord had requested. Do you remember the setting for the conversation? God was speaking to Moses from the midst of a burning bush! This alone is enough to produce a good deal of fear. Considering God's instructions and how they were issued, almost any of us would've experienced a panic attack if we'd been in Moses' position.

The future leader of the Israelites understood what God required, looked at himself realistically, and concluded he just didn't have what it would take to fulfill the Lord's call. His series of excuses was simply a humble acknowledgement that he wasn't up to the task. (See Exodus 3-4.) This is reinforced in Numbers 12:3: "Now the man Moses was very humble, more than any man who was on the face of the earth."

When God explained He'd work in and through the prophet and his brother Aaron, Moses consistently tried to do everything the Lord commanded. Through his successes and failures, Moses remained humble. As his life of faithful service came to an end, Moses twice spoke to the nation. He didn't mention what he'd accomplished. Moses praised the Lord that he'd witnessed God's mighty miracles, many of which He did through Moses. (See Deuteronomy 32-33.)

As we lead, our every thought, word, and deed must be filled with humility. Peter encourages us to "humble yourselves, therefore, under the mighty hand of God, that He may exalt you at the proper time."[12] The Lord will reward our humble service how and when He feels is best for us.

Naaman: An Obedient Leader

Naaman was the highly respected captain of the army of Aram, which today is Syria. The valiant warrior, a leper, pleased the king by leading his troops to victory over the nation's enemies. Because the God of Israel richly blessed Naaman's leadership of the Aramean forces, he demonstrated a deep sense of obedience when the Lord, through Prophet Elisha, called on him to do something strange.

When the army of Aram captured a young Jewish girl, the captain took her home as a servant for his wife. The slave suggested that Elisha could cure the officer of his leprosy. When the powerful military leader arrived at the home of the prophet, Elisha remained indoors. He sent a man to tell Naaman to wash seven times in the Jordan, and he'd be healed. The captain's fury eased when his servants suggested he'd have completed a much more challenging requirement to be returned to health. Should he not accomplish this simpler task? When Naaman did so, his flesh was restored![13]

It's sometimes difficult for a person of significant authority to obey the direction of others, especially when the demand seems to defy logic. Leaders rise to their lofty positions because they can determine how to react to challenges that confront them. Often, though, God wants to take us beyond our comfort zones. He wants to place a situation before us that can be resolved only with His help. He wants us to rely on Him and not on ourselves. As we see in the story of Naaman, when we obey God's direction, He stands ready to bless us.

In leading the Lord's warriors, we must diligently seek His path in overcoming problems beyond our control. When we know what He'd have us do, we must set aside our doubts and airs of self-importance, and we must simply obey. This trust and obedience demonstrate our love for God and result in a triple blessing: the Father loves us, and Jesus loves us and reveals Himself to us.[14]

Isaiah: An Available Leader

Isaiah demonstrates another quality required for leadership: availability. The prophet was eager to serve God. On many occasions, the Lord had revealed to him what He was planning to do in Israel. God had expressed His sorrow at the immorality throughout the nation. The people were corrupt, and their land lay barren.

The Lord proclaimed His frustration with the Israelites' sacrifices. His heart's desire, He said, was that His children "'cease to do evil, learn to do good; seek justice, reprove the ruthless; defend the orphan, plead for the widow.'"[15] Even in the midst of the people's rebellion, God's mercy was apparent. He pleaded with them to repent and promised forgiveness. Sadly, these divine pleas fell on deaf ears. The Lord's offer of compassion turned to a promise of vengeance for those who continued to ignore Him.

It would have been understandable if Isaiah had decided to take an extended vacation from his duties as prophet. Listening to and transcribing God's words must have been a heavy burden. Imagine what would race through your mind if God paid a call on you and described in graphic detail the wickedness of your nation and His plans to take revenge on the vast majority of the country's citizens.

Isaiah chose not to flee, but he did opt to get away for a while. Working through a supernatural travel agent, the prophet booked a holiday in heaven. In Isaiah's vision, following a brief guided tour, God had a question for His guest. "'Whom shall I send, and who will go for Us?'" Isaiah wasted no time in responding, "'Here am I. Send me!'"[16] Only then did the Lord tell the prophet what He wanted him to do.

Apostle Peter addressed a spirit of availability similar to that of Isaiah when he encouraged his readers to "... always [be] ready to make a defense to everyone who asks you to give an account for the hope that is in you."[17] Being prepared to allow God to use us in His way and His timing is essential as we lead others. Of course, it's equally crucial before we become leaders. Our labor for the Lord at lower levels also requires us to listen for and to obey His call to duty. As God works in and through us as we follow other spiritual leaders, He builds in us an awareness that we're to be available to Him and an understanding of how to respond when He decides it's time for us to take on leadership roles.

The Centurion: A Leader of Faith

During the time of Christ, Roman military officers were among the most influential residents of Israel. One day, a centurion met Jesus in the town of Capernaum. Their interaction demonstrated an important trait of a godly leader: faith. The soldier initiated contact with Christ, and his first word illustrates the foundation for his faith and the reason he felt he could approach Jesus with a request. The centurion called Jesus "Lord." Someone as powerful as this official in the emperor's army rarely showed respect to a Jewish citizen. Even before he made his request, the centurion's humility demonstrated he trusted Christ was able to do what he was about to ask.

The Roman then explained his servant, who was paralyzed, was experiencing great pain. Jesus volunteered to visit the officer's home and heal the suffering man. In humility, the military leader revealed tremendous faith in Christ. "'Lord,'" he said, "'I am not worthy for you to come under my roof, but just say the word, and my servant will be healed.'"

Jesus marveled at this response. The simple trust of a man from another country serving temporarily in Israel proved greater than the faith Jesus had observed among natives of the land. After commending the centurion as the witnesses to this exchange looked on, Jesus sent the man home to rejoice with his healthy servant.[18]

As this Roman military officer exhibited the faith that led to his servant being healed, Christian leaders must trust God completely as they guide those the Lord has placed in their care. We must have faith in God as He works in and through us as we seek to conform to the image of Christ. In addition, we must trust Him as we carry out the significant responsibility of discipling others. As we work to accomplish our duties as leaders, we can take confidence knowing our faith produces the victory that overcomes our worldly foes.[19]

Leadership isn't easy. We must tap into God's view of our disciples, seeing them as He sees them. We must appreciate His course for their Christian development. From this spiritual vantage point, we must motivate and encourage our followers. Only through faith in God's supernatural help can we aid others in reaching the next level in their spiritual lives.

Strong leaders possess a number of qualities beyond the nine we've reviewed here. We can gain a better appreciation for the traits required for leadership by studying more than simply biblical examples. Captains of industry and generals of the armed forces, champions of social change and great sports managers provide examples of how to guide others to significant achievements.

Wouldn't it be helpful, though, if we could wrap all their strong points into a single prototype who could serve as an example as we carry out our leadership duties? As you may have guessed, we're a little late in offering this idea. God thought of this before the creation of the world. His Son's earthly leadership—laying the foundation for what's blossomed into a global movement that's had an eternal impact on millions of people for more than 2,000 years—provides an outstanding model for those who lead His followers in the 21st century. Let's consider how Jesus reflected these nine traits of a godly leader.

Jesus Was a Visionary Leader

On more than one occasion, Jesus summoned His 12 closest followers and laid out a plan. After equipping them with the power and authority they'd need to complete their tasks, Christ issued the disciples' marching orders. They were to proclaim the kingdom of God, cast out unclean spirits, and heal the suffering. The Master also provided very specific instructions for what His followers should do in each town they visited. He told them whom to seek and what to say. He outlined the logistics that would be required and offered intelligence on the hostile reaction they'd receive. Christ also encouraged them with news of how the Holy Spirit would help them in their duties. (See Matthew 10.)

Jesus also sent out 35 pairs of followers with similar detailed instructions and warnings.[20] In His final meeting with the 12 disciples, Christ prayed for them, specifically mentioning the persecution He knew was in store and asking His Father to protect those He'd handpicked and trained to carry on His work. (See John 17.)

Christ's vision was not limited to an awareness of the opportunities and challenges awaiting His followers. Jesus also was fully aware of how His final days on Earth would play out. He foretold:

- His betrayal[21]
- Peter's denial[22]
- His suffering, death, and resurrection[23]
- His eventual return (see Mark 13)
- The judgment all mankind would experience[24]
- The rewards His faithful followers would receive[25]

The vision He received from His Father—both concerning Himself and those who'd continue His ministry—conditioned every decision Jesus made, every action He took, and every word He spoke.

Jesus Was a Courageous Leader

Christ spent a lot of time relieving the suffering of the folks He met on His travels. As He did, He exposed Himself to great physical harm. At the risk of contracting leprosy, Christ touched and healed lepers.[26] Disregarding His own safety, Jesus exorcised evil spirits from demoniacs.[27] Unconcerned about being thrown into jail and publicly condemned by Roman or Jewish leaders, Christ healed on the Sabbath in full view of Pharisees[28] and threw tradesmen from the temple.[29]

As courageous as these acts were, Jesus' fearlessness was most apparent in the suffering leading up to and including His death. Weak and exhausted, Christ stood valiantly as the Jewish religious leaders, Pilate, and Herod tried Him on trumped up charges.[30] Despite His innocence, He experienced horrible physical torture at the hands of cruel soldiers.[31] Jesus' ultimate act of courage, one that reflected heroism unmatched through the history of mankind, was to allow Himself to be nailed to a wooden cross carved from a tree He'd created,[32] knowing this intense pain and the death that would follow would enable every person who placed faith in Him to avoid even more excruciating pain for eternity.

Jesus Was a Leader Who Persevered

Leading is complicated by the inability or unwillingness of those being led to follow. This was a challenge for Jesus. His closest followers often failed to see the "big picture." Teaching through lecture and by example, Jesus revealed truth to His disciples that was hidden from everyone else. He must have been tremendously frustrated as they failed to understand His lessons. Even after years following Christ, the disciples didn't grasp some of what He shared with them at their final meal together.[33]

This lack of understanding was evident also among the masses. Several times He was saddened by the "unbelieving," "perverted," or "wicked" generation who wanted a supernatural sign.[34] Once when Christ was teaching a group of Jews who'd believed in Him, He remarked, "'Why do you not understand what I am saying? It is because you cannot hear my word.'"[35]

Not only did the "common man" often turn away from Christ perplexed, He also was constantly challenged by the religious elite of the day. Jealous and afraid He'd continue to "steal" their followers, the Pharisees went on the offensive to discredit Jesus. They criticized the lack of spirituality among Jesus' disciples,[36] His healing on the Sabbath,[37] and His association with sinners.[38] The chief priests, scribes, and elders tested Jesus.[39] Through this lack of understanding and downright hostility, Jesus never wavered; He continued to teach.

Jesus Was a Wise Leader
Apostle Paul wrote that in Jesus "are hidden all the treasures of wisdom and knowledge."[40] This conclusion reinforces what Jesus prayed for His disciples the night He was arrested. The Son of God confirmed His Father's word—the word He'd proclaimed through His ministry—was truth.[41] The first evidence of the wisdom of Christ came when Satan tempted Him at the end of His 40-day fast in the wilderness. Three times Satan attempted to deceive Jesus, and each time He defeated His wily adversary by referring to God's word. Christ's wisdom in quoting scripture preserved His sinless nature.[42]

Between Jesus' encounter with Satan and His final prayer with the disciples, His wise counsel was on view for those who were with Him constantly as well as for those whose time with the Savior was measured in minutes rather than days, weeks, or months. Jesus shared God's truth in lengthy sermons (see Matthew 5-7) as well as in brief encounters, such as when He explained the essence of worship to a sinful woman.[43] He revealed keen insight into His Father's kingdom as He taught multitudes, as He explained complex issues to His inner circle, and as He addressed concerns of searching individuals.

Whether Jesus' advice was universal—as when He pronounced the two greatest commandments[44]—or intensely personal—as when He told a rich, young ruler to sell all his possessions and follow Him[45]—His instruction clearly reflected His Father's perspective. The true test of the wisdom of Christ is that it's as applicable today, more than 2,000 years after it was spoken, as it was on the day He shared it.

Jesus Was a Leader of Integrity
Long before Christ arrived on the scene, Isaiah attested to His integrity. In his prophecy concerning the Messiah Who was to give up His life for all mankind, Isaiah explained the Savior would be a guilt offering. (See Isaiah 53.) This sacrifice, as the sons and daughters of Israel knew, was required by God to be "without defect."[46]

Two New Testament writers confirm Christ fulfilled this requirement. Paul reminds us Jesus was without sin,[47] while Peter describes Christ as "unblemished and spotless."[48] Since the days of Adam and Eve, lapses in integrity—immorality, impurity, greed, anger, untruthfulness—have been common to all mankind. Only the Son of Man has lived a pure and holy life. Had He not, He couldn't have died on the cross for our salvation.

Jesus Was a Humble Leader
Two thousand years ago, the God Who created Earth spent three decades residing upon His creation. In an act of tremendous humility, He stepped out of heaven and arrived on this planet as a helpless child born to unwed parents. He laid aside immortality to become mortal. He gave up royalty to live as a common craftsman. He completed a life of service by submitting to a painful execution. All Jesus accomplished on our behalf reflects a humility never equaled by anyone else. Apostle Paul captures the significance of Jesus' humility through the simple phrase He "emptied Himself."[49]

Christ's humility is evident not only in His ordinary birth and gruesome death. He humbled Himself when He allowed John to baptize Him.[50] He humbled Himself in seeking His Father's direction when confronted with tough decisions, such as choosing His disciples.[51] He humbled Himself by taking time to minister to youngsters.[52] He humbled Himself when He washed the disciples' feet as a demonstration of how they should treat their followers.[53] And through His humble leadership, Jesus became the greatest servant-leader the world has ever known.

Jesus Was an Obedient Leader
In Jesus' humility, He obeyed His Father's call to die for the sin of mankind.[54] This was simply a continuation of the obedience He'd displayed throughout His ministry. In fact, at the outset of the work He'd been called to do, Christ announced His intention to fulfill the prophecy that required Him to meet the spiritual needs of the poor, captive, blind, and downtrodden. He acknowledged the Father's purpose for Him was to preach the kingdom of God.[55] In obedience, He set about completing this task while preparing others to continue His work after He was gone.

Throughout His ministry, Jesus reminded others that He must obey His Father's call.

- "'My food is to do the will of Him Who sent Me and to accomplish His work.'"[56]
- "'I have come down from heaven, not to do My Own will, but the will of Him Who sent me.'"[57]
- "'He Who sent Me is with Me; He has not left Me alone, for I always do the things that are pleasing to Him.'"[58]

After faithfully obeying all God required of Him, Jesus looked back on His efforts with great thanksgiving because He'd "'glorified [the Father] on earth, having accomplished the work which Thou hast given Me to do.'"[59]

Jesus Was an Available Leader

The first three decades of Jesus' life had been devoted to preparing to serve His Father. Although we have no record of Christ's life between the ages of 12 and 30, we assume He was engaged in, and possibly took over, His earthly father's carpentry trade. In this line of work, Jesus undoubtedly learned discipline and precision. He also must have developed the ability to build strong relationships among those who called upon His skills. In addition, Christ knew the word of God and how to apply it. After 40 days of fasting and prayer, Jesus defeated Satan's attempts to get Him to reject His Father. This demonstrated His readiness to lead.[60] The Father recognized His Son's availability and immediately pressed Him into service. "From that time Jesus began to preach."[61]

Christ spent more time ministering to the outcasts of society than He did assisting influential citizens. His availability to dine with despised tax-gatherers and sinners served as proof that God was interested in the affairs of the lowly as well as those of a higher station.[62] As the crucifixion drew near, Jesus addressed His Father in prayer. He reported He'd been available for every task laid before Him on Earth, and He proclaimed His readiness to glorify the Father through His death. (See John 17.)

Jesus Was a Leader of Great Faith

It might have been very easy for Jesus to rustle up a miracle any time the mood dictated, but Christ preferred to demonstrate His reliance upon the Father when a need arose. Jesus was a man of prayer, and His prayers illustrate His faith in the Father.

Christ prayed prior to performing great miracles, as when He fed more than 5,000[63] and later repeated the feat for more than 4,000.[64] Before Jesus raised Lazarus from the grave, He looked to heaven and thanked His Father for hearing Him.[65] Christ prayed in a lonely place early in the morning[66] and often after slipping away from His companions.[67] Apostle Peter recognized Jesus' faith. The Savior's close friend reminds us that in all Christ's suffering, "He uttered no threats, but kept entrusting Himself to Him Who judges righteously."[68]

As we serve as spiritual leaders, we must be men and women of vision, courage, perseverance, wisdom, integrity, humility, obedience, availability, and faith. Only as we allow God to fashion these qualities in us will we be able to lead others in their quest to become what God wants them to be and to do what He wants them to do. These traits also serve as an excellent foundation as we develop and employ the skills required of a leader.

Lessons Learned

- Leaders in God's army are ordinary men and women the Lord has called and equipped to do extraordinary things.
- As we guide other followers of Christ, we must employ traits identical to those of earthly leaders: vision, courage, perseverance, wisdom, and integrity.
- Additionally, Christian leaders must be humble, obedient, available, and faithful.
- We will never be successful in developing these qualities through human wisdom and strength. We must rely on God's Holy Spirit to build these characteristics in us.
- We gain great inspiration and instruction for our roles as leaders as we regularly review the leadership of Christ and others in scripture.

Unit Analysis

To download Unit Analysis and Personal Battle Plan material, please go to www.forwardintobattle.com.

It's not easy being a leader in God's army. It's much less challenging to join the ranks of the anonymous, blending in with the masses who are following a solitary leader marching in front of the troops. It's safer to be a spiritual corporal than a general. Satan and his evil henchmen don't spend nearly as much time trying to pick off those hidden deep in the formation as they do attacking and crippling the leader. Why would anyone want to take charge of a platoon, a battalion, or a division? As undesirable as such duty seems, we must rise to the occasion when God promotes us into leadership positions. Fortunately, from Joseph to Jesus, the Lord has provided some exceptional models for us to follow. We can take heart, too, in the knowledge that as spiritual leaders, we don't serve in isolation. The Holy Spirit leads us as we lead others, and together we can achieve victory!

1. Who's the best leader you've served? What character traits did this leader exhibit consistently? How have you copied these qualities in your leadership?
2. Both Joseph and Jesus were blessed with the vision to see present and future events from God's perspective—a valuable quality for a leader. As modern-day spiritual leaders, what can we learn from James 4:13-17? Does James's caution suggest we can't discern the spiritual dimension of what's happening around us? What does I Corinthians 2:11-16 tell us about the vision we need as we lead others?
3. Joshua displayed tremendous courage on the battlefield. Jesus was courageous in the face of physical and verbal abuse that eventually ended in His death. In the spiritual warfare we're engaged in, we may be subject to a variety of negative responses, from passive indifference to downright hostility. Read Acts 3:12-26. How can Peter's example encourage us as we seek to be faithful in leading others to Christ? According to Matthew 10:17-20, what was the source of Peter's courage? How is the same strength available to us today?
4. Nehemiah labored with great perseverance to rebuild the wall around Jerusalem. Jesus persevered in explaining His Father's kingdom to

people who couldn't—or chose not to—understand His lessons. Apostle Paul also endured hardship in the cause of Christ. How does his instruction in II Corinthians 4:7-9 spur us on as we carry out our duties as leaders? In John 15:7, when the going gets tough, what actions does Jesus tell us to take? What results does He guarantee?

5. The tremendous wisdom of Solomon and Jesus is evident in scripture. Upon Solomon's coronation as king, he asked the Lord for understanding and discernment. To lead effectively, we need the same qualities. According to I Corinthians 1:20-25, how is God's wisdom different from man's wisdom? How does James 1:5 tell us we may obtain the same wisdom that was available to Solomon? Read Colossians 1:9. In helping our followers become wise, what does Apostle Paul model?

6. While we won't achieve the perfection of Jesus in this life, we can call on God to help us to do what is right consistently. According to II Corinthians 7:1-2, what can we learn about integrity from Paul's life and teaching? Spiritual leaders are subject to intensified attack as Satan tries to destroy our credibility and make us ineffective in our ministries. What confidence may we take from I Corinthians 10:13, and how should we apply this verse in our lives?

7. Moses was humble enough to know he was unqualified to take on the heavy responsibility God thrust upon him. Jesus' humility as a servant-leader provides a wonderful example for us thousands of years later. According to Matthew 18:4, what standard of humility did Christ suggest? What do you think He means by this? Read Ephesians 4:1-2 and Colossians 3:12-13. What do these verses tell us about the significance Paul placed on humility? How does Philippians 3:4-14 reveal the apostle's credibility to discuss this subject?

8. Naaman obeyed some seemingly foolish instructions and was healed. Jesus' obedience in completing the tasks His Father assigned Him was absolute. Read John 14:21 and 23. What does Jesus say is a prerequisite for obedience? How can we learn what God requires of us?

What are the results of our obedience? Knowing what God expects and wanting to do it aren't enough to ensure we'll obey. According to Philippians 4:13, what can we do to make sure we'll be successful in our attempts to follow the Lord's commands?

9. Isaiah expressed his availability even before he knew his mission. Jesus was available to live for us and to die for us. One of the great challenges of leadership is stepping outside our comfort zones. Skim through Hebrews 11. How does the availability of these great warriors inspire you to be available to be used by God? How were they challenged to serve, and what did God accomplish through them?

10. The centurion's faith was evident in recognizing Jesus could heal his servant. Jesus' faith was evident as He continually requested His Father's help in matters ranging from the mundane to the miraculous. How does Hebrews 11:1 define faith? What does this mean in your own words? In Mark 12:22-24, what does Jesus tell us about the faith we'll need as leaders? How does Abraham's faith, as described by Paul in Romans 4:20-24, serve as a model for you? Turn back to Hebrews 11. How were these brave heroes able to achieve what God set out for them?

11. Jesus spent His final night of freedom in the Garden of Gethsemane. This brief but deeply passionate event illustrates many of the qualities a great leader must possess. Read Luke 22:39-54, and discuss what this incident reveals about Christ's vision, courage, perseverance, wisdom, integrity, humility, obedience, availability, and faith.

Prayer Points

- Praise our wise and sovereign God for the wonderful examples of spiritual leaders He's provided in scripture
- Thank the Lord for Christian leaders you've been able to serve and who've provided living models of the principles contained in His word

- Ask God to help you to become a leader who consistently exhibits the character traits He expects of those He's called into positions of authority
- Commit to seeking God's direction on serving as a leader, willing to step outside your comfort zone by tapping into the Holy Spirit's wisdom and strength to accomplish everything God lays before you

Personal Battle Plan

If you haven't yet had the opportunity to lead, review the following plan to prepare for when you are called to be a leader. As you gain experience in leadership, use these questions to evaluate your character as you guide your followers to achieve the goals of the unit.

1. Recall the two best leaders and the two worst leaders you've worked with through the years. **List the character traits of each group** you'd like to copy or avoid.

Good Leaders – Traits to Copy	Bad Leaders – Traits to Avoid
a.	a.
b.	b.
c.	c.
d.	d.
e.	e.

2. **Evaluate leadership experiences you've had in the past.** These may have been in a Christian or a non-Christian context. List what you perceive to be your character strengths as well as your weaknesses. (Don't worry about performance; we'll look at how you do on leadership tasks in the next session.) Pray for God's help in identifying how

you can capitalize on strengths and eliminate weaknesses, and list any ideas He brings to mind.
   a. Strengths:
   b. Weaknesses:
3. In this chapter, we looked at nine qualities of several leaders from the Bible. **Assess where you stand in applying these traits in your leadership opportunities** by placing an "X" on each of the lines below.

I usually see things_____I have trouble understanding
from God's view   God's perspective

I stand up courageously_____I tend to be low on courage,
to all challenges   so I often back down

Nothing deters me; _____I try my best, but sometimes
I always achieve my   enough is enough
goal

I have a great grasp of_____I don't seem to know what to
the best way to go   do without seeking advice

Although tempted often,_____I often do what's best for me
I never give in   rather than doing what's
                                   right

I'm quite happy not to take_____I like to boast about what I do
credit for what I achieve   so everyone knows

My greatest pleasure is_____No one really expects me to
obeying what I'm told   do everything I'm asked

When the chips are down, _____ I'm ready, willing, and able	My first priority is to take care of myself
I can do all things through _____ Christ and call on Him often	I really don't feel good about bothering God for help

4. Based on the answers to question 3, **list areas in which you consistently display good leadership traits.** Pray that God would allow you to further develop these qualities and to use them in leading others.
5. Based on the answers to question 3, **list areas in which you need to improve**. Jot down some ideas on how you can do a better job. Pray for God's direction and strength as you seek to overcome shortcomings and become a stronger leader.
6. **Make an appointment** to discuss your answers to these questions with a Christian mentor. Ask for an honest assessment of your leadership potential and performance. Seek advice on how you can best use your gifts and abilities to lead others, and ask your trusted friend to pray with you that God would reveal when, where, and how He desires you to exercise spiritual leadership.
7. **Prepare for the next session** by listing what you think are the most important duties of a godly leader. Consider the actions the leader must take to get the best out of the troops.

Chapter 10

Getting the Most from the Troops

Leadership is the art of getting someone else to do something you want done because he wants to do it.

General Dwight D. Eisenhower[1]

GREAT LEADERS POSSESS outstanding character. We must allow God to work in us as we develop and use the traits modeled by Jesus and other biblical examples. Great leaders also lead. They get the most from their troops, and working together as a team, leaders and followers achieve their units' goals.

One of the best leaders I've served with was an Air Force colonel and former Rhodes Scholar. As commander of the 48th Tactical Fighter Wing at RAF Lakenheath, England, in the mid-1980s, Colonel Sam Westbrook consistently demonstrated the character traits we reviewed in the previous chapter. He was a man of vision, constantly seeking to set in motion projects that would benefit the base and its people long after his two-year assignment was done. He was a man of wisdom, not just with respect to the technical requirements of the job, but also in how to deal with the people under his command. He was a man of integrity, unyielding in his determination to maintain an honorable course. He was a humble man who seemed more interested in elevating those around him than in gaining recognition for his own achievements. In these and other attributes, Colonel Westbrook was a superb leader.

In addition to these virtues, the commander also possessed another necessary trait: the skill to transform a collection of several thousand individuals—each with unique abilities, knowledge, experiences, and attitudes—into a fighting force capable of defeating any foe that threatened the United States or its allies. Colonel Westbrook's rare combination of character and competence set him head and shoulders above leaders who lack one or the other of these essential elements.

Leading with Competence

As we lead other followers of Christ—whether they're our families, members of our Bible study or outreach groups, folks at church, or people serving in national or global Christian ministries—we must do so with character and competence. We've seen examples of outstanding character from the pages of scripture, but what can God's word teach us about the competence we need as we lead other warriors in His army?

A leader's competence can be measured in two ways. First, we can evaluate technical ability by the organization's output. In a military sense, it might be fighter missions flown compared to those scheduled. It might be bombs on target. It could be a sufficient number of trained crewmembers to conduct operations aboard a battleship. Perhaps it's having sufficient weapons and ammunition to hold enemy forces at bay for 90 days. It all boils down to whether or not the unit is prepared to achieve victory in combat. The commander is responsible for ensuring the troops' readiness. Regardless of the leader's skills, experience, dedication, and potential, if the unit is judged to be unfit for combat, the commander is quickly replaced.

In addition to technical ability, a leader must be competent in getting the most from the troops. Humans are complex, emotional beings. What motivates one may have absolutely no impact on another. Problems at home may prevent one from doing the job, while another facing similar challenges may be completely unaffected at work. Some strive for awards and promotion, and others serve out of a sense of duty. The leader's job is to know people well enough to meet their professional and personal needs while spurring them to excellence in accomplishing their piece of the organization's mission.

In the case of spiritual leaders, the two types of competence overlap. Christian groups want to produce changed lives among those who've decided to follow Christ and those who don't yet know Jesus as Savior. Technical competence in spiritual leaders is measured by how well they motivate their subordinates to employ their collective gifts and abilities so people inside and outside the organization are transformed into what God wants them to be. At the same time, Christian leaders must be competent in developing a deep rapport with their followers so they'll grow in their faith and be fruitful in helping to change the lives of others.

In building relationships that will produce transformed lives, the spiritual leader may benefit from a point Jesus made during His final meal with the disciples. When His followers began to argue about who among them would go down in history as the greatest, Christ explained they were way off base. He said the greatest should become as the youngest, and the leader as the servant. Jesus pointed to Himself as the model for this advice, explaining He'd come into the world to serve others.[2] If our Commander's ministry was focused on serving others, those in positions of authority in God's army ought to follow His example. A Christian leader **serves** his or her people in six key ways. The leader:

- **S**hepherds
- **E**ducates
- **R**ebukes and restores
- **V**alues

- Encourages
- Sends out

The Spiritual Leader Shepherds

Men and boys who care for their flocks—both literally and figuratively—play a significant role in scripture. When Moses realized his days leading the Israelites were drawing to a close, he sought the Lord's direction in appointing a man to guide the congregation so they wouldn't be like sheep without a shepherd.[3] God answered Moses' prayer by calling Joshua to take charge.

Later, when Israel's first king disobeyed God, the Lord regretted His choice. God sent Prophet Samuel to scold King Saul and to discover the Lord's replacement. God directed Samuel to visit Jesse in Bethlehem, and he introduced the prophet to seven of his sons. Realizing the future king wasn't among them, Samuel asked Jesse if the boys had any brothers. The father replied his youngest son, David, was out tending the sheep.

The man who'd one day sit on the throne began life as a humble shepherd. In fact, David described to King Saul one aspect of these duties when he offered to fight Goliath. "'Your servant was tending his father's sheep. When a lion or bear came and took a lamb from the flock, I went out after him and attacked him, and rescued it from his mouth.'" David attributed his success to the Lord, "'who delivered me from the paw of the lion and from the paw of the bear.'"

Carrying only a slingshot, and armed with total confidence in God's ability and desire to deliver him from Goliath, the valiant youngster killed his nine-foot-tall adversary, thus launching an overwhelming victory for the Jews over the Philistines. (See I Samuel 16-17.) Years later, when David was anointed king, his subjects repeated words God had spoken about him during Saul's reign: "'You will shepherd My people Israel, and you will be a ruler over Israel.'"[4]

David's years shepherding his flocks and the nation of Israel were vivid in his mind as he described how our heavenly Shepherd cares for His human sheep in the 23rd Psalm. He provides for our nourishment, rest, and comfort. He restores us when we're downhearted. He guides us in doing right and avoiding wrong. He casts out fear and anxiety, even as we approach our final days on Earth. We receive His tremendous love and kindness in this life and will receive even greater blessings for eternity in His presence.

The writer to the Hebrews describes Jesus as the great Shepherd.[5] This can be traced back to Christ's own words to a crowd of followers and doubters. Jesus began with a parable explaining a shepherd calls his sheep by name. The animals follow because they know his voice. When His audience failed to grasp Christ's message, He became more direct. "'I am the good shepherd; and I know My own, and My own know Me. ... I lay down My life for the sheep.'"[6]

Jesus demonstrated His shepherding skills at a time when He and the disciples were so busy in reaching out to those in need that they didn't have time to eat. He led them to a lonely place where they could rest a while before undertaking any further ministry.[7]

What can we learn from these human and divine shepherds about how spiritual leaders are to shepherd their sheep? One duty of a servant-leader is to provide for followers' needs. Colonel Westbrook demonstrated this superbly after assuming command. He called me into his office and gave me an assignment. I was to prepare a summary of my unit's priorities and a list of everything I'd need to achieve these goals. He promised to provide as many resources as he could and to judge my efforts only on the tasks these provisions would allow me to work on.

As we survey the spiritual battlefield, our followers' needs will take many forms. As a shepherd leads his flock to a place of nourishment, we may have to ensure our troops' physical needs are met, both personally and in the ministries we send them to perform. We'll have to protect them as a shepherd ensures the security of his sheep. This will include cover during attacks by Satan and his demonic forces as well as in times of persecution by human foes. Sheep follow their herdsman because they know his voice and know he cares for them. Likewise, our followers need to know us and to be sure they can trust us, that they can turn to us in challenging times and we'll listen and help.

A shepherd can't drive his flock without scheduling times along the way for rest, and we must provide times of refreshment for those who follow us. We must ensure our followers don't become "burned-out Christians." Overworked and ineffective followers of Christ are all too common, and this is largely because leaders don't place a premium on balancing ministry with rest.

The Spiritual Leader Educates

In the military, senior leaders are often assisted by executive officers. They sit just outside their bosses' offices, casting an eagle eye over reams of paperwork to ensure perfection. They pass judgment on who's allowed to meet with the leader and assure their senior officers arrive where they're supposed to be, when they're to be there. They're usually the first to arrive in the morning and the last to depart at night.

These posts are seldom filled with the most administratively gifted. Executive officers usually have demonstrated the skills and character to one day assume the lofty jobs filled by the senior officers they serve. These potential leaders are placed in close proximity to current leaders to prepare them for the high positions they'll assume down the road. Their bosses invest time in them, explaining their decisions, modeling the character required to lead, and demonstrating how to work with other senior leaders to get the job done. The leaders are working to reproduce themselves so their branch of the armed forces will remain in good hands for years to come.

Probably very few military leaders through the centuries have realized this practice is biblical. Jesus selected 12 disciples to be with Him, men

He would prepare to preach and to cast out demons.[8] Christ wanted His disciples to be close so He could teach them and they could watch Him in action. Telling and showing these special followers what God wanted them to be would produce leaders who'd continue the work Jesus started long after He returned to heaven.

The gospels are filled with stories of Jesus' teaching. In Mark 4, Jesus taught a multitude a parable about a man who sowed seed upon various types of soil. When the crowd dispersed and Jesus was alone with His disciples, He explained it fully to them. The 12 often had the benefit of insight their Teacher chose not to share with the masses.

Jesus' lectures covered a range of topics. He taught the disciples about manmade tradition, human nature, and sin. He made them aware of how strong relationships are built within families and among friends and associates. He helped them understand His Father's power, plans, and perspective on life and death. He instructed them on heaven. He lectured them on love, grace, mercy, compassion, forgiveness, and humility. He encouraged them to share God's word with others. He warned them about persecution—His and theirs. He revealed the future. The disciples' spiritual education was thorough and reliable.

In addition to instruction from the greatest Professor the world has known, the disciples benefited from Jesus' demonstrations in the laboratory of life. Christ modeled how to maintain a deep and loving relationship with His Father. He showed compassion always leads to action as He healed the sick, raised the dead, and encouraged the hopeless. Jesus exhibited a range of miracles and astounded the disciples with the news that they'd accomplish similar extraordinary feats.[9]

Jesus' kindness knew no boundaries based on race, religion, age, or gender; all in need received help in equal measure. Christ showed the disciples how to confront and eliminate discrimination, injustice, false religious beliefs, and deceit by never backing down to those who practiced these evil behaviors. When their three-year education was complete, the disciples had heard or seen every lesson they'd need to duplicate Jesus' ministry. He'd successfully reproduced Himself, not once but 11 times. Only Judas proved unqualified to carry on in the footsteps of Christ.

Others in the Bible educated their followers. Joshua spent many years as an aide to Moses. The future general was privy to the prophet's verbal instruction—which Moses had received in conversations with God—and to his leader's example in extremely challenging circumstances. His work as Moses' right-hand man led to Joshua being chosen for several field exercises that enabled him to develop the character and skills he'd need when God called him to replace his mentor.

After Christ's death, Apostle Paul modeled the importance of education in leadership. As he crisscrossed the Mediterranean on his missionary journeys, Paul always ministered with at least one close associate. Barnabas, John Mark, Silas, Timothy, and many others who either traveled with or were visited by Paul learned a great deal from the words God inspired in him as well as the acts he performed in spreading the good news of Christ. Although some of these men were mature Christians, all of them must have been encouraged as they witnessed or heard about Paul's miraculous conversion, his bold proclamation of the gospel, his recovery following attempts to kill him, his steadfastness despite persecution, his faithful witness even while sitting in a dingy prison cell, and his willingness to speak out to members of every level of society.

In educating those we lead, we should follow the examples from God's word. As we do, we should consider the words of Ralph Waldo Emerson: "What you are stands over you the while, and thunders so that I cannot hear what you say to the contrary."[10] A consistent, Christ-like character and devoted service empowered by the Holy Spirit will complement our words of instruction and ensure those who follow us will be well prepared when God calls them to serve Him and to lead others.

The Spiritual Leader Rebukes and Restores

Just short of two years into my Air Force career, I attended the wing commander's daily staff meeting. As a second lieutenant, I was surrounded by a sea of colonels. Just prior to the meeting, I had a private audience with the commander, a man who'd always encouraged me. On this occasion, he'd very emphatically corrected me for a relatively minor error. Red-faced, I'd shamefully slunk into the conference room and assumed my position at the far end of the massive table where senior officers had already assembled. The commander marched in on my heels with a scowl on his face, nestled into the huge chair at the head of the table, and instructed the first briefer to begin his presentation.

After a handful of briefings, the commander instructed those at the table to report on the activities of their units. With great pride, each colonel provided a synopsis he hoped would impress the boss. When the commander called on me, still stung by his earlier scolding and with my eyes fixed firmly on the small notebook in front of me, I mumbled in a barely audible voice, "Nothing, sir." Immediately, the boss responded, "Terry, I'll see you in my office as soon as this meeting is over!" Twenty pairs of eyes flashed from one end of the table to the other, and 20 men twice my age were certain this would be the last time they'd see me at a staff meeting. My short and undistinguished Air Force career was about to come to a premature end, they reasoned. So did I.

Upon entering the holy of holies for a one-on-one confrontation with a man I greatly respected, I was greeted with the question, "What was wrong with you in there?" Suspicion confirmed. "Sir, I was upset about what you said before the staff meeting," was all I could say. "Let me tell you something," the commander quickly replied. "I corrected you earlier because I can see great potential in you. You'll be an excellent officer when you mature a bit. It's only when a leader has given up on a subordinate that he chooses not to mention a mistake and firmly challenge him to buck up. Now, get back to work. I'm expecting great things from you."

Whew! That wasn't as bad as I'd expected. In fact, I left his office more motivated than before any of this had occurred.

This was a lesson I recalled many times in the 27 years that followed. Occasionally, a leader must take a subordinate to task. To ignore a follower's shortcomings is to invite unit failure. As Christian leaders, we must lovingly confront those we lead when they fail to measure up to the standards we've set. Whether their offenses are a matter of character or performance, we're responsible for "speaking the truth in love,"[11] clearly yet gently explaining their words or actions were inappropriate. In addition, we must make our followers aware of the damage they caused, both to themselves and to the organization. Finally, our rebuke must be followed by restoration. We must ensure by our words and deeds that our followers realize their value as individuals and as members of a team.

Jesus modeled this approach several times in His dealings with Peter. The disciple must have felt on top of the world when, in response to Peter's recognition that Jesus was the Messiah, Christ commended him with these words: "'Blessed are you, Simon Barjona, because flesh and blood did not reveal this to you, but My Father Who is in heaven.'" Imagine the fisherman's delight when Jesus promised to build His church using Peter as its foundation.

Highs can become lows very suddenly; peaks of joy can change to valleys of despair overnight. Peter discovered this when he suggested Christ shouldn't have to suffer and be executed. His comments produced Jesus' well-known rebuke: "'Get behind Me, Satan! You are a stumbling block to Me; for you are not setting your mind on God's interests, but man's.'"[12]

A few days later, Jesus' restored Peter as a valuable member of His inner circle. The disciple joined James and John as witnesses to Christ's conversation with Moses and Elijah, and the three men heard the Father's voice coming from a bright cloud above them.[13] It's safe to say that after this divine appointment, Peter didn't fret much over the scolding he'd received earlier.

Peter was merely mortal, so this lesson didn't sink in totally, as an incident just prior to Christ's crucifixion reveals. When Jesus once again predicted His betrayal—this time adding that one of the disciples would be involved in the plot—Peter proclaimed he was prepared to lay down his life for Christ. Jesus then told Peter the bad news: The disciple would deny Him three times.[14] Within hours, Peter told a slave girl, a small group of soldiers and slaves, and a slave of the high priest that he wasn't associated with Jesus.[15] Following his final denial, Jesus turned and looked at Peter. In great humiliation, the disciple wept bitterly.[16]

Fortunately for Peter, this wasn't his last encounter with his beloved Master. After Jesus' resurrection, He visited seven of His followers at the Sea of Galilee and had a personal counseling session with Peter. Three times—one for each denial—Christ encouraged His disciple to care for His sheep. This final restoration was the boost Peter needed to carry out his work as leader of the new church.[17]

The discipline Jesus exercised among His disciples reflects God's discipline for the troops in His army. Paraphrasing Proverbs 3:12, the author of the letter to the Hebrews explained the Lord disciplines those He loves. This is for our good, "that we may share His holiness." Though God's discipline may be painful as we experience it, it will produce righteousness in us.[18] As we rebuke and restore as Christian leaders, we'll help those we lead to move forward in their pursuit of holiness and righteousness.

The Spiritual Leader Values
During an assignment at the Pentagon in the late 1980s, I served as a personal assistant to a top Air Force general. One of my duties was to sit in when reporters interviewed the senior officer. Toward the end of my time in Washington, I received a call from Bob Woodward, the Pulitzer Prize-winning *Washington Post* journalist who, with colleague Carl Bernstein, uncovered President Richard Nixon's involvement in the Watergate scandal. Mr. Woodward explained he was working on a book that would reveal the

complex relationship between the nation's political and military leaders as they planned combat operations. The reporter asked if he could meet with the general to get some details for his new volume.

In three wide-ranging interviews, Mr. Woodward probed the inner workings of the Pentagon's preparations for Operation Just Cause, the U.S. invasion of Panama in December 1989. Of the many issues discussed, one sticks out vividly in my mind. It concerned the advice top military officials provide the President and other political officials who are contemplating sending U.S. troops into combat.

The general explained that senior military leaders strongly believed the commitment of military forces must ***always*** be the last possible option. These officers felt the responsibility for sending young Americans into combat in which many might give up their lives rested squarely on them. They didn't want to risk losing even one soldier, sailor, airman, or Marine if other means of resolving international crises existed. These top leaders truly valued the nation's men and women in uniform.

As spiritual leaders, we must value those we lead. Just as we desire our subordinates to respect us, we must respect them. God's word contains many examples of leaders recognizing the value of their people, expressing their gratitude, and elevating these outstanding contributors to positions in which they, too, became great leaders.

When a famine loomed on the horizon in Egypt, Pharaoh summoned a 30-year-old Jew locked away in prison to seek his advice—not concerning the challenges ahead but to interpret dreams featuring cows and grain. Acknowledging God as the source of his wisdom, Joseph interpreted the dreams, described the coming catastrophe, and suggested a plan to preserve the lives of the Egyptians over the seven years the land would fail to sustain crops.

Pharaoh expressed the value he placed on Joseph, telling him no one was as discerning and wise. He then elevated the former prisoner to the second-highest position in his kingdom, sealing the promotion with fine linen clothes and assorted jewelry. Joseph rewarded Pharaoh's trust by stockpiling food that saved the lives of the people, and in the process, he also shrewdly acquired all the land of Egypt for the ruler. (See Genesis 41 and 47.)

History repeated itself more than 13 centuries later when Babylon conquered Judah and several young Jewish men "in whom there was no defect, who were good-looking, showing intelligence in every branch of wisdom, endowed with understanding, and discerning knowledge" were selected for service in King Nebuchadnezzar's court. Among these superb specimens of Hebrew youth was Daniel.

When the ruler had puzzling dreams his magicians, conjurers, and sorcerers couldn't figure out, Daniel was hurriedly brought before the king. The young man humbly gave credit to the Lord for the insight He'd imparted. Daniel then outlined the future of several great kingdoms, ending in the kingdom of Christ. Nebuchadnezzar fell on his face praising God and Daniel, presented many gifts to the young man, and promoted him to rule over the entire province of Babylon. (See Daniel 1 and 2.)

If you're concerned with these examples, don't worry: Spiritual leaders don't have to possess the ability to interpret dreams! When God calls us to lead, He'll give us the vision, wisdom, and perspective we need to accomplish the tasks He lays out for us. In these examples, our focus is on Pharaoh and Nebuchadnezzar. The two leaders valued the contributions of their people, ensured their young advisers were publicly recognized, and elevated them to positions of greater responsibility. Today, Christian leaders must value their followers, commend them often, and ensure they serve in duties that best employ their gifts and abilities.

The Spiritual Leader Encourages

In the military, successful commanders are respected for their ability to motivate their forces on the eve of battle. In a 1970 movie, actor George C. Scott starred as General George Patton. Standing in front of a huge

Getting the Most from the Troops

American flag as the film opens, the general rallies his troops with a speech that rivals the most stirring pep talk by an athletic coach just prior to a championship game.

Several years later, Mel Gibson portrayed William Wallace, his face sporting blue and white war paint as he urged Scottish warriors to crush the English forces of King Edward I. His passion was so intense that many viewers of "Braveheart" wanted to turn back the clock, jump out of their theater seats, and enlist to fight alongside the charismatic leader!

What many have seen in films, I experienced following a terrorist bombing in Germany that killed a number of American soldiers in the mid-1980s. In retaliation for Libyan involvement in these deaths, U.S. leaders decided to attack several targets in the African nation. As fighter pilots and their weapon systems officers at RAF Lakenheath plotted flight routes and tactics, generals and colonels representing various levels of command—from the Pentagon down to our unit—visited the aircrews to tell them of the importance of their mission and urge them on to success.

When Moses was preparing to send the Israelite army into Canaan to conquer the land God had promised them, more than half a million troops served under his command. Throughout the buildup to their operations, Moses gave a series of spiritual pep talks that serves as a wonderful example for Christian leaders today. Though it stretches across 30 chapters in the book of Deuteronomy, a few themes surface again and again.

Moses began his rallying speech by reminding his army of all the Lord had done for the Israelites. "'For the LORD your God has blessed you in all that you have done; He has known your wanderings through this great wilderness. These forty years the LORD your God has been with you; you have not lacked a thing.'"[19]

In their earlier battles, Moses explained, God had delivered all their foes into their hands. The leader then urged his army to keep the Lord's commands as they took possession of the land He'd promised their fathers. He encouraged them to pass on to their children all they'd learned

255

about the Lord's provision and protection. Moses instructed the people not to forget God's promises to them. He added they'd find the Lord if they searched for Him with all their heart and all their soul.[20]

In addition to reminding the troops of the Lord's blessings and the obedience He desired, Moses told them God would give them "'great and splendid cities which you did not build, and houses full of all good things which you did not fill, and hewn cisterns which you did not dig, vineyards and olive trees which you did not plant, and you shall eat and be satisfied.'"[21] You can just imagine 600,000 soldiers hooting and cheering, thrusting their weapons over their heads in great expectancy, knowing the Almighty was assuring them victory.

Throughout His ministry, Jesus encouraged His closest disciples—individually, in a group of three, or the entire dozen—to follow Him, to pray, to trust in His Father, to deny themselves, and to reach out to others in His name. Jesus also urged them with a peek into the future, describing His second coming and revealing the disciples would sit on thrones with Him in heaven.[22]

Jesus encouraged Philip to devise a plan to feed thousands who'd gathered to listen to His teaching[23] and later suggested he look for the Father by observing His Son.[24] When Mary anointed Jesus with expensive perfume, He urged the disapproving Judas to give a higher priority to worship than to raising money for ministry.[25] Christ encouraged Peter to walk on water,[26] to forgive others as often as they ask,[27] and to feed His sheep.[28] He challenged Peter, James, and John to pray with Him in Gethsemane.[29] And He allowed the doubting Thomas to be encouraged by touching His resurrected body.[30]

Before He ascended into heaven, Jesus encouraged the men who'd build His church. Christ reminded the disciples they'd receive supernatural power from the Holy Spirit so they could take His message to the farthest reaches of the world.[31] The disciples encouraged new believers in their faith, bringing people together for study, fellowship, meals, and prayer. This allowed their followers to develop the strength and courage they'd need to apply their leaders' teaching in a hostile environment.[32]

Following his dramatic conversion, Paul was encouraged by the Christian leaders in Damascus, and he quickly began to share the gospel in the city's synagogues.[33] The apostle provided great encouragement for fellow missionaries as they walked together along dusty paths or accumulated a load of frequent-sailing miles traversing the Mediterranean carrying the good news from Asia to Europe and back.

Paul encouraged Timothy, who he called his true child in the faith, to "fight the good fight, keeping the faith and a good conscience;" to "discipline yourself for the purpose of godliness;" and to "show yourself an example of those who believe."[34] The apostle further challenged Timothy to "present yourself approved to God" and to "preach the word; be ready in season and out of season; reprove, rebuke, exhort, with great patience and instruction."[35] These words inspired Timothy as he led the church in Ephesus.

The writer to the Hebrews reminds us of the importance of building up those who serve under us: "Let us consider how to stimulate one another to love and good deeds, ... encouraging one another; and all the more, as you see the day drawing near."[36] As the day of Christ's return approaches, spiritual leaders must encourage their followers to grow closer to the Lord and to employ their gifts and abilities in helping others to develop a deeper relationship with God.

We must remind those God has entrusted to us of all He's done for Jesus' followers. We must know what type of encouragement each needs. While some are spurred on by dramatic pep talks, others respond better to quiet, individual inspiration. Whatever tactic is appropriate, leaders must motivate their troops to don the armor of God, depart the protection of the fortress we call the church, and engage the enemy in the ferocious spiritual war around us.

The Spiritual Leader Sends Out

If the result of a leader's shepherding, educating, rebuking and restoring, valuing, and encouraging is merely a collection of people who know more than when they began the process, feel loved and cared for, and have a positive self-image, the leader will have failed. This is exactly what a conference speaker had in mind when she suggested, "If you think you're leading but no one is following, you're just out for a nice walk."

All the care and preparation you provide won't be fully effective unless your followers take action on what they've learned. True, their knowledge and faith may have grown significantly along the way. But remember: If we are who God wants us to be, we'll do what He wants us to do. The Lord uses human leaders to help others become what He wants them to be and to launch their troops into doing what He wants them to do.

In his gospel, Luke tells about Jesus sending His followers into action. Previously, Christ had recruited His disciples and provided on-the-job training for the 12. They listened to His instruction, publicly and privately, understanding some but unable to comprehend much. They observed Him healing the sick and casting out demons from the possessed. They wondered about His frequent absences from the group as He slipped away to pray. They were uncomfortable when He spent time with unpopular and rejected people and worried as He ruffled the feathers of the rich and influential. And they feared for their lives when their little boat nearly capsized during a gale on the lake.

Of course, Jesus knew what He was doing, and He knew what impact it was having on His disciples. There was nothing random in all this; these activities didn't happen by chance. One of the reasons for Christ's words and actions was that He was preparing His followers for the day they'd do exactly what He was doing. They'd pray and teach. They'd heal and cast out demons. They'd spend time with society's undesirables and stand up to powerful officials. And all but two—one who betrayed Him and another who died of natural causes after years of imprisonment—would, as martyrs, give up the lives they feared they'd lose during a storm on a lake years earlier. This ragtag band of men from assorted backgrounds would carry on Jesus' ministry to transform the world by transforming men and women one by one in the power of the Holy Spirit!

Following His initial training for the disciples, Jesus decided it was time to field-test what they'd learned. He called the 12 together, gave them instructions and the power they'd need to complete their tasks, and sent them on their way. The disciples traveled from village to village, preaching and healing. At a designated time, Jesus' followers returned and gave Him a thorough rundown on all the Lord had done through them.[37]

Through the remainder of his book, Luke describes Christ's continuing preparation of these dozen men through teaching and modeling. Following His resurrection, Jesus had his final earthly conversation with the 11 who'd remained loyal. After "[opening] their minds to understand the scriptures," Christ sent them out to proclaim to all nations repentance for forgiveness of sins in His name.[38] Jesus' example at the end of His earthly ministry reflects one of the greatest responsibilities a leader faces: sending out those who've been identified and prepared to carry on the ministry.

Jesus departed this world satisfied He'd been faithful to His Father's call to shepherd, educate, rebuke and restore, value, encourage, and send out His disciples. He calls us to do the same as we serve those He has placed under our leadership. As we faithfully accomplish our spiritual duties on Earth, we can expect to be handsomely rewarded when our service in God's army on this planet comes to an end.

Lessons Learned

- If we're to lead effectively, we must possess outstanding character and competence.
- A leader in God's army shepherds his or her troops, nourishing them, protecting them, developing intimacy with them, and ensuring they get the rest they need.
- Those who guide other spiritual warriors must educate them through words and deeds.

- Another important role for a leader is to rebuke followers when they go astray and then to restore them to a position of confidence and courage.
- In addition, we must value those we lead, recognizing their significant contributions to the unit and commending their outstanding performances.
- A leader must encourage each subordinate with the specific style of motivation that brings out the best from the follower.
- The final task of a leader is to send combat-ready forces into battle so they can put their preparation into action as they become what God wants them to be and to do what God wants them to do.

Unit Analysis
To download Unit Analysis and Personal Battle Plan material, please go to www.forwardintobattle.com.

Satan's greatest desire in his attacks on followers of Christ is to make us totally ineffective in carrying out the orders God has given us. Our adversary wants to prevent us from sharing the love of Jesus with others, and he's just as determined to ensure we don't lead other believers to become more like Christ. God's desire, though, is that we constantly grow in our faith and service so we may guide others in spiritual pursuits. When He calls and equips us for this role, we must follow in Christ's steps in serving those we lead. Tapping into the Lord's strength and wisdom, we can overcome Satan's tactics to throw us off track.

1. Consider the leaders you've served under as you worked toward a common objective. How well did they shepherd, educate, rebuke and restore, value, encourage, or send out their followers? How did those in the organization respond to their leadership?

2. Servant leadership is often illustrated by the example of Jesus washing the disciples' feet during His final meal with them. Read John 13:1-20, and imagine you were there. What do you think would have been going through your mind as Christ set down His basin and knelt before you? What lesson was He trying to impart? Is the idea of serving those we lead relevant in the 21st century? If so, how can we follow Jesus' example?
3. What thoughts come to mind when you consider how a shepherd cares for his sheep? How are these responsibilities illustrated in each of the following passages? As spiritual leaders, how can we move beyond the shallow relationships we often have with those we lead and build an intimacy that will allow us to understand our people's needs and help our troops to meet them?
   a. John 10:3-4
   b. John 10:9-11
   c. Luke 15:4-6
   d. Psalm 23
4. According to Mark 3:13-15, what was the first task for the 12 Jesus chose as His closest disciples? As these men listened to the Messiah's teaching and watched His interaction with people, how do you think they felt? What were some of the most important lessons they learned from this firsthand education?
5. It's easy to be a model for others when things are going well. It's much more difficult to be a good example when everything around us seems to be in turmoil. Often, though, it's during these challenges that our followers are watching most closely. What can modern leaders learn about how to deal with adversity from Jesus' example in I Peter 2:21-23?
6. Read Matthew 16:13-23. What range of emotions do you suppose Peter felt as Jesus first commended him as having special insight into

God's ways and then criticized him for failing to consider the Lord's perspective? What thoughts may have gone through Peter's mind over the six days between Jesus' rebuke and His invitation for the disciple to join Him as He met with Moses and Elijah? What impact did this event have on Peter's future ministry? What does this passage reveal about how we're to rebuke and restore those we lead?

7. When Nehemiah discovered the desperate situation in his homeland, he knew he had to do something to help the people of Jerusalem. According to Nehemiah 1:4, what was his first course of action? Read Nehemiah 2:1-9. What did the servant do prior to making a request of the king? How did Artaxerxes respond? To what did Nehemiah attribute the king's favor? What do the ruler's actions reveal about the value he placed on his servant? What would Nehemiah have had to do to earn this response? How can we recognize the value of those who serve under us, and how can we reward them for their devoted service?

8. The Lord spoke to Joshua as he assumed leadership over the people of Israel. How did God's encouragement in Joshua 1:1-9 prepare the general to carry out his responsibilities? Read Joshua 1:10-18. In his initial act as commander, Joshua called on the tribes that already had received their inheritance to leave families and property behind and join their countrymen in conquering the land across the Jordan. What was their response? What could they see in Joshua's leadership that led to this reaction? How can we encourage our followers to serve the Lord with courage?

9. Some Christians seem to be involved in a lifetime of spiritual booklearning with little application of what they've studied. Why is it important for a leader to help followers move from the training ground onto the battlefield? Prior to sending troops into combat, what must a Christian leader do to ensure they're prepared? What lessons can we learn from the example of Jesus as described in Luke 9:1-6 and 10:1-11 ?

Prayer Points

- Praise our kind and loving Father for His Son's consistent demonstration of how to be a servant for those we lead
- Thank the Lord for the opportunities He's given or will give us to help other Christians become the people He desires them to be
- Ask God to help you recognize and accept the leadership positions He's prepared you for and through which He intends to bless others
- Commit to following the example of Christ in shepherding, educating, rebuking and restoring, valuing, encouraging, and sending out those God calls you to lead so they may serve faithfully and eventually become leaders in their own right

Personal Battle Plan

If you haven't yet had the opportunity to lead, review the following plan to prepare for when you are called to be a leader. As you gain experience in leadership, use these questions to evaluate how well you serve your followers as you work together to achieve the goals of the unit.

1. As you've served the Lord using the gifts and abilities He's blessed you with, has He allowed you to lead? If so, **evaluate your overall effectiveness as a spiritual leader** by filling in specific positions of authority you've held in the following general areas—now or in the past—and then indicate how well you feel you performed your duties.

	Poor	Fair	Good	Excellent

   a. Family
   b. Workplace
   c. Church

                    Poor   Fair   Good   Excellent

   d. Community
   e. Other
2. To be a shepherd for those you lead, you must develop strong relationships with your followers. If you've had the opportunity to lead a group of Christians, use the scale below to **assess the depth of your relationships with those on your team**. Consider how well you've been aware of what's been happening in the lives of your followers and your understanding of what they've felt their needs were. Also reflect on the likelihood your followers would approach you to ask for your support. Jot down some ideas about how you might better shepherd your subordinates in the future.

   Intimate_____Shallow
   Relationships   Relationships

3. We educate our followers through teaching and modeling. An effective leader maintains consistency between words and deeds. As you look back on your leadership, **determine how well what you said matched what you did**. Have you demonstrated your competence in the tasks you've asked your followers to perform, or have you required them to do things you wouldn't do yourself? Have you encouraged them with biblical examples and then acted contrary to your verbal lessons? If you note inconsistency between words and deeds, make a note of what you can do to correct this.
4. Christians in general and leaders in particular often have a great deal of difficulty in confronting other followers of Christ when mistakes are made. Because we're sensitive to the feelings of others, we don't want to say anything that might discourage someone who has

fallen short, so we say nothing at all. Our leadership roles sometimes require us to rebuke and restore those in error. **Review how you've dealt with followers who've missed the mark.** Has your response been to criticize without offering suggestions for improvement? Have you been so wishy-washy that your subordinates had no idea they'd made mistakes? Have you avoided saying anything to the offending parties for fear of hurt feelings? Or have you respectfully outlined the problem, proposed and possibly demonstrated a better way to get the job done, and then affirmed your troops for their vital contribution to the team? Pray for God's help where you need to improve.

5. Many people working in the "trenches" within churches and other Christian organizations become disillusioned because their leaders never pass along thanks for a job well done. Hours of hard work, in some cases while enduring significant satanic attack, are met with seeming indifference as leaders are so heavily involved in their own tasks they fail to provide constructive feedback to their troops. **Assess how well you communicate value** to your subordinates. If you need to improve, schedule feedback appointments with your people now and follow up with them periodically. Determine how you can reward them for their outstanding performance in a meaningful way, and follow through as often as commendation is warranted.

	Never	Sometimes	Often	Always
a. I review my followers' performance regularly and provide constructive feedback.				

	Never	Sometimes	Often	Always

- b. I express gratitude for team members' contributions to our goal.
- c. I am aware of how I can reward my people, and I do so in a timely manner.
- d. I regularly commend my troops in front of others.
- e. My subordinates are sure I respect their commitment and results.

6. Although in our roles as Christian leaders we may not urge huge armies to fight the good fight, members of the smaller units we're responsible for need regular encouragement. In addition to group pep talks for our teams, we must determine how to "get inside the heads" of our subordinates to learn how best to motivate them toward the goal. Make a list of those you lead at home or in other ministry, and with God's help, **note how you'll motivate each of your followers** individually.

7. A leader's work of readying troops culminates in sending them into combat. In some churches and ministries, however, leaders choose to protect their subordinates by continually extending their preparation periods. The schedule of planning meetings and training sessions is often prolonged as more and more discussions are added prior to ministry getting under way. **Plan to launch your**

subordinates into ministry soon, and continue to SERVE them as they go.
8. **Prepare for the next session** by considering what you think it will be like to spend eternity in God's presence in heaven.

Completing the Mission: A Final Transition

IN TODAY'S MILITARY, deployments around the globe separate families for many months. Members of the armed forces engage in combat to protect the interests of their nation and allied countries much more frequently than they did during the Cold War era. These duties require them to make great sacrifices. In some cases, they lay down their lives to establish the foundation for democracy for people who've rarely, if ever, experienced freedom.

Often men and women in uniform serve for less pay than they'd command in civilian jobs. In addition, they're bombarded regularly with media coverage of groups within the country and around the world expressing great hostility about military forces being sent to international hotspots.

As they work 12-hour shifts—or longer—daily, deploy halfway around the world leaving spouses and children behind, and serve in areas where sniper fire and suicide bombers have killed hundreds of their contemporaries, many questions fill their minds. "How well am I carrying out my duties?" "Is what I'm doing worthwhile?" "Does anyone appreciate my sacrifice?" "How will my contribution be recognized—now, throughout my time in uniform, and when I complete my dedicated service?" The military answers these questions in three ways: performance evaluations, awards and decorations, and compensation for those who serve a full career.

During my nearly 30 years in the Air Force, officer evaluation systems changed often. The one constant was that when rating time rolled around, the anxiety level rose dramatically. I was particularly concerned while assigned to a base in Italy. For two and a half years, the colonel passing final judgment on captains at my base was located at a headquarters in Germany. He evaluated us without seeing us in action, merely rubber-stamping the ratings of lower-ranking officers in the chain of command.

The ultimate reward at rating time was to have done such a superb job that the evaluation was shipped to a three- or four-star general for endorsement. With his comments and signature included in the report, the future was secured: advancement ahead of contemporaries, assignment to the most important positions, and, eventually, promotion to general. If this competition for success didn't get the adrenalin flowing, nothing would!

Because advancement in rank doesn't happen often, military members receive awards and decorations for faithful service. At the end of each tour of duty and for performance of heroic proportions at any point during an assignment, a troop is awarded a medal—a small, round piece of metal at the end of an inch-and-a-half strand of ribbon—that's presented with much pomp and circumstance.

Finally, those who serve at least 20 years receive several retirement benefits. Among these are a monthly pension; medical care; and the use of military commissaries, recreation areas, and other facilities. These rewards compensate those who gave up safer and better-paying opportunities and instead devoted themselves to the service of their nation.

As the military recognizes its members, God rewards Christians for faithful service in His army. While the Lord blesses His spiritual warriors throughout their earthly lives, scripture tells us God's ultimate recognition comes upon arrival at their eternal home.

Jesus' words to the disciples at their last supper together give us a hint of what awaits us. "'In My Father's house are many dwelling places; ... I go to prepare a place for you. And if I go and prepare a place for you, I will come again, and receive you to Myself; that where I am, there you may be also.'"[1] Jesus now sits at the right hand of His Father, so **our eternal retirement home is in heaven** with the Lord.

In addition to telling His closest followers He was going to make ready a residence they'd enjoy forever, Jesus asked His Father to reunite them with Him in heaven when they'd fulfilled their earthly duties. Just prior to His arrest, Jesus prayed, "'Father, I desire that they also, whom Thou hast given Me, be with Me where I am, in order that they may behold My glory, which Thou hast given Me.'"[2]

Isaiah was blessed with a vision of heaven before the Lord commissioned him for duty. The prophet describes God's throne room and the angelic beings who worship Him continually.[3] God also allowed Daniel and Ezekiel to view His dwelling place. (See Daniel 7 and Ezekiel 1.)

During his exile on the island of Patmos, John had a similar vision. The apostle reports One sitting on the throne had the appearance of a jasper stone and a red quartz. John also noted a rainbow around the throne; 24 elders occupying their own thrones; and four fantastic, six-winged creatures circling overhead singing praises to God. (See Revelation 4.) What a scene, and we'll reside there forever!

Paul tells us that in this magnificent setting, we'll receive a debrief on our time as warriors in God's army. He explains all Christians have the same foundation for our service: Jesus Christ. **God will reward the achievements** of those He judges to have performed with distinction in building on this foundation. The prize: treasures that will never be destroyed or taken from us. While all Jesus' followers will enjoy the pleasures of heaven forever, those whose performance fails to measure up to what our Commander calls us to accomplish will forfeit certain honors the Father wishes to bestow upon us.[4]

The promise of all God has in store should provide great incentive for us to complete our duties on this planet with excellence. As we toil in His service in this life, Jesus is watching our every action. He provides all the strength and wisdom we need to achieve the mission He's set for us.

At the same time, He's preparing a heavenly home for us where we'll enjoy Father, Son, and Holy Spirit for eternity. Before we know it—in God's perfect timing when Jesus' preparations are complete—Christ will invite us to join Him in the paradise He's created specifically for each of us. Jesus will escort us to heaven and reveal to us how we've done in His service on Earth. I can't wait!

CHAPTER 11

Retiring From Active Duty

Did you ever stop to think that God is going to be as pleased to have you with Him in Heaven as you are to be there?

A. W. Tozer[1]

TWENTY-EIGHT YEARS, SEVEN months, 18 days, and 14 hours after I'd been commissioned a second lieutenant in the Air Force—less than a week prior to my last official day in uniform—I was in the spotlight during another ceremony. Standing in a conference room in the Pentagon alongside the general I'd worked for during the final three years of my career, I was retired from military service.

For many years, I'd downplayed significant milestones. When given the option, I'd always had a medal sent to me through the base distribution system rather than taking part in a formal presentation. Promotion ceremonies had been extremely small affairs, usually attended only by my family and my boss.

When I retired, I wasn't given a choice. The general told me when, where, and how the ceremony would happen. As when I'd become a cadet and when I was commissioned onto active duty, my retirement was a rite of passage that marked a dramatic change in my life. Following nearly 33 years as a cadet and officer, I was about to return to the civilian ranks I'd departed in 1968.

It was a very nice event. After a few kind words of gratitude for my service, the general presented me one last medal. Many in the crowd were there because they felt it would have been inappropriate to attend the catered reception afterwards without putting in an appearance at the ceremony. They were polite and seemed to pay attention when I spoke at great length about the tremendous support I'd received from family, co-workers, and friends through the years and even greater length about the role Christ had played in my life.

The most memorable aspect of the day was spending a few minutes with many people who'd blessed me through my career. My wife and children. My wife's parents. My secretary during my first assignment and her husband. Men and women I'd served with at one base or another. My pastor. Men from Pentagon Bible studies. Members of our church. All shared words of encouragement—between bites of hors d' oeuvres—that launched me into the next phase of life.

A Heavenly Retirement Home

Unlike earthly professions, our service in God's army has no end. As long as we're healthy, we represent the King of kings and Lord of lords, carrying out the mission He's given us. Our orders change throughout our lives, but we serve until God calls us to join Him in heaven. We can look forward to a spiritual retirement ceremony when we pass from this life to the next.

Five and a half years before I retired, I received an unexpected assignment to the Pentagon for a second tour of duty. God's providence in this move was clearly visible. Within a few weeks of our arrival in northern Virginia, my uncle, who lived nearby, fell and broke his hip. Ray's daughter and her family resided in Connecticut, so we offered to help when the 76-year-old required assistance.

One of Ray's first requests was that we look into the details of a retirement home west of Washington, D.C. Nestled in a beautiful, wooded area near the Potomac River, the facility had been built for former military senior officers. Its brochure was filled with photos of distinguished-looking gentlemen in coats and ties with glamorous ladies on their arms. The common areas were splendid and the quarters warm and inviting.

Upon reviewing the marketing literature, I had visions of daylong gatherings featuring tales of how the home's residents had led charges up hills, navigated powerful warships, or shot down adversaries in aerial dogfights. Could there be any better way for military leaders and their spouses to spend their last few years? No; this was as good as it gets! As lovely as this home might have been, it pales by comparison to the setting in which Christians will spend eternity.

What We Think about Heaven
When our children were young, they sang a song in Sunday school that went like this: "Heaven is a wonderful place, filled with glory and grace. I want to see my Savior's face. Heaven is a wonderful place. I want to go there!"[2] It was one of those songs that seemed to have no end; the kids simply repeated these words over and over until they grew tired, and then they stopped—or we made them stop!

Over time, children's interest in heaven seems to decline. Perhaps this is because with increasing age come increasing responsibilities that demand time and attention, diverting focus away from spiritual things. Perhaps adults become skeptical when they see the evil and suffering that exist in the world, wondering if all the talk about a loving God in heaven is just a myth. Whatever the reason, heaven isn't usually high on the list of topics discussed among family, friends, or business associates.

In 2003, the Barna Group surveyed the American public on the topic of life after death. More than three quarters (76%) claimed to believe in the existence of heaven. Of these, 64% thought they'd go to heaven when they die, 5% said they'd cease to exist, 5% felt they'd come back as another life form, and one half of 1% said they'd go to hell. Almost one in four (24%) admitted they had no idea what would happen to them when they die.[3]

Eleven years later, the Pew Research Center conducted a Religious Landscape Study. The 2014 findings were very similar to those of the Barna Group, with 72% of Americans expressing a belief in heaven, which was defined by the researchers as "a place where people who have lived good lives are eternally rewarded."[4]

Heaven has been written and sung about for all time. In 428 B.C., Greek philosopher Euripides wrote that the giant Atlas upheld heaven.[5] In *Hamlet*, Shakespeare lamented that "some ungracious pastors" called parishioners to tread "the steep and thorny way to heaven" while clergymen failed to practice what they preached.[6] In 1805, Sir Walter Scott, a Scottish novelist and poet, suggested, "Love is heaven, and heaven is love."[7]

In *The Scholar Gypsy*, written in 1853, Matthew Arnold proposed that on the topic of heaven, little difference exists between those who are deeply religious and those who aren't. He wrote:

> Thou waitest for the spark from heaven: and we,
> Light half-believers of our casual creeds,
> Who never deeply felt, nor clearly willed …
> Who hesitate and falter life away,
> And lose tomorrow the ground won today –
> Ah! do not we, wanderer! await it too?[8]

Over the years, a vast number of songs has featured lyrics about heaven. I remember my parents listening to "Pennies from Heaven" and "Thank Heaven for Little Girls." Rock-and-roll artists have picked up this theme, turning out such hits as "Stairway to Heaven," "Knockin' on Heaven's Door," "Tears in Heaven," and "Wear Your Love Like Heaven." Country-and-western artists have joined in with "Will There Be Sagebrush in Heaven?" and "You Can't Haul a U-Haul into Heaven." And then there are "Made in Heaven," "Hands in Heaven," "Eyes of Heaven," "Starlight up in Heaven," "So Close to Heaven," and "Monkey Gone to Heaven."

Heaven also features prominently in Christian literature. In his classic book *The Pilgrim's Progress*, John Bunyan describes the scene when his primary character, Christian, approaches heaven. The city in which the Almighty resides was built of pearls and precious stones, and its streets were paved with gold. These produced a glorious reflection in the sun. Outside the gates were orchards, vineyards, and gardens belonging to the King.

To enter heaven, Christian had to cross a deep river. At first fearful, the pilgrim was encouraged by the thought that Jesus would be with him as he passed through the waters. As Christian came up out of the river on the opposite shore, two angels greeted him and led him into his eternal home.[9]

What the Bible Says about Heaven

The words heaven, heavens, and heavenly appear more than 700 times in the Bible. We find at least three different meanings for the concept in scripture.

In the very first verse of the Bible, we're told, "In the beginning God created the ***heavens*** and the earth."[10] In this context, the word refers to the expanse that stretches above Earth and contains the moon, stars, clouds, thunder, and lightning. From the heavens descended rain, dew, and the manna God provided to the Israelites on their journey to the Promised Land.

King David rejoices in the beauty of the heavens in several of his psalms. He explains they display the Lord's splendor[11] and declare His glory.[12] David proclaims, "The LORD has established His throne in the heavens; and His sovereignty rules over all."[13] Asaph, author of some of the psalms, tells us God's righteousness is evident in the heavens.[14]

During His ministry on Earth, Jesus spoke often about the ***kingdom of heaven***. As God's children, the Jews eagerly anticipated its coming. They looked forward to the arrival of the Messiah because they knew He'd usher in the long-awaited kingdom. When Christ announced, "'The time is fulfilled, and the kingdom of God is at hand,'"[15] He was making the bold assertion that through Him, the wait was over. Jesus had arrived not to help people become better people but to call them to a radical decision to become part of the kingdom of heaven.

A quick tour through Matthew's gospel reveals Christ addressed God's eternal kingdom much more than He discussed rules for life on Earth. Jesus fasted for 40 days in the wilderness and then began His ministry. Matthew summarizes His initial sermons in one sentence: "'Repent, for the kingdom of heaven is at hand.'"[16]

In His Sermon on the Mount, Jesus taught the kingdom of heaven belongs to the poor in spirit as well as to those who are persecuted for the sake of righteousness.[17] Christ also cautions that to gain entry into the kingdom, one must be more righteous than the religious leaders of the day.[18]

His instruction also included a warning. Many, He said, will expect to gain access to the kingdom of heaven. Unfortunately, not everyone who lives a "godly" life and takes part in "godly" activities will be allowed entry. Our "righteous" actions alone don't ensure the kingdom will be open to us.[19] According to God's Son, we must do the will of the Father to be admitted, and the single entry requirement is that we must receive Christ as Savior.

Many of Jesus' parables deal with the kingdom of heaven. Jesus assured His disciples that unlike all those who were perplexed by His teaching, the 12 would understand the mysteries of the kingdom of heaven.[20] He then shared with the disciples and others several stories that compared the kingdom with everyday items: wheat and weeds, a mustard seed, yeast, hidden treasure, a valuable pearl, and a fishing net.[21] Christ's goal was to stimulate His listeners to think beyond their earthly activities and to understand eternity in God's presence was much more preferable than eternity apart from Him.

Christ told His disciples a person must become like a child to enter the kingdom of heaven.[22] He wasn't suggesting we become childish; many adults do fine at this without the Lord's direction. What Jesus was getting at is that entry into His kingdom is reserved for those who humbly recognize their insignificance compared to the almighty, all-knowing, ever-present, loving Creator of everything that exists. This childlikeness also means followers of Christ must depend totally on our Father to provide for all our needs and must accept graciously His leadership in our lives.

Jesus compared entry into the kingdom of heaven to a king willing to forgive the debt of his slave.[23] He also instructed a rich, influential young man to follow Him if he truly desired to receive eternal life. When the fellow declined His invitation, Christ was saddened that those who had great wealth would set their possessions above intimacy with Him—in this life and for eternity.[24]

Further teaching and answers to the questions of priests and paupers suggest Jesus wished to discuss nothing more than eternal life in His Father's kingdom. In fact, the final words of Jesus in Matthew's gospel highlight His passion for men and women in all nations knowing about and gaining access to the kingdom of heaven. Claiming the authority of His Father, Christ sent out His followers—the initial warriors in God's army—to carry on His instruction so others would learn of Him, receive Him as Savior, and spend eternity in His presence.[25]

John provides additional insights on God's eternal kingdom. He mentions Christ told Nicodemus spiritual rebirth was necessary for entry. (See John 3:1-21.) The apostle also tells how Jesus revealed to a Samaritan woman that He's the source of eternal life.[26] Christ made the same claim to Jews who were persecuting Him.[27]

Jesus said He'd been dispatched to Earth from His heavenly home to make it possible for people to enter God's kingdom. (See John 6:26-58.) Before His crucifixion, He prays that those who've placed their faith in Him would be with Him in heaven so they could behold His glory.[28] It's obvious how much Jesus wants mankind to experience the blessing of being part of the kingdom of heaven.

God's Dwelling Place
In addition to the heavens and the kingdom of heaven, scripture reveals the splendor of **God's dwelling place in heaven**. Many years before Jesus proclaimed the kingdom of God had come, Prophet Isaiah was allowed a vision of heaven. He reported seeing the Lord seated on a throne, high and exalted, wearing a majestic robe that filled the temple. Above Him were heavenly beings called seraphs, each with six wings. With two wings they covered their faces, with two they covered their feet, and with two they flew. They called to one another, "'Holy, holy, holy, is the LORD of hosts. The whole earth is full of his glory.'" At the sound of their voices, the foundations and thresholds shook, and the temple was filled with smoke.[29]

Prophet Ezekiel also was permitted a vision of heaven. He reports seeing four living beings, each with four faces (a man, a lion, a bull, and an eagle) and four wings, gleaming like shined bronze. Over their heads was an expanse like crystal, and above that was what appeared to be a man sitting on a throne surrounded in radiance. Ezekiel described the scene as the glory of the Lord, and as the prophet fell on his face, God ordered him to take a message to the people of Israel. (See Ezekiel 1.)

Daniel, too, was blessed with a look into God's residence. In the midst of some dramatic heavenly action, Daniel caught a glimpse of God sitting on a throne. He also saw "'One like a Son of Man'" coming in the clouds of heaven, and He received from His Father an everlasting kingdom "'that all the peoples, nations, and men of every language might serve Him.'" (See Daniel 7.)

In the book of Revelation, John describes the vision of heaven Jesus shared with him. Upon walking through an open door, the apostle saw a throne, and the Person sitting on it appeared like precious gems. A rainbow resembling an emerald encircled the throne, and around it, 24 elders dressed in white and wearing golden crowns sat on other thrones. From the throne came flashes of lightning and peals of thunder. Before the throne, seven lamps—the seven spirits of God—were blazing.

In addition, John saw what looked like a sea of glass, clear as crystal. In the center, around the throne, were four living creatures, each with six wings, and they were covered with eyes all around. The first was like a lion, the second was like an ox, the third had a face like a man, and the fourth was like an eagle. Day and night they continually sang, "'Holy, holy, holy, is the Lord God, the Almighty, Who was and Who is and Who is to come.'" As the creatures glorified God, the elders fell down before Him in worship, laying their crowns before the throne and saying, "'Worthy art Thou, our Lord and our God, to receive glory and honor and power; for Thou didst create all things, and because of Thy will they existed, and were created.'"[30]

Later in the revelation, John saw "a new heaven and a new earth; for the first heaven and the first earth passed away." The apostle records his vision of a holy city—the New Jerusalem—coming down out of heaven from God, "made ready as a bride adorned for her husband."[31] Saints from across the centuries will reside eternally in this city with Father, Son, Spirit, and legions of angels who remained true to God when Lucifer rebelled.

John reports he "heard a loud voice from the throne, saying, 'Behold, the tabernacle of God is among men, and He shall dwell among them, and they shall be His people, and God Himself shall be among them, and He shall wipe away every tear from their eyes; and there shall no longer be any death; there shall no longer be any mourning, or crying, or pain; the first things have passed away.'"[32] The apostle says those who dwell in the New Jerusalem will see Jesus face to face. They won't need the light of a lamp or the sun because God will be their illumination, and the Father and Son will reign forever.[33]

In addition to proclaiming the kingdom of heaven during His earthly ministry, Jesus also taught about God's dwelling place. As one of its three eternal Residents, Christ had left the splendor of heaven to spend three decades on Earth. He describes it not from limited exposure in dreams but having existed there with His Father and the Holy Spirit from before the world began.[34]

He encourages good works among His followers, explaining His Father in heaven is glorified by these actions.[35] As Jesus taught His listeners to pray, He instructed them to praise His Father in heaven and to do God's will on Earth as it's accomplished in heaven. Additionally, Jesus suggested heavenly treasures were far more valuable than anything they'd accumulate throughout their earthly existence.[36] Christ also explained, "'Everyone therefore who shall confess Me before men, I will also confess him before My Father who is in heaven. But whoever shall deny Me before men, I will also deny him before My Father Who is in heaven.'"[37]

Jesus told the story of Lazarus, a poor but righteous man who'd exist eternally in the presence of God, and a rich man who had no faith in God and was cast away from Him forever. This parable illustrates both the huge gulf between the two eternal states as well as the torment that will befall those who, during their earthly lives, fail to give Jesus first place.[38]

Christ discussed heaven during His last meal with the disciples. Before the group headed to the Garden of Gethsemane, Jesus' followers—clueless as to what was about to happen—began to debate their status. Christ used the occasion to give them a preview of their significant responsibilities in heaven: "'Just as My Father has granted Me a kingdom, I grant you that you may eat and drink at My table in My kingdom, and you will sit on thrones judging the twelve tribes of Israel.'"[39]

Jesus also spoke about His return to heaven.[40] He explained He'd prepare a place there for all who come to the Father through His Son and said He'd personally escort His followers to their eternal home.[41]

Jesus' Greatest Desire

Why did Jesus put such significant emphasis on God's eternal kingdom? Why did He speak constantly about heaven? He did so because His greatest desire was to awaken men and women with the startling news of the paradise His Father had created for them and to shake them from their spiritual laziness brought on by a shortsighted focus on the pleasures of this life. He wanted to encourage them to choose God's abundant, everlasting blessings over the limited, fleeting happiness they thought they'd experience by shutting the Lord out of their lives on Earth.

The orders Jesus received during His earthly ministry directed Him to share this good news with a variety of people in a variety of locations throughout Israel. Whether He was greeted with cheers or jeers, Christ completed this duty with courage and passion. He was totally consumed with the responsibility His Father had given Him, knowing His steadfast proclamation of the kingdom of heaven would have everlasting consequences.

Christ's teaching about eternal life hit the mark with John. In addition to his gospel account, the apostle penned a letter to ensure people who'd received Jesus as Savior were certain of their ultimate fate. To dispel all doubt from their minds, John wrote, "God has given us eternal life, and this life is in His Son. He who has the Son has the life; he who does not have the Son of God does not have the life. These things I have written to you who believe in the name of the Son of God, in order that you may know that you have eternal life."[42]

Paul wanted to help early believers live lives that honored God and to encourage them concerning their future. The apostle explains that those who exist apart from the Lord in this life are doomed to carry on this separation for eternity, but those who trust Jesus as their Savior receive the free gift of eternal life.[43]

On rare occasions, God allows us to get a glimpse of what heaven must be like. While stationed in Korea, I attended a weekend retreat in Seoul. In the midst of our Sunday worship, the doors of the small chapel suddenly burst open. In unison, 26 startled men turned abruptly to discover the retreat organizers had arranged for dozens of other Christians to come into the chapel singing, playing guitars, and waving bouquets of flowers. The "intruders" were young and old and of a variety of ethnic backgrounds. All were smiling broadly and singing praises to God.

A couple of years later, I took part in a men's conference in a huge football stadium in Washington, D.C. As tens of thousands rose to sing praises to God, I gazed around the stadium and saw men of various shapes, sizes, and colors standing in love and unity.

Eternal Life: Intimate Relationships

I learned a very important lesson about heaven at these events. More than the beauty, splendor, and majesty of our heavenly surroundings, the most wonderful aspect of our new home will be the relationships we experience there. Jesus makes this clear as He prays to His Father at the end of His last meal with the disciples. He lifts His eyes to heaven and says, "'This is eternal life, that they may know Thee, the only true God, and Jesus Christ Whom Thou hast sent.'"[44]

According to Jesus—the One Who devoted Himself to teaching people about God's kingdom and gave up His life to pave the way for us to reside in heaven—eternal life is an intimate relationship among Him, His Father, and His followers. The great British preacher Charles Haddon Spurgeon reinforced this concept as he described our eternal home. "As good Rutherford says, 'Heaven and Christ are the same thing.' To be with Christ is to be in heaven, and to be in heaven is to be with Christ. That prisoner of the Lord very sweetly writes in one of his glowing letters—'O my Lord Christ, if I could be in heaven without you, it would be a hell; and if I could be in hell, and have you still, it would be a heaven to me, for you are all the heaven I want."[45]

The importance of considering eternal life as intimacy with the Lord can't be overemphasized. You see, this relationship actually begins on this planet when we receive Christ as our Savior. For the remainder of our days on Earth, we are a part of God's kingdom. We grow into a deeper communion with the Father and the Son as the Spirit lives within us and helps us to achieve our mission of becoming more like Jesus.

When we pass from this life to the next, our relationship with God becomes fuller and more vibrant as we experience the very presence of the Almighty. This challenges us to devote ourselves now—in the very early days of our eternal lives—to drawing closer to the Lord as we await a glorious reception when we, like Bunyan's pilgrim, pass through the waters, come up out of the river, and enter our heavenly home.

A Reunion in Heaven

I was a lieutenant stationed at McGuire Air Force Base in New Jersey, when the brave Americans who'd spent years in North Vietnamese prison camps were repatriated to the United States in what was called Operation Homecoming. Our unit was one of three major airlift wings on the east coast, so a number of former prisoners of war were ferried from Southeast Asia to McGuire before eventually traveling to their homes in the U.S.

When flights carrying POWs arrived on the base, reporters, photographers, and camera crews took up positions a hundred yards from where C-141 cargo aircraft came to rest on the flightline. The only people allowed to breach the gap between journalists and the planes were the official military greeting party, families of the POWs, and a handful of other men and women who'd served alongside the returning soldiers, sailors, airmen, and Marines.

As the passenger doors of a C-141 opened, a parade of several gaunt men in new uniforms began. When POWs spotted their loved ones in the crowd, they quickly broke ranks and raced toward the open arms of the small contingents that were rushing toward them. As these folks met, they locked in embraces that lasted several minutes. Then arm in arm and beaming through the tears, each cluster wound its way to the nearby terminal and the cars that would take them to their next destinations.

In much the same way, our entry into heaven will be marked by a reunion with the warriors in God's army we've served with on Earth. Some will be members of our families. Others will be folks from the churches we attended. We'll be excited to see the person or people who led us to faith in Christ. Our crying and hugs will be filled with joy as we realize these closest relationships will have no end. We'll be united with our comrades in heaven—and with hundreds of thousands of soldiers who preceded us in serving God over the centuries—to enjoy intimacy with the Lord for eternity!

In a letter to the believers in Thessalonica, Paul describes Jesus' return to Earth. "The Lord Himself will descend from heaven with a shout, with the voice of the archangel, and with the trumpet of God; and the dead in Christ shall rise first. Then we who are alive and remain shall be caught up together with them in the clouds to meet the Lord in the air, and thus we shall always be with the Lord." Paul encourages his readers to comfort one another with this description of our eternal union with God.[46]

While being in the presence of Father, Son, Spirit, and fellow warriors is an exciting prospect, this isn't all we can anticipate. God also has something special ahead for each of us: the presentation of awards for faithful service.

Lessons Learned

- The most crucial issue we face during our days on Earth is not how to enjoy our 70 to 80 years but what we can expect for eternity when we pass from this life to the next.
- As soldiers in God's army, we serve on active duty fulfilling the orders He issues us until our earthly lives come to an end.
- Death brings with it a spiritual retirement ceremony in which the Lord's warriors enter into His presence in heaven.
- Jesus even now is preparing a dwelling place for us in His Father's house. When it's ready, He'll return to escort us to the home in which we'll reside forever.

- The splendor of this heavenly home far outshines even the most spectacular natural beauty of this planet.
- Christ's earthly existence was characterized by a single-minded passion to help men and women understand the joy that awaits all who receive Him as Savior and to encourage them to place their faith in Him.
- As citizens of God's eternal kingdom, we now enjoy intimate relationships with Father, Son, and Spirit. We look forward to eternity with them and the legion of warriors who've served in the Lord's army.

Unit Analysis

To download Unit Analysis and Personal Battle Plan material, please go to www.forwardintobattle.com.

Many people today think of Christianity as nothing more than a set of rules designed to limit their enjoyment in life. These folks might consider Jesus the ultimate spoilsport, telling men and women what's allowable and what's forbidden. A review of the gospels reveals Christ wasn't as interested in putting out restrictive guidelines for life as He was in helping people enter God's kingdom. Although heaven awaits those who place their trust in Christ as Savior, we sometimes mistakenly believe eternal life begins at the moment we die. Actually, eternal life is a relationship between God and humans that starts when we become Jesus' followers, continues through the remainder of our lives on Earth, and then carries on eternally in the presence of Father, Son, and Holy Spirit.

1. Have you ever attended an event to honor someone who was retiring from his or her job? If so, what emotions did you observe or feel? After all the excitement wore away, what thoughts do you suppose were going through the mind of the person who was about to begin a new and very different phase of life?

2. Read Psalm 19:1 and Psalm 8:1-9. How do the heavens declare the glory of God? In Romans 1:19-20, what does Paul tell us is revealed through God's creation? What is the apostle's warning in verse 25?
3. Jesus' discussions and parables often were focused on what people had to do to enter the kingdom of God. What are some of the requirements He mentioned? Explain each of these in your own words.
   a. Matthew 5:3, 8, 10
   b. Matthew 13:44-46
   c. Matthew 18:1-4
   d. John 3:1-8
4. On occasion, God has allowed His most trusted servants a guided tour of heaven. How do the following passages describe His dwelling place? What seems to be the main activity for the supernatural beings and humans gathered there?
   a. Isaiah 6:1-7
   b. Daniel 7:9-10, 13-14
   c. Ezekiel 1:4-10, 22, 26-28
   d. Revelation 4:1-11
   e. Revelation 22:1-5
5. John 17:5 reminds us Jesus was present with the Father in heaven before the world was created. According to Acts 1:9-11, where did Christ go when His ministry on Earth ended? Read John 14:1-6 and Romans 8:34. What is Jesus doing in heaven? When did He tell His disciples they'd join Him?
6. Before His crucifixion, Jesus provided an excellent definition of eternal life as He prayed to His Father. In John 17:1-3, Christ describes eternal life as a relationship, not a destination. As we grow closer to God during our lives as followers of His Son, how do we develop a greater appreciation for what heaven must be like? How does our earthly relationship with God prepare us for living eternally in His presence?

7. Some people claim to want eternal life, but when confronted with the decision to begin a relationship with Jesus, they reject the offer. Read Matthew 19:16-26. In verse 21, what did Jesus tell the young man to do if he wanted to join Him? What attitudes of the heart would be reflected by these actions? What does Jesus ask people to give up today? What reasons do some give for refusing to follow Him?
8. While many people deny Christ during their lives on Earth, others truly believe they're on the road to heaven through faith in Him. Jesus' warning in Matthew 7:21-23 suggests that at least some are in for quite a surprise. According to Christ, who will enter heaven? What do you think He means by "the will of My Father"? What does this passage tell you about activities being the key that opens heaven's door? How does Ephesians 2:8-10 help you understand the connection between entry into the kingdom of God and good works?
9. Jesus began His ministry by telling those who'd listen about the kingdom of God. (Matthew 4:17) He kept His focus on this theme for the next three years. When Christ was about to return to heaven, He told His disciples to take the message to as many as they could influence throughout the world. (Matthew 28:18-20) Every day we come into contact with many people who either have rejected Jesus, who mistakenly believe they're headed for heaven, or who've never heard of Christ. What should be our attitude about sharing the gospel with others?

Prayer Points

- Praise God for the splendor and majesty of heaven, which outshine even the most spectacular sights across Earth
- Thank the Lord that Jesus is preparing an eternal dwelling place for you in heaven and that He'll escort you to it when the time is right

- Ask God to prepare you for the intimate moments you'll share with Him in heaven by developing an increasingly closer relationship with Him in this life
- Commit to renewing and maintaining your enthusiasm for helping others to appreciate the heavenly home that awaits all who trust Christ as Savior

Personal Battle Plan

1. **Take the poll below.** If you believe heaven doesn't exist, or if you're not *certain* your ultimate destination after death is heaven, arrange to talk with a more mature Christian about the Bible's teaching on these topics.
   a. Do you believe in the existence of heaven, where people live forever with God after they die?
      ____ Yes ____ No
   b. If you responded "Yes" above, immediately after death, which of the following do you think will happen to you?
      ____ Go directly to heaven
      ____ Go to purgatory
      ____ Be reincarnated
      ____ Be the end of your existence
      ____ Go to hell
2. Are you absolutely sure Jesus will escort you to heaven the moment you breathe your last on Earth? Is anything holding you back from trusting Him to be your Savior? Or is there any possibility, no matter how remote, that you *think* you're His follower because of all the "good things" you do for Him? If you have never received Christ as Savior, read I John 5:11-13, **commit your life to Jesus** through a prayer something like the one below, and be confident your reservation in heaven for eternity is secure.

Father, I acknowledge I've fallen short of being the person you want me to be, and my rebellion separates me from You. Jesus, thank You for taking on the penalty for my sin by dying on the cross for me. I now open my heart to You and receive You as my Savior. Lord, thank You for forgiving me and allowing me to become part of Your family. Holy Spirit, through the strength and wisdom you provide, help me to become more and more like Jesus in this life and to rejoice in the certainty that I'll spend eternity in heaven when my days on Earth end. In Jesus' name I pray. Amen.

3. Many people, when they become followers of Christ, immediately begin to focus on the here and now. What do I have to ***do*** now that I'm a Christian? What do I have to ***stop doing***? What must I ***learn***? Our spiritual lives can become extremely hectic, but this isn't what Jesus modeled. As you conform to the image of Christ, **plan a special time to reflect on the kingdom of God**. Arrange for a day away—just you and God. Take your Bible and search the scriptures for passages on the majesty and character of the Father, the love and sacrifice of the Son, and the comfort and friendship of the Holy Spirit. Read about God's kingdom—on Earth and in heaven. And then praise the Lord for Who He is and for all He's done through the ages.

4. Because eternal life is a relationship and not a destination, **evaluate how well you "know the only true God, and Jesus Christ**, Whom God has sent." List two specific actions you'll take immediately to improve your relationship with God, and review your progress once a month. Continue to work on these until you're consistent in these areas, and add other actions you need to improve.

	Strongly Disagree	Somewhat Disagree	Neither Agree nor Disagree	Somewhat Agree	Strongly Agree
a. I have a very consistent time in God's word regularly, and I'm getting to know Him and what He requires of me.					
b. I have a very consistent prayer time daily. Not only do I make requests, but I also express deep praise and thanks. I often experience God communicating something to me during my prayers.					
c. Worship is not a rote, hollow event for me. God really touches me deeply					

	Strongly Disagree	Somewhat Disagree	Neither Agree nor Disagree	Somewhat Agree	Strongly Agree
	and personally during these services. I feel free to express my love and gratitude to Him inwardly and outwardly in worship.				
d.	I constantly feel Jesus' presence in everything I do. Whether it's a spiritual activity or not, He's always with me.				
e.	Because I have such a deep, deep love for Jesus, I can't wait to introduce Him to others. Everyone I know knows I'm a follower of Christ, and I've shared the gospel with most of them.				

5. **List three people you think will be in your greeting party when you arrive in heaven.** Obviously, we may be so awestruck being in the very presence of God that we won't have time for conversation with family members or friends who've preceded us. But if the opportunity presents itself, what would you like to say to each of these three people?
6. **List three people you believe aren't headed to heaven.** After praying for the Lord's wisdom, strength, and courage, arrange to meet with each of these people to tell them about God's kingdom and how they may begin to experience eternal life now. Think and pray through what you'll say in advance, and ask a Christian friend to listen to what you plan to share and to provide feedback.
7. **Prepare for the next session** by listing what you believe will be your rewards for the Christian duties you perform on Earth. Consider how these rewards compare with what you've received for outstanding contributions in worldly endeavors.

CHAPTER 12

Receiving Recognition for Service

When armies return from victorious war, the loudest cheers are not for those who have fought the fewest battles, nor for the flags which are cleanest, but for the regiments which are cut down to a few men, and for the colors that are shot to pieces. So it will be in heaven when the redeemed are welcomed home: those who have fought the most battles, and bear the most 'marks of the Lord Jesus,' will receive the highest honors.

J. R. Miller[1]

THROUGHOUT THEIR SERVICE, the performance of military troops is observed frequently. As in any occupation, soldiers, sailors, airmen, and Marines want to be rewarded when they've done well, but official recognition doesn't happen often. When it comes, it generally takes one of two forms: a high rating on an annual evaluation or a medal for outstanding achievement.

I labored under several evaluation systems during my time in the Air Force. Some required a rater to determine a priority listing of the officers serving in the unit. In at least one of the rating schemes, regulations dictated the percentage of officers who could receive the top mark, how many could be assigned the second-highest rating, and so on. Officers quickly learned how to impress the boss. Their goal became doing all they could to ensure their raters appreciated the valuable contribution they were making to the unit's mission. A few young officers seemed to spend as much time trying to determine how to impress the brass as in completing assigned tasks!

In addition, officers tried to earn more prestigious medals than their contemporaries. They also wanted to accumulate as many awards as possible. This was important because at the front of an officer's record was an official photo. A uniform jacket awash in the bright colors of dozens of medals for superb contributions to the Air Force and the nation would impress the members of a promotion board.

Early in my career, I was amused to see the reaction of several older, combat-tested officers as they spotted the many medals worn by younger troops whose service had taken place only in the peaceful days of the Cold War. Having served when these awards weren't distributed so freely, the senior officers wore a modest number of medals, but a couple of them had come as a result of heroic deeds in air-to-air dogfights. Wonder and cynicism often crossed the face of a veteran whose junior wore twice as many awards, the most significant for having survived a two-year tour of duty in the Azores!

Outstanding ratings and significant medals weren't an end in themselves but a means to an end. The more glowing the evaluation and the more prestigious the medal, the more likely an officer was to be promoted ahead of contemporaries. The goal was to be recognized as the best in your field so, down the road a couple of decades, you'd wear the stars of a general.

God's Rewards for Faithful Service

God's word outlines how followers of Christ will be rated and rewarded, and we don't have to worry about how the Lord sees us compared to anyone else. Additionally, we don't have to impress other humans as we perform our duties as God's warriors. In the words of Apostle Paul, "Whatever you do, do your work heartily, as for the Lord rather than for men; knowing that from the Lord you will receive the reward of the inheritance. It is the Lord Christ Whom you serve."[2] Our job is simply to carry out with excellence the orders God gives us as we complete the mission He's entrusted to us.

Unlike human bosses who observe our work only on occasion, God knows all we do in His service. If, in the words of an old hymn, "His eye is on the sparrow, and I know He watches me," we can be sure nothing slips past His notice. Contrary to our present leaders who witness only our actions, God's analysis goes much deeper: He also sees our motivation.

The Lord informed Prophet Samuel that while man looks at others' outward appearance, He looks at our hearts.[3] Apostle Paul echoed these words when he warned that God would disclose the motives of men's hearts and would praise those who deserved it.[4]

As military officers wish to please their commanders, Christians should desire to obtain a good evaluation from our heavenly Commander. Acknowledging we work for the Lord rather than earthly masters and realizing our ultimate reward comes from Him, Paul's assessment of his ministry stands as a noble goal for all followers of Christ: "I have fought the good fight, I have finished the course, I have kept the faith."[5]

The apostle could look forward with confidence to appearing before Jesus upon his entry into heaven. Paul knew Christ would judge and reward him for his years in God's service. We can join generations of spiritual warriors since the days of Paul in the same confidence because Jesus promised His Father would honor anyone who served Him faithfully.[6]

The Lord's Judgment
Knowing God will evaluate our deeds and the reasons behind them, it's helpful to understand how this process works. Christ warned His disciples

that all mankind will one day get what they've earned during their time on Earth. Jesus explained He would come in the glory of His Father with His angels to repay every person according to his or her deeds.[7] Years later, Christ confirmed this for Apostle John: "'Behold, I am coming quickly, and My reward is with Me, to render to every man according to what he has done.'"[8]

Those who have the option of joining God's army but decide they'd be better off fighting against Him rather than for Him will pay the consequences for their rebellion. Paul says these enemy soldiers—the unrighteous—won't receive the inheritance the Lord will bestow upon His warriors.[9]

In God's perfect timing, Satan and his forces will be vanquished. Spiritual warfare will cease. Our great enemy will be sentenced to eternity in a lake of fire and brimstone, where he'll be tormented day and night.[10] God has promised that on that day, He'll take no prisoners!

Since the beginning of time, the Lord has kept meticulous records of who has served in His forces. He's entered the names of His troops into a ledger He calls the book of life. Anyone not registered in the Lord's army will be punished alongside the devil. Listen to how Apostle John describes the scene.

> I saw a great white throne and Him Who sat upon it. ... And I saw the dead, the great and the small, standing before the throne, and books were opened; and another book was opened, which is the book of life; and the dead were judged from the things which were written in the books, according to their deeds. ... And if anyone's name was not found written in the book of life, he was thrown into the lake of fire.[11]

This is the fate of all who don't receive Christ as Savior. Through God's grace and mercy, soldiers in His army can look forward to another end.

While we, too, will be judged, the review of our service will result in rewards, not punishment. Unlike those who pledge their allegiance to Satan, God's warriors will receive a wonderful inheritance from our heavenly Father. Apostle Paul explains it this way:

> For no man can lay a foundation other than the one which is laid, which is Jesus Christ. Now if any man builds upon the foundation with gold, silver, precious stones, wood, hay, straw, each man's work will become evident; for the day will show it, because it is to be revealed with fire; and the fire itself will test the quality of each man's work. If any man's work which he has built upon it remains, he shall receive a reward. If any man's work is burned up, he shall suffer loss; but he himself shall be saved, yet so as through fire.[12]

As Christians, we can be confident that regardless of whether or not our spiritual deeds survive the test by fire Paul describes, all of us will be saved. In other words, each person who truly receives Christ as Savior is guaranteed a place in heaven for eternity. It's into this magnificent scene, into the presence of our Savior, we'll step when our days on Earth end. There, before the throne of Almighty God, we'll receive eternal rewards.

An Inheritance Awaits God's Warriors
The theme of the Lord blessing His people with a spiritual inheritance appears often in scripture. King David cries out for salvation, pleading that God's inheritance would include everlasting care for His people. He praises the Lord that the inheritance of the blameless will endure forever.[13] We have no reason to be anxious about the Lord changing His "last will and testament." He's promised us blessings, and He'll deliver!

Many years after David expressed his hope in the inheritance to come, Jesus assured His disciples that all who serve Him will be richly blessed when He sits on His throne in heaven. Christ promised the 12 they'd join

Him on thrones of their own, assisting in judgment. Though the reward of lower-ranking officers and foot soldiers in God's army is not as grand, Jesus tells us everyone who gives up earthly relationships and possessions for His sake "'shall receive many times as much, and shall inherit eternal life.'" In a later conversation, Christ explains the kingdom we'll inherit was prepared for us from the foundation of the world.[14]

When a man asked Jesus to settle a dispute concerning the division of the family inheritance, Christ instead told a parable. He shared the story of a rich man who determined he'd build larger barns for his grain and other goods. This, the man reasoned, would allow him to live the good life—eating, drinking, and partying. Unfortunately, God had other plans. The good life became no life at all as the Lord didn't allow him to see dawn the following day. Jesus warned we should avoid laying up earthly treasure but rather seek an unfailing treasure in heaven, reinforcing a lesson He taught during His Sermon on the Mount.[15]

Paul goes to great lengths to help the Galatians understand the inheritance the Lord has set aside for followers of Christ. All who put their faith in Jesus, he says, become sons and heirs of God. When we're adopted into God's family, we become eligible to receive an inheritance from our heavenly Father, and His blessing doesn't depend on our obedience to the Law of Moses.[16]

These explanations of who'll receive an inheritance from the Lord stand in stark contrast to the prevailing wisdom of the Jewish religious leaders of the day. The Pharisees believed the Lord materially blessed those He loved. In their view, wealth was God's reward for keeping the law. The formula for becoming heirs of God's blessings for eternity was total obedience to His commandments during this life, not faith in His Son. Paul disputed this conventional wisdom.

The apostle points out that God—not man—will reward us with an inheritance. Paul adds we'll receive fabulous riches, and the first of these wonderful gifts—God's pledge of our inheritance—is the Holy

Spirit, Who dwells within our hearts from the moment we receive Jesus as Savior.[17] Finally, the apostle tells us our inheritance will never end. The victory Christ gives us over death—and in death—should spur us on as we serve in the combat zone of planet Earth. As Paul reminds us, "[Our] toil is not in vain in the Lord."[18]

During Peter's years with Christ, he learned a great deal about what we can expect in the future. The apostle points to God's mercy as the source of our hope of what's to come, and he goes on to explain the blessings we'll receive as heirs will not perish, be defiled, or fade away. He adds our inheritance is reserved for us in heaven.[19]

I've known a few old folks who, when they realize their days on Earth are winding down, walk around the house placing small labels bearing names of relatives and friends on all their worldly possessions. These treasures are then reserved for those who'll outlive them. Based on our earthly service, the Lord has labeled the eternal riches He'll present to His warriors in heaven. When you think about it, this is a great tradeoff. We'll leave behind a few manmade articles that eventually will fall apart and receive rewards selected just for us from God's limitless and glorious wealth!

The writer to the Hebrews tells us Jesus created the world and inherited "all things" from His Father. Similarly, those who've served in God's army are guaranteed an eternal inheritance. We also learn that those who'll receive an inheritance from the Lord are not limited to saints who've lived during and following Jesus' walk on Earth. The faith of Old Testament warriors—Noah, Abraham, Isaac, and Jacob among many others—has earned them eternal rewards.[20]

While Apostle John was living in exile on the island of Patmos, he received a vision of what God's warriors could expect upon retiring to heaven. His teacher on this occasion was our Commander Himself. In letters Jesus dictated to John for distribution among seven churches in Asia Minor—present-day Turkey—He outlined the heavenly rewards "overcomers" would receive.

Our Physical Needs Will Be Met

First, Christ explained that our inheritance will include provision for all our physical needs. That's right: We'll exist physically in some form. When we die, we don't become bodiless spirits darting through space eternally. Our arrival in heaven will coincide with Christ transforming our humble human bodies to conform with His glorious, resurrected body.[21]

We should look forward to this event with great joy. Think back to our mission as we serve our Commander in this life: We're to be conformed to the image of God's Son. While the resemblance will be imperfect throughout our days on Earth, God has promised this mission will be accomplished fully when we join Him in heaven.

Paul says our heavenly bodies will be indestructible, glorious, and powerful.[22] Although scripture doesn't provide a description of what they'll look like, we can assume they'll be different from our earthly bodies because God will design them for life in heaven for eternity. We'll undoubtedly be strong and healthy; we'll never again endure the pain of illness, disease, injury, or death. In addition, we won't experience tears, mourning, or crying.[23]

God's word seems to indicate our heavenly bodies will require physical sustenance, and Jesus explained the Lord will provide us nourishment, clothing, and a place of residence. At the direction of Christ, John wrote to Christians in Ephesus that Jesus would permit those who overcome to "'eat of the tree of life, which is in the Paradise of God.'" Similarly, Jesus promised His followers in Pergamum they'd be nourished by hidden manna—divine food.[24] A glorious beverage is also on the menu. Toward the end of the book, John learns the Lord will freely give to those who thirst from the spring of the water of life.[25]

As God nourishes our bodies, He'll also provide our apparel. In John's dispatch to Sardis, Christ pledged to clothe residents of heaven in white garments.[26] This seems to be the uniform of the day for God's heavenly army. In one of Daniel's visions, the Lord was arrayed in a robe as white as snow.[27] As Peter, James, and John witnessed Jesus' meeting with Elijah and Moses, Christ's garments "became radiant and exceedingly white, as no launderer on Earth can whiten them."[28]

In John's vision, seven angels stepped out of a heavenly temple en route to pouring the wrath of God across Earth. Their uniforms? Clean, bright linen. The apostle also observed another group wearing similar attire: 24 elders sitting on thrones around God's throne. Each of the elders was clothed in white garments and golden crowns.[29] We'll check out the crowns in a minute.

John specifies two additional groups clothed in white. All who've been martyred because of their faith in Christ will be issued white robes, as will a great multitude who endure the tribulation described in the book of Revelation. The apostle looked on as this immense group, waving palm branches, worshiped before the throne of God, serving Him around the clock in His temple.[30]

Jesus' revelation to John includes two final descriptions of His followers adorned in white. In what promises to be the wedding of all weddings, Christians from throughout the ages will be united in marriage to Christ, the Lamb of God. The bride, as believers are called, will wear fine, bright, clean linen.[31]

Our celebration may be short-lived. According to the apostle, immediately following the feast, heaven will open and Jesus will ride out on a white horse to judge and to wage war. Right behind Him, also mounted atop white horses, will be the armies of heaven. Each soldier will be clothed in fine linen, white and clean. Having served during various eras in God's army on Earth, these warriors will now unite to become the fiercest combat team ever assembled, overwhelming and defeating Satan and his kings, commanders, and mighty men.[32]

It may well be—but we can't be sure—the soldiers in God's army, arrayed in their glistening, white robes, will make an appearance well in advance of this ultimate battle in the war between the Lord and the devil. In

God's revelation to Daniel, the prophet saw an event that's predicted several times in the New Testament. "'I kept looking in the night visions, and behold, with the clouds of heaven One like a Son of Man was coming. … And to Him was given dominion, glory and a kingdom, that all the people, nations, and men of every language might serve Him. His dominion is an everlasting dominion which will not pass away; and His kingdom is one which will not be destroyed.'"[33]

Jesus repeats this prophecy on at least a couple of occasions. He says all the tribes of Earth will see Him coming on the clouds with power and great glory. While on trial before the Jewish high priest and other religious officials, Christ testifies, "'You shall see the Son of Man [Jesus] sitting at the right hand of power, and coming on the clouds of heaven.'"[34]

Three New Testament writers mention these clouds. Paul suggests that when Christ returns to Earth with His followers who've died earlier, Christians alive at the time will be caught up with them in the clouds to meet the Lord in the air.[35] The author of the letter to the Hebrews tells his readers a great cloud of witnesses surrounds us.[36]

John predicts every eye will see Jesus when He returns in the clouds. The apostle also observed Christ on a white cloud, carrying a sharp sickle and heading to Earth to punish those who'd rejected Him.[37] Do you think it's simply a coincidence that we see all the divisions of God's army arrayed in brilliant white linen and the Commander being spotted so often in the "clouds"? My bet is that what appears to be a mass of tiny, condensed water droplets from the perspective of those viewing the scene from ground level are actually members of the Lord's forces traveling with the King of kings.

And what about the crowns? Jesus promised the faithful at Smyrna a crown of life would complement their white robes and round out their wardrobes. He also warned the saints at Philadelphia to guard their crowns so no one could take them.[38] Our royal headgear will signify how well we've used the gifts and abilities God has blessed us with in carrying out our orders. Three authors of five separate New Testament letters describe these rewards.

- ***An imperishable crown***: The writer who has the most to say about heavenly crowns is Paul. In his first letter to the Corinthians, the apostle uses the term "wreath" to describe a saint's eternal reward. Paul compares our efforts as followers of Christ to athletes who compete in a race. Only one runner receives the prize for finishing first, and in Paul's day, it was a wreath made of leaves. Our reward, though, will be with us forever; it will be an imperishable crown.[39]
- ***A crown of exultation***: Paul tells Jesus' followers in Thessalonica about a crown of exultation. The apostle suggests it's emblematic of our hope and joy. He asks an interesting question: "Who is our ... crown of exultation?"[40] Notice Paul doesn't ask ***what*** the crown is. We tend to think of this reward as something material. In fact, when Christians perform noteworthy deeds in serving the Lord, we sometimes say they've earned another jewel in their crowns. It's easy to picture the scene in heaven as great martyrs, preachers, and evangelists stroll along the streets of gold carefully balancing huge, jewel-covered crowns atop their heads while lesser saints sport beanies that feature only a small, precious stone or two.

    The apostle's response to his question reveals our "crowns" may not be something we wear. He told his readers that ***they***, in the presence of Jesus when He returns, would compose this special crown. Paul said these humans were his glory and joy.[41] This reinforces a similar thought the apostle shared with Christ's followers in Philippi. Paul wrote that he couldn't wait to be with these brothers and sisters, referring to them as his joy and crown.[42]

Perhaps the visible recognition of our spiritual service will be the beaming faces of those we've touched for Jesus during our days on Earth. It may well be that none of us will parade around heaven in precious headgear and that the only jewel-like sparkle we'll notice will be the radiance of friends and family members God allowed us to bless in some small way during our earthly travels. Surely this will far outshine even the most glittering diamonds, rubies, and emeralds! This would confirm the words Zechariah wrote around 520 B.C. The prophet, speaking about the deliverance of God's warriors in the tribes of Judah and Ephraim, compared these folks to "the stones of a crown, sparkling in His land."[43]

- *A crown of righteousness*: A third reward mentioned by Paul is a crown of righteousness, which the Lord will present to all who've looked forward to His appearing.[44] Their hope will be rewarded for the righteous living it produced. If we allow the Spirit to mold us into holy people, if we allow Him to share the love of Christ with others through our words and deeds, and if we tell those around us about Jesus and His return to Earth, we'll receive this crown.

- *A crown of life*: James explains the Lord has promised a crown of life to those who love Him. As with the crowns Paul mentions, an outward action must accompany this inner love. Men and women who receive this crown will have persevered under trial.[45] As we've seen, our earthly lives are marked by a constant battle against a persistent and powerful adversary. Satan will pull no punches in tempting us to rebel against God. In fact, the more we tap into the Holy Spirit to become like Christ, the more our enemy will intensify his attacks. The crown of life will be ours only if we use the means of escape God provides when Satan tries to lead us astray. Through the Lord's strength and wisdom, we can persevere and emerge victorious when under trial.

- ***A crown of glory***: A final crown is set aside for a very specific group who'll spend eternity with the Lord. Apostle Peter mentions an unfading crown of glory the Chief Shepherd will present to elders who've shepherded flocks of believers on Earth. Leaders who've performed this role voluntarily, eagerly, and humbly are destined for this special recognition. Peter suggests one additional requirement for receiving the crown of glory: The elders' service must coincide with God's will.[46]

In addition to nourishment and clothing, the Lord will provide an eternal home for His warriors. Prior to His death, Jesus briefed His disciples on a heavenly construction program. He explained He'll prepare dwelling places for His followers in His Father's house. When these quarters are ready, He'll personally escort their residents to heaven.[47]

In His revelation to John, Christ assured members of the church in Philadelphia that each of His followers will become "'a pillar in the temple of My God, and he will not go out from it anymore.'" Later John explains the temple Jesus referred to was not a large, stone building. God the Father and His Son are the temple in the new Jerusalem.[48]

The letter Christ dictates to the church at Smyrna illustrates His followers will reside for eternity in the presence of God. Those who overcome won't be hurt by the second death—the punishment of eternal separation from God.[49] When the forces of God overwhelm and capture the enemy's camp at the last battle between the two adversaries, Satan and his allies will be thrown into a lake of fire and brimstone. (See Revelation 20.) Followers of Christ, on the other hand, avoid this fate.

Paul looked forward to an intimate, eternal union with his Savior. In his letter to Jesus' followers in Philippi, the apostle writes, "To me, to live is Christ, and to die is gain." This wasn't the testimony of a man who was worn out with his earthly ministry and therefore eager to escape its challenges. Paul looked forward to fruitful labor in the name of Jesus, assisting the Philippians—and the members of other churches—to experience joy in their faith. At the same time, he knew without a doubt it would be "very much better" for him to dwell in the presence of Jesus forever.[50]

The apostle's earthly association with Christ lasted only minutes as the Lord chatted with him on the road to Damascus. The thought of Jesus preparing a heavenly home for him must have sustained Paul through his missionary adventures. God's warriors today should be filled with the same joyful expectation as they engage in their spiritual duties.

Christians in Thyatira are told another element in our inheritance is "'the morning star.'" This promise isn't as easily understood as Jesus' other pledges. Christ refers to Himself as "'the bright morning star.'"[51] As such, Jesus will produce the light that will illuminate heaven. John reports the new Jerusalem does not require the sun or moon because "the glory of God has illumined it, and its lamp is the Lamb. And the nations shall walk by its light."[52]

We'll Receive New Identities

Christ's letters to the seven churches reveal that in addition to caring for our physical needs, He'll provide His followers new identities. Upon our arrival in heaven, Jesus will acknowledge our names before His father and the angels.[53] This will fulfill what He predicted in a conversation with His disciples. He told them He'd confess before God's angels everyone who confesses Him before men.[54]

More than just announcing our presence, our Commander may brief the Father on our earthly service, outlining the victories we achieved in our battles with Satan. Perhaps it will be during this meeting, if our labor as God's soldiers has been fruitful, that we'll hear a response similar to what Christ mentioned in one of His final parables.

Jesus told His disciples about a man preparing to set out on a journey. Before departing, he entrusted varying numbers of talents to his slaves. A talent was a unit of weight for metals such as gold, silver, bronze, and brass. It's estimated one talent of silver weighed around 94 pounds, and historians suggest the talent was equal to what a person would earn in 20 years. In Matthew's account, the man distributed five talents to one slave, two to another, and one to the third.

Upon the master's return, he discovered the first two slaves had doubled the amount he'd given them. The first servant presented 10 talents to the man; the second laid out four talents. The final slave, afraid his master would be furious if he failed to produce a return on the investment of the man's money, had hidden the talent and returned only the amount he'd received.

As we consider our heavenly inheritance, perhaps the most exciting lesson from this story comes from the master's words as he commended slaves one and two: """Well done, good and faithful slave; you were faithful with a few things, I will put you in charge of many things, enter into the joy of your master."""[55]

When Jesus confesses us before the Father and His angels, it will be evident whether or not our investment of spiritual "talents" has produced a return that survives when tested by fire. If God's soldiers have built on Christ's foundation with gold, silver, and precious stones, He'll look into their eyes and repeat the words all of us should long to hear from our Commander: "Well done, good and faithful [warrior]; enter the joy of your Master."

When this introduction is complete, Christ tells the saints at Philadelphia, He'll write upon us three names: His new name, His Father's name, and the name of the city of God—the new Jerusalem. At this point, we'll begin an eternal identification with the Lord. In addition, Jesus asks John to write to the church at Pergamum about another element of our inheritance: a new name written on a white stone that no one knows but the recipient.[56]

Name changes in the Bible, while not common, occurred on at least three significant occasions. In the Old Testament, the Lord called a man named Abram—which means high father or the father is exalted—to leave his family and head to a land God would show him. The reason: "'I will make you a great nation, and I will bless you, and make your name great; ... and in you all the families of the Earth shall be blessed.'"[57]

Abram obeyed the Lord's call and took his wife, nephew, and a band of others to Canaan. Twenty-four years later, Abram and Sarai were still childless. Although he'd fathered a child by his wife's maid, Abram—at the age of 99—was probably wondering how he got his name. These thoughts were interrupted when God once again came calling. The Lord announced He was changing Abram's name to Abraham, which means the father of a multitude or the father of nations.[58]

While Abraham may have thought the new name had a literal meaning, we know God was talking about all those who'd become members of His spiritual family through faith in Christ. Abraham didn't know it at the time, but the Lord had chosen his bloodline to bring Jesus into the world. Abraham's new name reflected his faithfulness and obedience, qualities that produced the opportunity for all future generations to receive an eternal inheritance.

Jacob—Abraham's grandson—also became known by another name. After Jacob had deviously stolen older brother Esau's birthright, Isaac banished his younger son to what today is Syria. Over the years, Jacob amassed two wives, 11 children, and great wealth. He eventually decided to return to his homeland and set out with his family and livestock. As the large entourage approached Esau's home in Edom, Jacob's fear factor rose dramatically.

The night before he was to meet his brother, Jacob spent some time alone. A mysterious stranger joined him, and the two began to wrestle. Their match continued until dawn, and the intruder—the Captain of the Lord's army—was unable to defeat His adversary. He asked Jacob to release Him, but Jacob demanded to be blessed.

The blessing was quite unorthodox. The Commander said, "'Your name shall no longer be Jacob, but Israel; for you have striven with God and with men and have prevailed.'" Jacob was astounded and realized his opponent had been the Lord.[59] So Jacob's name was changed from "he who supplants" to "he who strives with God" or, according to other translations, "he prevails with God." Previously known for deceiving his father and wronging his brother, Jacob's new name also would become the name of the Jewish nation.

In the New Testament, Jesus changed the name of His most well-known follower. When Andrew first introduced his brother to Christ, He immediately announced Simon would be called Peter. The future apostle's given name meant "he who listens," particularly to the words of God. Jesus chose to call him Peter—which means "rock"—because He had a special mission in mind for His new companion. As Christ later revealed, Peter would become the foundation upon which He'd build His church when He departed Earth to return to heaven.[60]

You might suggest Saul's name was changed to Paul. In the book of Acts, Luke writes that in the church's early days, Saul was also known as Paul. Actually, these are the Hebrew and Greek versions of the same name. We have no evidence the switch was divinely inspired.

In the Air Force, aircrew flight suits and some other uniforms feature patches with the airman's name and unit. During my stint in England, I wore a patch bearing the words 48th Tactical Fighter Wing under a drawing of the Statue of Liberty, which was the nickname of our organization. A second patch displayed my name, and on my shoulders were symbols of my rank. Anyone from any Air Force base across the globe who saw me in this uniform could have identified me: "You're Major Tyrrell, and you're assigned to the 48th TFW." In addition, I carried in my wallet an identification card that listed my name, rank, serial number, and the date my commission was to end.

The white stones we'll receive upon entry into heaven will be our means of identification. They'll bear names different from what we were called on Earth. These stones, coupled with the names Christ will write upon us, will serve as evidence God has accepted us and considers us worthy to exist in His presence. Unlike my military ID card, we'll have no labels indicating when our commissions will no longer be valid as our new identities will last for eternity.

Military units maintain what's referred to as an alpha roster. As its name suggests, it's an alphabetical listing of those who serve in the organization. Jesus directed John to inform church members in Sardis, "I will not erase [the names of His followers] from the book of life."[61] This eternal alpha roster will bear the new names of all who've served in God's army and will be a written record of our new identities.

We'll Be Assigned New Orders

These new names will bring new responsibilities as we're elevated to positions of authority. Jesus' message to the church at Thyatira informed its members, "'He who keeps My deeds until the end, to him I will give authority over the nations; and he shall rule them with a rod of iron … as I also have received authority from My Father.'"[62]

This promise is another reference to Old Testament prophecy. The psalmist predicted the future reign of the Lord's Anointed with these words of the Father: "'"Thou art My Son, today I have begotten Thee. Ask of Me, and I will surely give the nations as Thine inheritance, and the very ends of the Earth as Thy possession. Thou shalt break them with a rod of iron, Thou shalt shatter them like earthenware."'"[63]

Do you see what Jesus is saying to His followers at Thyatira? Having been promised He would inherit authority over the nations, Christ explains He's decided to share this responsibility with us! We'll actually assist in ruling over Jesus' enemies and will reign with Him as He judges evil. Paul understood this as he reminded the believers at Corinth that the saints would judge the world and angels.[64]

Part of our rule and judgment will occur when Christ descends from heaven to judge and wage war. "From His mouth comes a sharp sword, so that with it He may smite the nations; and He will rule them with a rod of iron."[65] And we'll be right there with Jesus, wielding the rods He's issued to us.

Our new identities and orders provide one additional fringe benefit. Jesus tells the Laodiceans that not only will we reside in the house of God, we'll also be able to sit with Christ on His throne.[66] Talk about an elevated position! You can't get much higher than sitting next to the King of kings and Lord of lords, the Creator and Sustainer of the universe.

God allowed my family one of those brief encounters that revealed something of heaven in September 1985. My commander at RAF Lakenheath put me in charge of a special event that was to be held at Cambridge University. He asked me to select and invite a guest speaker to deliver an after-dinner talk. My choice was Prince Charles. It took a few months for our invitation to make its way through a maze of bureaucracy, but eventually we received the terrific news that the prince would visit us. Because he was already scheduled for another event on the night of our dinner, he agreed to put in an appearance at our base a few days earlier.

On the day of the visit, school was suspended, and children waving miniature Union Jacks lined the route Prince Charles would travel. His limousine pulled in at a pre-arranged stop, and our royal guest emerged to walk through a crowd of several hundred excited Americans. As the prince turned the corner for the final leg of his walk, he came face to face with my children. He walked up to them, chatted for a moment, and accepted a picture Trevor had drawn for him. Elapsed time: less than one minute.

Prince Charles's next stop was a reception for base officials and their spouses. Elizabeth and I stood with eight other people, the second or third of a dozen groups the prince would meet. After his ice-breaking question—"Have you seen the film *Rambo*?"—we engaged in a lively discussion for about 10 minutes. The consensus of group members as our guest moved on to the next cluster was that our time with him had been delightful. For the Tyrrells, these few minutes with the future king of England was an exciting time.

This event pales by comparison to what warriors in God's army have in store. A day is coming when we'll meet our King face to face, and He'll present us with a great inheritance: refreshing nourishment, regal clothing, a heavenly home, identities as His special ones, and positions of tremendous authority. And our time with the Lord won't last a few minutes. We'll walk and talk with our Savior and Commander forever.

Ironic, isn't it? We'll receive from Jesus the eternal equivalent of what Satan's forces—those who choose not to enter into a relationship with the Father through faith in His Son—work so diligently to accumulate during their lives. As God's warriors move forward into battle through the days we have remaining on Earth, we can derive great encouragement knowing God will bless us with heavenly treasures in recognition of our faithful service.

Lessons Learned

- The Lord has promised to reward us handsomely for our service in His army.
- When our time on Earth is done, we'll receive an inheritance that will never end, is undefiled, and is reserved for us in heaven.
- Our ultimate rewards will be based upon how well we used the gifts and abilities we received from the Lord.
- As a part of our inheritance, God will provide us nourishment, clothing, and dwelling places for the new bodies we'll receive when we check into our eternal home.
- We'll also receive new identities that demonstrate we belong to God and are worthy to exist in His presence forever.
- As joint heirs with Christ, we'll be called upon to assist Him in reigning over and judging the nations.

Unit Analysis

To download Unit Analysis and Personal Battle Plan material, please go to www.forwardintobattle.com.

Everyone who lives on this planet ultimately faces God's judgment. The Lord will judge those who were soldiers of Satan's evil forces to punish them for their rebellion. He'll judge warriors in His army to distribute rewards for faithful service. Upon arrival at our eternal, heavenly home, we'll begin to fully experience the wonderful inheritance God has set aside for us. Followers of Jesus will receive blessings based on how well we've accomplished God's orders. These rewards will be accompanied by a new set of duties we'll carry out not just in the name of Christ, but serving alongside our Savior and Lord.

1. What has been the most significant prize or recognition you've earned in your life? What feelings did you experience as you accepted the award? How did others treat you for having distinguished yourself in such a notable way?
2. Read Colossians 3:23-24. How does the knowledge that the Lord will reward your day-to-day spiritual performance affect the effort you put forward? While earthly leaders assess the results we produce, what does I Samuel 16:7 suggest is most important as God reviews our actions? According to Hebrews 4:12, on what basis will the Lord make His evaluation?
3. Apostle Paul says we're saved through faith as a gift of God. (Ephesians 2:8-9) James, the brother of Jesus, asks if someone with no good works can be saved. (James 2:14) How would you answer this question? What is the relationship between faith and works? Ephesians 2:8-10 might help as you ponder this issue. What did Jesus say about our deeds in Matthew 16:27?
4. In I Corinthians 3:10-15, Apostle Paul outlines how followers of Christ are to be judged on their service in God's army. According to verse 15, what can all Christians expect? What does the remainder of this passage suggest will be the criteria for the Lord's decision on how to reward His warriors?
5. What do the following verses tell us about the inheritance that awaits us in heaven?
    a. Galatians 4:1-7
    b. Ephesians 1:18

c. I Peter 1:3-4
   d. Hebrews 9:15
6. How are our future bodies described in I Corinthians 15:42-44? According to Philippians 3:20-21, how will these glorious bodies represent the ultimate fulfillment of the mission for soldiers in God's army? What do Revelation 2:7 and 17 and Revelation 21:6 tell us will be on our menu for eternity?
7. Various passages throughout scripture describe Jesus, angels, elders, and martyrs clothed in bright, white garments. In Revelation 19:7-8, what are we told Jesus' followers will wear in heaven? What do you think about the idea that when Christ is pictured in the Bible as returning to Earth "in the clouds," (Matthew 24:29-31) He'll actually be descending with legions of Christians in their glistening robes?
8. What do we learn in these verses about the crowns that will be presented to those who spend eternity with the Lord?
   a. I Thessalonians 2:19, Zechariah 9:16-17
   b. II Timothy 4:8
   c. James 1:12, Revelation 2:10
   d. I Peter 5:4
9. Jesus told His disciples He'd prepare a place for them in His Father's house. How does Apostle John describe this in Revelation 21:1-22:5? Try to put into words the feelings you'll have when you sit down with Jesus on His throne. (Revelation 3:21)
10. When you depart this planet, your loved ones will have a few words engraved on your tombstone. Read Luke 12:8 and Revelation 3:5. When you arrive in heaven, Jesus, the Commander of God's army, will commend your accomplishments in His service before His Father and the angels. What will He say? What would you like Him to say? Encourage other Christians to move forward into battle in the power of the Holy Spirit so you will be certain to hear those precious words from Jesus: "Well done, good and faithful [warrior]."

Prayer Points

- Praise God for the wonderful inheritance that awaits followers of His Son in heaven
- Thank the Lord that He'll judge His soldiers not for punishment but for rewards
- Ask God to help maintain your focus on pleasing Him in all you do rather than pleasing your human audience
- Commit to serving faithfully in God's army so the work you build on the foundation of Christ will endure and not be burned up when tested by fire

Personal Battle Plan

1. God's desire is that we please Him in all we do. **Honestly assess whom (or Whom) you serve** in the various aspects of your life using the chart below. If adjustments are necessary, ask for God's help in rearranging your priorities.

	Never	Sometimes	Often	Always
a. At work, I'm more interested in serving as God's ambassador than in earning the favor of my boss.				
b. In my relationships with friends and co-workers, I put aside what the Lord wants me to do so I can enhance my reputation.				

	Never	Sometimes	Often	Always

c. At home, my highest priority is being the spouse and parent God wants me to be, not pleasing the family.

d. At church, I seek to gain the acceptance of my pastor and other leaders, knowing that if they're satisfied, God will be happy with my performance.

2. We mortals sometimes do the right things for the wrong reasons. If God judges our hearts, it's important we understand what's motivating our actions. Write down the activities through which you currently seek to draw closer to the Lord or help others to draw near to Him. For each, **indicate why you do what you do**. Pray regularly that you'll be motivated simply by a desire to be the person God wants you to be and to do the things God wants you to do.

3. Go back to your Personal Battle Plan for Chapter 7 and write down the spiritual gifts you feel God has given you. **Evaluate the results of your use of these gifts**. When your ministry is tested by fire, will you discover you've had a significant, eternal impact on the lives of those you've served, or will your actions have made no appreciable difference in their lives? If you conclude your work has enabled others to receive Christ as Savior and make Him Lord, press on with diligence and enthusiasm. If your assessment reveals your work will be consumed in the fire, talk with a more mature Christian about how you can be more effective in the use of your gifts.

Forward into Battle

No Impact - Everything Consumed	Some Impact - A Few Rewards in the Ashes	Significant Impact - Great Rewards

   a.

   b.

   c.

4. List the "riches" you've accumulated on Earth. Now jot down the riches you can look forward to in heaven. **Compare the happiness you experience now with the joy that awaits you** in the presence of God. Express your gratitude daily for all God has done and is doing in your life on this planet, and thank Him for the tremendous inheritance you'll receive when Jesus escorts you to your eternal home.

Riches on Earth	Riches in Heaven

5. Soldiers in God's army can look forward to glorious and powerful bodies; nourishment; and dazzling, white garments upon taking up residence in heaven. What will vary among us is the headgear we'll be issued. **Review the criteria God will use in awarding various crowns.**

   a. Crown of righteousness: for consistently doing what's right in God's eyes (II Timothy 4:8)

   b. Crown of exultation: for having an eternal impact on the lives of others (II Thessalonians 2:19-20)

c. Crown of life: for faithful service, even through suffering and tribulation (Revelation 2:10); for loving God and persevering under trial (James 1:12)

d. Crown of glory: for distinguished service leading other followers of Christ (I Peter 5:4)

Ask the Lord to help you place your first priority not on possible rewards but on accomplishing the mission He's given us: being conformed to the likeness of His Son. Continually seek the Lord's direction and strength, and don't miss an opportunity He gives you because you're distracted by worldly matters. As you tap into the Spirit's power and wisdom to fulfill our primary goal, God will provide opportunities for you to grow in your faith, and He'll determine which of these crowns to award you.

6. Apostle Paul said, "For to me, to live is Christ, and to die is gain." **Plot where you stand on this issue**. Is your life fully devoted to your Savior, and can you think of nothing better than to see Him face to face. Or would you prefer to enjoy the pleasures of this life for a lot longer, safe in the knowledge you'll have plenty of time with Jesus when you get to heaven. Ask God to help you adopt His perspective on this challenging statement. If wrestling with this assessment provokes anxiety or confusion, talk with a trusted Christian mentor or friend.

To live is Christ;_____To live is gain;
to die is gain   to die is Christ

7. During our lives on Earth, the Lord encourages us to confess—to make an open, bold, and courageous proclamation—our faith in His Son. In return, Jesus promises to confess us before His Father and the angels of heaven. When Jesus announces your entry into your

eternal home, what open, bold, courageous proclamation would you like Him to make about you? **Write the script for His remarks**. Now pray daily God will empower you to move forward into battle as a warrior in His army in such a manner that these words will be justified.

Epilogue

WHEN I ARRIVED at the Air Force Academy nearly five decades ago, I had only a vague notion of what it would be like to serve in the armed forces. Although I had a general idea of what life at the Academy was all about, nothing could have adequately prepared me for the rigorous military, academic, and physical challenges I'd experience over the next four years. I honestly didn't know if I'd make it through the demands of the Academy.

Likewise, I was even less aware of what my time on active duty would entail. Whether I'd serve five years or five times that long in the Air Force was anyone's guess. I realized I'd never be a pilot, but I had no idea what specialty I'd go into upon my graduation. About the only thing I knew for sure was that I was entering the military at a time when tens of thousands of young Americans were fighting and many were dying in the jungles of Southeast Asia.

Despite spending all my youth and the majority of my teen years attending and participating in three different churches, I was equally unprepared for service in God's army. I had memorized quite a few children's songs, knew a vast number of Bible stories, and sincerely believed Jesus was the Son of God, but I'd heard nothing about receiving Him as my Savior. As far as I could tell, I was a Christian, and the standard God expected of me was perfection. I had no idea what I was supposed to do as a follower of Christ—beyond going to church every Sunday and trying my hardest to please God day in and day out.

I learned almost everything you've read in *Forward into Battle* **after** becoming a Christian. I'd like to report that much of this knowledge came rapidly following my decision to receive Jesus as Savior. Sadly, that wouldn't be true. While I learned some lessons quickly, others took decades to sink in. By God's grace and persistence, I'm still learning important concepts today, and with God's help, I'm trying to put them into practice rather than simply store them in my bank of Christian knowledge.

When I began working on *Forward into Battle*, I had only one goal in mind. My desire was to pass on to you lessons that took me many years to appreciate so you'd understand them more quickly than I did. If you can pick up the important Christian concepts I've learned through victories and defeats—and thousands of hours listening to sermons, hearing conference speakers, participating in Bible studies, and reading Christian books—then my hope is that you'll be better prepared to serve faithfully as a warrior for God.

Of course, the proof of the fruitfulness of this book isn't that your brain will be packed with a great deal more Christian knowledge than it was before you read it. What's crucial is that you apply in your day-to-day service in the Lord's army what you've learned in the book. If the words you've read, the discussions you've had, and the personal goals you've set enable you to serve God more honorably and effectively, the time I've put into preparing this material will have been worthwhile.

In 1858, in the midst of a great revival in Pennsylvania, a Presbyterian pastor preached a sermon that included a tribute to a minister who'd died a few days earlier in a tragic accident. Nearly 160 years later, the words of George Duffield, which became the hymn "Stand Up, Stand Up for Jesus," perfectly summarize the combat and rewards we'll experience as warriors in God's army.[1]

> Stand up, stand up for Jesus, ye soldiers of the cross;
> Lift high His royal banner, it must not suffer loss:

From vict'ry unto vict'ry, His army shall He lead,
Till ev'ry foe is vanquished, and Christ is Lord indeed.

Stand up, stand up for Jesus, the trumpet call obey;
Forth to the mighty conflict, in this His glorious day:
Ye who are men now serve Him against unnumbered foes;
Let courage rise with danger, and strength to strength oppose.

Stand up, stand up for Jesus, stand in His strength alone;
The arm of flesh will fail you, ye dare not trust your own:
Put on the gospel armor, each piece put on with pray'r;
Where duty calls, or danger, be never wanting there.

Stand up, stand up for Jesus, the strife will not be long;
This day the noise of battle, the next the victor's song;
To him who overcometh a crown of life shall be;
He, with the King of glory, shall reign eternally.[2]

As you stand up for Jesus, putting into practice what you've learned through *Forward into Battle* and anticipating the rewards that await you in heaven, I trust you'll serve the Lord fruitfully and passionately as a warrior in His army.

Acknowledgements

I'M GRATEFUL TO a number of people who've helped and encouraged me as I've developed the material in *Forward into Battle*. In the very early days of my writing, Lieutenant Colonel Jim Fishback (U.S. Army, Retired) and his wife, Bea—who worked with us in what was then called the Military Ministry of Campus Crusade for Christ—reviewed a much shorter draft and suggested I expand it into a full-fledged book. Without their encouragement, the manuscript wouldn't have evolved into its published form.

Several folks cast a critical eye over the material, and each of them provided valuable feedback that I've tried very hard to apply to the final edition. Among them were Brigadier General (U.S. Air Force, Retired) David Warner, the current Executive Director of the Officers Christian Fellowship; Colonel (U.S. Army, Retired) Joe Terry; and Chaplain (Lieutenant Colonel, U.S. Air Force, Retired) Bruce Arnold. David Preston and Chris Adsit, who were serving with Military Ministry at the time, both made helpful suggestions and were most encouraging as the project developed. Phil Knowles, Michael Apichella, and Rev. Scott McAlister also offered thoughtful comments and assured me I was heading in the right direction.

Major General (U.S. Air Force, Retired) Jerry White, an accomplished author who for many years served as the International President of the Navigators parachurch ministry, encouraged me and shared his wisdom on the publishing process. Campus Crusade staff member and author

Randy Newman also helped me understand the range of publishing options to consider when the manuscript was completed.

Christians at two U.S. Air Force bases in England—RAF Lakenheath and RAF Mildenhall—field-tested *Forward into Battle* in 12-week Bible studies. Their feedback enabled me to fine-tune the material in both the readings and the unit analyses.

Special thanks go to Dan and Linda Barker and John and Vicki Gingrich. Their very generous financial contributions made possible the printing of *Forward into Battle*.

Pat Pearce, the director of Cru's New Life Resources, was extremely helpful in pointing me to a publisher and in helping me understand the value of launching a website to support the book. I owe a huge debt of gratitude to Drew Swartz, a member of our Cru Military Bible study in England, for helping me prepare my material for the publisher and setting up an extremely attractive and functional *Forward into Battle* site on the Internet.

Thanks also go to my wife Elizabeth, who constantly encouraged me during the writing of the book and spent many hours proofreading the manuscript, pointing out mistakes and offering suggestions to make it clearer. I appreciate her reminders that what I'd created would help many warriors in God's army to serve Him more faithfully.

References

Foreword

1. Sabine Baring-Gould, "Onward, Christian Soldiers," in *Book on Worship for United States Forces* (Washington, D.C.: U.S. Government Printing Office, 1974), 412.

Section 1 Introduction

1. John 15:18-19
2. John 17:14-15
3. John 14:6
4. John 17:3

Chapter 1

1. Francis Chan, *Crazy Love: Overwhelmed by A Relentless God* (Colorado Springs, Colorado: David C. Cook, 2008), 34. Francis Chan is an American preacher, speaker, and author. He is the former teaching pastor of Cornerstone Community Church in Simi Valley, California, a church he and his wife started in 1994. He is also the founder and chancellor of Eternity Bible College.
2. Psalm 148:2, 5, II Peter 2:11, II Samuel 14:17, 20

3. Ezekiel 28:12, 15, Isaiah 14:12-13, Revelation 12:3-4
4. Romans 5:12, I John 5:19, II Timothy 2:26
5. Genesis 1:1-5
6. Job 10:21-22, Job 24:13-16
7. John 1:4-5
8. John 3:19-20, John 12:35
9. II Corinthians 4:4
10. Romans 1:18-26
11. II Peter 2:2-3, 7-8
12. Matthew 15:19
13. I John 2:15-17
14. Galatians 5:19-21, II Corinthians 12:20, Romans 13:13, Romans 1:29-31
15. Romans 3:10, Psalm 14:3
16. Romans 3:23
17. James 4:4
18. Isaiah 29:15
19. Ecclesiastes 2:14
20. Romans 5:12, 6:23
21. James 1:14-15
22. Genesis 1:27
23. John 4:24
24. Genesis 3:19
25. Romans 2:9
26. C.S. Lewis, *The Great Divorce* (New York, New York: HarperCollins Publishers, 2001). (Quoted at www.goodreads.com.)
27. Leviticus 11:44-45, 19:2, 20:26, 21:8
28. Psalm 5:4-6
29. I Samuel 16:7
30. Genesis 8:21

Chapter 2

1. W.E. Sangster, *The Pure in Heart* (London, England: The Epworth Press, 1955), xi. W.E. Sangster was a Methodist pastor who served as senior minister at Westminster Central Hall in London during World War II. He later was elected president of the Methodist Conference of Great Britain. Throughout his ministry, his talks, workshops, and books were designed to equip his congregation and the larger church family to invite others to join them as followers of Christ. Sangster was known for his efforts to instill a passion for the Christian life among those he viewed as lukewarm pew-sitters.
2. John 1:12
3. John 8:12
4. John 12:35-36
5. John 12:46
6. John 3:3
7. Acts 26:18
8. Ephesians 5:8, 11, Colossians 1:13, 21
9. I John 4:8, 16
10. Romans 3:23
11. John 3:16
12. Psalm 145:8
13. Matthew 15:32-38
14. Luke 7:11-17
15. Psalm 86:5
16. Luke 7:36-50
17. I Timothy 1:15
18. Romans 3:10
19. I John 3:1
20. Romans 5:8
21. Psalm 100:5

22. Romans 8:38-39
23. Ephesians 3:19
24. Ephesians 2:4-5
25. I Peter 1:3
26. I John 4:9-10, 14b
27. Colonel W.N. Nicholson, *The History of the Suffolk Regiment 1928-1946* (Uckfield, England: Naval and Military Press, 2009). (Reviewed at www.naval-military-press.com.)
28. Ernest Gordon, *Miracle on the River Kwai* (Glasgow, Scotland: Collins, 1963). (Cited at www.josh.org/miracle-on-the-river-kwai.)
29. Medal of Honor Recipients, www.cmohs.org/recipient-detail/2920/o-brien-william-j.php.
30. Medal of Honor Recipients, www.cmohs.org/recipient-detail/2623/baker-thomas-a.php.
31. Ephesians 2:8-9
32. Ephesians 1:7-8
33. Romans 5:1-2, 18-19
34. II Corinthians 5:18-20
35. Galatians 4:4-5
36. Philippians 3:20
37. Romans 6:17-22
38. Galatians 5:22-23
39. I Corinthians 2:16
40. Ephesians 2:10

Section 2 Introduction

1. John 14:15, 21, 23
2. John 15:1-11
3. John 14:26
4. John 16:7-15

5. Acts 5:17-20
6. Acts 12:1-10
7. Hebrews 12:1
8. John 13:34-35
9. John 15:12-13, 17
10. John 17:21-23
11. John 17:18

Chapter 3

1. Joni Eareckson Tada, *A Place of Healing: Wrestling with the Mysteries of Suffering, Pain and God's Sovereignty* (Colorado Springs, Colorado: David C. Cook, 2010). (Quoted at www.goodreads.com.) Joni Eareckson Tada, the founder and chief executive officer of Joni and Friends International Disability Center, is an international advocate for people with disabilities. The author of more than 50 books, she also hosts a radio program aired on more than 1,000 outlets.
2. Joshua 5:13-6:21
3. Isaiah 55:4
4. Exodus 15:3, 6-7
5. Revelation 19:11-21
6. Matthew 10:34
7. I John 3:8
8. I Corinthians 15:25
9. Ephesians 1:19-23
10. Colossians 1:16-18, 2:10
11. Matthew 22:37-38
12. John 21:15-17
13. John 14:1-3, 10-11, 16-17, 20
14. John 14:15, 21, 23
15. Brother Lawrence, *The Practice of the Presence of God* (White Plains, New York: Peter Pauper Press, Inc., 1963), 18.

References

16. Luke 7:36-50
17. Matthew 10:1-15
18. Matthew 28:18-20
19. John 17:3
20. Matthew 26:36-39
21. Philippians 2:8
22. Matthew 28:18
23. Colossians 1:18
24. I Peter 5:6
25. Luke 10:1-20
26. Acts 2:1-41
27. Acts 3:1-10
28. John 15:16
29. Colossians 1:10
30. John 14:12
31. Acts 1:8
32. Luke 10:1
33. Matthew 18:20
34. Matthew 16:16
35. John 2:19-22
36. Matthew 19:16-22

Chapter 4

1. John C. Maxwell, *The 17 Indisputable Laws of Teamwork* (Nashville, Tennessee: Thomas Nelson Publishers, 2001), 2. John Maxwell is an author, speaker, and pastor who has written more than 60 books, primarily focusing on leadership. His books have sold millions of copies, with some on the *New York Times* Best Seller List.
2. Romans 8:11
3. Matthew 28:19

4. II Corinthians 13:14
5. Acts 5:3-4
6. Genesis 1:2
7. Hebrews 9:14
8. I Corinthians 12:6, 11
9. Luke 1:35
10. I Corinthians 2:10-11
11. Psalm 139:7-12
12. John 14:16-17, 26
13. John 15:26
14. John 16:13
15. John 16:8-11
16. Daniel 7:10, Zechariah 1:10-11
17. Genesis 19:1, 12-25
18. II Samuel 24:1, 15-17
19. II Kings 6:8-23
20. Hebrews 1:13-14, Luke 20:36, Revelation 5:11-13
21. Psalm 103:20
22. Hebrews 1:14
23. Genesis 24:7
24. Acts 8:26-27
25. I Kings 19:1-8
26. Matthew 4:1-11
27. Daniel 6:22
28. Acts 12:7-10
29. Luke 22:43
30. Acts 27:22-26
31. Acts 12:5-17
32. Psalm 34:7
33. Hebrews 12:1
34. Ecclesiastes 4:9-12

35. Luke 10:1-16
36. Luke 10:17-19
37. I Corinthians 12:12, 14-20, 27-31

Section 3 Introduction

1. John 15:16
2. Romans 8:29
3. John 13:14-15
4. John 13:34-35, 15:12
5. John 17:3
6. John 14:21,23, 16:23-24
7. John 15:1-6
8. John 15:8
9. John 14:12
10. John 17:13
11. John 14:30, 17:15
12. John 13:2, 26-27
13. John 15:18-25
14. John 15:20
15. John 17:14
16. John 17:25
17. John 16:33
18. John 17:15

Chapter 5

1. Jim Reimann, *Morning by Morning: The Devotions of Charles Spurgeon* (Peabody, Massachusetts: Hendrickson Publishers, Inc, 1998), 42. Charles Haddon Spurgeon was the pastor of the New Park Street Chapel (later the Metropolitan Tabernacle) in London for 38 years in the mid- to late-1800s.

It's estimated that in his lifetime, Spurgeon preached to around 10,000,000 people. He was a prolific author of many types of works, including commentaries, books on prayer, devotionals, magazines, poetry, and hymns.

2. Ephesians 2:19
3. John 18:36
4. Ephesians 2:19, Philippians 3:20
5. John 14:30
6. Ephesians 2:2
7. I Timothy 1:17
8. Genesis 6:5-8
9. Deuteronomy 34:9
10. Isaiah 6:1-2, 4
11. Matthew 4:18-22
12. John 1:43-44
13. Matthew 19:16-22
14. Acts 9:1-19
15. Romans 8:28
16. Romans 8:29
17. Genesis 1:26-27
18. II Corinthians 3:18
19. Romans 12:2
20. John 14:21
21. Matthew 22:37-39
22. Matthew 14:13-23
23. Mark 1:35
24. Luke 5:16
25. Luke 6:12
26. Luke 22:39-46
27. Luke 4:16
28. C. Austin Miles, "In the Garden," www.namethathymn.com.
29. John 14:13-14

30. John 15:7-8
31. John 16:23-24
32. I John 1:9
33. Psalm 46:10
34. Proverbs 8:17
35. Hebrews 1:3
36. John 14:7, 9
37. Psalm 119:105
38. John 17:17
39. Matthew 4:1-11
40. II Timothy 2:15
41. II Timothy 3:16-17
42. Acts 17:10-12
43. Psalm 4:4
44. John 4:1-26
45. John 17:17
46. John 8:31-32
47. Hebrews 10:24-25
48. William J. Reynolds, *Companion to Baptist Hymnal* (Nashville, Tennessee: Broadman Press, 1976), 26.
49. Henry Francis Lyte, "Abide with Me: Fast Falls the Eventide," in *Book on Worship for United States Forces* (Washington, D.C.: U.S. Government Printing Office, 1974), 152.
50. Mark 3:13-15
51. Mark 4:33-34
52. Mark 6:30-32
53. John 14:1-6
54. Mark 6:7-13
55. John 15:12-13
56. *Today in the Word*, April 1, 1992.
57. I Corinthians 14:1, Ephesians 5:2

58. John 13:34-35
59. Matthew 9:35-38
60. Matthew 8:14-17
61. Luke 7:11-17
62. Mark 10:13-16
63. Mark 11:15-18
64. Galatians 5:13, 6:10

Chapter 6

1. Sun Tzu, *The Art of War* (New York, New York: Classic Books International, 2009). (Quoted at www.goodreads.com.) Sun Tzu was a Chinese military general, strategist, and philosopher who is thought to have lived in the mid- to early 500s BC. He is traditionally credited as the author of *The Art of War*, an extremely influential ancient Chinese book on military strategy.
2. Ephesians 6:12
3. "Barna's Annual Tracking Study Shows Americans Stay Spiritually Active, but Biblical Views Wane," The Barna Group, www.barna.com, (May 21, 2007).
4. "Most American Christians Do Not Believe that Satan or the Holy Spirit Exist," The Barna Group, www.barna.com, (April 13, 2009).
5. "Majority of Americans Surveyed Believe Heaven and Hell Exist, the Devil and Angels Are Real and God Is Not Responsible for Recent U.S. Tragedies," The True Life in God Foundation, www.prnewswire.com, (May 29, 2013).
6. "YouGov Poll Says Nearly 60% of Americans Believe the Devil is Real," www.patheos.com, (September 21, 2013).
7. Genesis 3:4
8. Revelation 20:1-3
9. Matthew 12:24-29
10. Matthew 13:19
11. John 8:44
12. John 14:30

References

13. II Corinthians 4:4
14. II Corinthians 6:15
15. Ephesians 2:2, 6:12
16. I Peter 5:8
17. Revelation 9:11
18. Revelation 12:10
19. Galatians 5:22-23
20. I John 5:19
21. Mark 4:1-20
22. John 13:2, 27
23. Acts 5:1-11
24. II Corinthians 11:3
25. Luke 13:10-16
26. Genesis 3:1-7
27. II Corinthians 11:14
28. II Corinthians 2:11
29. Psalm 91:11-12
30. Matthew 4:1-11
31. John 17:21-23
32. Revelation 12:9
33. Judges 9:1-25
34. I Samuel 16:13-15
35. I Kings 22:1-23
36. I Timothy 4:1
37. Romans 8:38-39
38. Ephesians 6:10-17
39. Leviticus 17:7
40. Psalm 106:35-39
41. Luke 8:26-39
42. Matthew 17:14-21, Mark 9:14-29
43. Matthew 12:22, Luke 13:10-13

44. Luke 11:24-26
45. Matthew 10:1
46. Luke 10:1-17
47. Acts 16:16-18
48. Matthew 25:41
49. Revelation 20:10

Section 4 Introduction

1. John 15:5, 8
2. John 14:21, 23-24
3. John 14:11-14
4. Winston Churchill, speech entitled "Never Give In, Never, Never, Never," delivered at Harrow School, London, October 29, 1941, www.churchill-society-london.org.uk.
5. II Corinthians 5:20

Chapter 7

1. Francis Schaeffer, *Death in the City* (Downers Grove, Illinois: InterVarsity Press, 1969), 142. Francis Schaeffer was an American evangelical Christian theologian, philosopher, and Presbyterian pastor. He wrote 22 books on a range of spiritual issues. He also established the L'Abri community in Switzerland in 1955. Today there are L'Abri study centers in Europe, Asia, and America where guests can seek answers to their questions about God and the significance of human life.
2. II Corinthians 10:4
3. I Kings 3:1-15
4. Proverbs 1:7, 2:2
5. Proverbs 3:5-7
6. Colossians 3:1-2

7. Acts 1:8
8. II Corinthians 12:7-10
9. Matthew 19:26
10. Philippians 4:13
11. Romans 12:7-8
12. I Corinthians 12:8-10
13. I Corinthians 12:10
14. Ephesians 4:11
15. Ephesians 4:15
16. Ephesians 6:11, 13-16
17. Isaiah 59:17
18. II Corinthians 10:4-5
19. John 14:6
20. John 17:17
21. Philippians 3:9
22. Philippians 4:13
23. I Corinthians 15:3-4
24. Romans 10:9-10
25. Acts 4:12
26. Romans 10:17
27. I John 5:11-13
28. Hebrews 4:12
29. Discussion on these six weapons was inspired by chart in the *Life Application Study Bible*, New International Version (Wheaton, Illinois: Tyndale House Publishers, Inc., 1984), 2142.
30. Jamie Owens-Collins, "The Battle Belongs to the Lord," www.metrolyrics.com.
31. "Code of Conduct for Members of the United States Armed Forces," www.au.af.mil.
32. Galatians 5:19-21
33. Ephesians 4:17-24

34. Galatians 5:22-23
35. John 15:12
36. James 1:2
37. II Timothy 2:22
38. Ephesians 4:1-2
39. Colossians 3:12
40. II Peter 1:5
41. II Corinthians 5:7
42. I Timothy 6:11
43. II Peter 1:6
44. Philippians 2:3-4
45. Philippians 2:5-8
46. Mother Teresa interview with Edward W. Desmond for *Time Magazine*, December 4, 1989, www.servelec.net/motherteresa.htm.
47. Napoleon Bonaparte, www.azquotes.com/quote/1059244.
48. Micah 6:8
49. Mark 10:43-45
50. Adapted primarily from a list of spiritual gifts by Dr. Richard Krejcir, Into Thy Word Ministries, www.intothyword.org.

Chapter 8

1. Theodore Roosevelt, speech entitled "Citizenship in a Republic," delivered at the Sorbonne, Paris, France, April 23, 1910. Theodore "Teddy" Roosevelt was an American statesman, author, explorer, soldier, naturalist, and reformer who served as the 26th President of the United States. He was Assistant Secretary of the Navy under William McKinley, resigning after one year to serve with the 1st U.S. Volunteer Cavalry—the Rough Riders—during the Spanish-American War in Cuba.
2. Genesis 6:13-22
3. Genesis 12:1-4

References

4. Genesis 15:5
5. Exodus 3:10-4:17
6. Deuteronomy 34:10-12
7. Joshua 1:1-9
8. Joshua 24:15
9. Isaiah 6:1-8
10. Isaiah 6:9-13, 7:10-14
11. Matthew 4:19
12. Mark 3:14-15
13. John 1:40-51
14. Matthew 10:1-20
15. Matthew 28:19-20
16. Matthew 19:16-26
17. Acts 9:1-20
18. Acts 9:10-19
19. John 10:14
20. John 14:21
21. Romans 8:38-39
22. Matthew 18:20
23. Hebrews 12:2
24. Psalm 119:105
25. Philippians 4:6-7, 19
26. I Corinthians 2:16
27. Colossians 3:23-24
28. Ephesians 6:10-18
29. I Peter 5:9, I John 5:4-5
30. Matthew 4:1-11
31. Philippians 4:13
32. I John 4:4
33. Hebrews 10:24-25
34. Ecclesiastes 4:9-10, 12

35. Acts 13:1-6
36. II Corinthians 5:20
37. Ephesians 6:19-20
38. Deuteronomy 20:1-4
39. Deuteronomy 23:14
40. Joshua 6:2, 8:1
41. Joshua 10:14, 42
42. Joshua 23:8, 10
43. I Samuel 17:47
44. Psalm 20:7
45. Psalm 21:9, 11, 13
46. Psalm 60:11-12, 108:12-13
47. II Kings 6:14-17
48. II Chronicles 14:8-12
49. II Corinthians 2:14
50. II Corinthians 4:7-11
51. II Corinthians 10:3-5
52. I Corinthians 15:57-58
53. Ephesians 6:10-11, 13
54. I Corinthians 10:13
55. Hebrews 2:14
56. James 4:7
57. Martin Luther, "A Mighty Fortress Is Our God," in *Book on Worship for United States Forces* (Washington, D.C.: U.S. Government Printing Office, 1974), 123.
58. Philippians 4:13

Section 5 Introduction

1. John 14:12
2. Mark 3:14-15

3. Mark 6:7-13
4. John 13:1-15
5. Multiple sources, including "Edward Kimball—The legacy of a Sunday School teacher," uponthesolidrock.wordpress.com.

Chapter 9

1. James Charlton, *The Military Quotation Book* (New York: Thomas Dunne Books, 2002), 83. H. Norman Schwarzkopf was a four-star general in the U.S. Army. While serving as Commander-in-Chief, United States Central Command, he led all coalition forces in the Persian Gulf War in 1990-1991.
2. James 4:13-15
3. John 16:13
4. Deuteronomy 31:23
5. Joshua 1:1-9
6. I Corinthians 15:57
7. I Kings 3:3-14
8. I Kings 3:16-28
9. Psalm 41:12
10. Daniel 1:8-16, 2:48
11. Proverbs 16:18
12. I Peter 5:6
13. II Kings 5:1-14
14. John 14:21
15. Isaiah 1:16-17
16. Isaiah 6:1-8
17. I Peter 3:15
18. Matthew 8:5-13
19. I John 5:4
20. Luke 10:1-20
21. John 13:21-30

22. John 13:36-38
23. Luke 18:31-34
24. Matthew 25:31-46
25. Matthew 19:27-30
26. Mark 1:40-45
27. Matthew 8:28-34
28. Matthew 12:9-14
29. John 2:13-22, Mark 11:15-18
30. Luke 22:66-71, 23:1-25
31. Mark 15:15-20
32. John 19:16-30
33. John 14:7-9
34. Luke 9:37-45, 11:29-32
35. John 8:43
36. Luke 5:33-6:5
37. Luke 6:6-11
38. Luke 15:1-2
39. Luke 20:1-8, John 8:1-11
40. Colossians 2:3
41. John 17:7-8, 17
42. Matthew 4:1-11
43. John 4:7-26
44. Matthew 22:34-40
45. Matthew 19:16-26
46. Leviticus 6:1-7
47. II Corinthians 5:21
48. I Peter 1:19
49. Philippians 2:3-11
50. Mark 1:9-13
51. Luke 6:12-19
52. Mark 10:13-16

References

53. John 13:1-20
54. Philippians 2:8
55. Luke 4:14-21, 43
56. John 4:34
57. John 6:38
58. John 8:29
59. John 17:4
60. Matthew 4:1-11
61. Matthew 4:17
62. Mark 2:15-17
63. Mark 6:30-44
64. Mark 8:1-9
65. John 11:41
66. Mark 1:35
67. Luke 5:16
68. I Peter 2:21-25

Chapter 10

1. Dwight Eisenhower, speech delivered at the annual conference of the Society of Personnel Administration in Washington, D.C., May 12, 1954. Dwight David "Ike" Eisenhower was the 34th President of the United States. He was a five-star general in the U.S. Army during World War II and served as Supreme Commander of the Allied Forces in Europe. He later became the first Supreme Commander of NATO.
2. Luke 22:24-27
3. Numbers 27:15-17
4. II Samuel 5:2
5. Hebrews 13:20
6. John 10:1-18
7. Mark 6:30-32

8. Mark 3:14-15
9. John 14:12
10. Ralph Waldo Emerson, "Letters and Social Aims," quoteinvestigator.com.
11. Ephesians 4:15
12. Matthew 16:13-23
13. Matthew 17:1-6
14. John 13:31-38
15. John 18:15-27
16. Luke 22:54-62
17. John 21:1-17
18. Hebrews 12:4-11
19. Deuteronomy 2:7
20. Deuteronomy 4:29
21. Deuteronomy 6:10-11
22. Matthew 24:29-31, 19:28
23. John 6:5-6
24. John 14:8-10
25. John 12:1-8
26. Matthew 14:28-31
27. Matthew 18:21-35
28. John 21:15-17
29. Matthew 26:36-46
30. John 20:26-29
31. Acts 1:8
32. Acts 2:41-47
33. Acts 9:19-20
34. I Timothy 1:18-19, 4:7, 12
35. II Timothy 2:15, 4:2
36. Hebrews 10:24-25

37. Luke 9:1-10
38. Luke 24:36-49

Section 6 Introduction

1. John 14:2-3
2. John 17:24
3. Isaiah 6:1-4
4. I Corinthians 3:10-15

Chapter 11

1. A. W. Tozer, *The Attributes of God: A Journey into the Father's Heart* (Camp Hill, Pennsylvania: Christian Publications, 1998). (Quoted at www.goodreads.com.) Aiden Wilson Tozer was an American Christian pastor in West Virginia, Illinois, and Canada. He was also an author, magazine editor, and spiritual mentor. Among the more than 40 books he authored, at least two are regarded as Christian classics: *The Pursuit of God* and *The Knowledge of the Holy*.
2. O.A. Lambert, "Heaven Is A Wonderful Place," www.psalty.com.
3. "Americans Describe Their Views about Life After Death," The Barna Group, www.barna.com, (October 21, 2003).
4. Caryle Murphy, "Most Americans Believe in Heaven ... and Hell," Pew Research Center, www.pewresearch.org, (November 10, 2015).
5 Justin Kaplan, editor, *Familiar Quotations* (Boston, Massachusetts: Little, Brown and Company, 1992), 68.
6. Kaplan, 193.
7. Kaplan, 377.
8. Kaplan, 498.
9. John Bunyan, *The Pilgrim's Progress* (Oxford, England: Oxford University Press, 2003).

10. Genesis 1:1
11. Psalm 8:1
12. Psalm 19:1
13. Psalm 103:19
14. Psalm 50:6
15. Mark 1:15
16. Matthew 4:17
17. Matthew 5:3, 10, 12
18. Matthew 5:20
19. Matthew 7:21-23
20. Matthew 13:11
21. Matthew 13:24-52
22. Matthew 18:1-6
23. Matthew 18:21-35
24. Matthew 19:16-26
25. Matthew 28:18-20
26. John 4:14
27. John 5:24
28. John 17:24
29. Isaiah 6:1-4
30. Revelation 4:1-11
31. Revelation 21:1-2
32. Revelation 21:3-4
33. Revelation 22:4-5
34. John 17:5
35. Matthew 5:16
36. Matthew 6:9-13, 19-21
37. Matthew 10:32-33
38. Luke 16:19-31
39. Luke 22:29-30
40. John 7:33, 8:21-30, 13:33, 16:28

41. John 14:1-6
42. I John 5:11-13
43. Romans 6:23
44. John 17:3
45. C.H. Spurgeon, *Morning by Morning* (Springdale, Pennsylvania: Whitaker House, 1984), 19. Samuel Rutherford was a Scottish Presbyterian pastor, theologian, and author in the first half of the 17th century.
46. I Thessalonians 4:16-18

Chapter 12

1. J. R. Miller, *Come Ye Apart* (London: Thomas Nelson & Sons, 1906), reading for November 5. James Russell Miller was a popular Christian author, Editorial Superintendent of the Presbyterian Board of Publication, and pastor of several churches in Pennsylvania and Illinois.
2. Colossians 3:23-24
3. I Samuel 16:7
4. I Corinthians 4:5
5. II Timothy 4:7
6. John 12:26
7. Matthew 16:27
8. Revelation 22:12
9. I Corinthians 6:9-10
10. Revelation 20:10
11. Revelation 20:11-15
12. I Corinthians 3:10-15
13. Psalm 28:9, 37:18
14. Matthew 19:28-29, 25:34
15. Luke 12:13-21, 33, Matthew 6:19-20
16. Galatians 3:18, 26-29, 4:1-7
17. Colossians 3:24, Ephesians 1:13-14, 18

18. I Corinthians 15:50-58
19. I Peter 1:3-4
20. Hebrews 1:2, 9:15, 11:7-9
21. Philippians 3:20-21
22. I Corinthians 15:35-44
23. Revelation 21:1-7
24. Revelation 2:7, 17
25. Revelation 21:6
26. Revelation 3:5
27. Daniel 7:9
28. Mark 9:2-3
29. Revelation 15:5-16:1, 4:4
30. Revelation 6:9-11, 7:9-17
31. Revelation 19:7-8
32. Revelation 19:11-19
33. Daniel 7:13-14
34. Matthew 24:30, 26:64
35. I Thessalonians 4:16-17
36. Hebrews 12:1
37. Revelation 1:7, 14:14-20
38. Revelation 2:10, 3:11
39. I Corinthians 9:24-25
40. I Thessalonians 2:19
41. I Thessalonians 2:20
42. Philippians 4:1
43. Zechariah 9:11-17
44. II Timothy 4:8
45. James 1:12
46. I Peter 5:1-4
47. John 14:1-6
48. Revelation 3:12, 21:22

49. Revelation 2:11
50. Philippians 1:21-26
51. Revelation 2:28, 22:16
52. Revelation 21:23-24
53. Revelation 3:5
54. Luke 12:8
55. Matthew 25:14-30
56. Revelation 3:12, 2:17
57. Genesis 12:2-3
58. Genesis 17:1-8
59. Genesis 32:22-30
60. John 1:35-42, Matthew 16:18
61. Revelation 3:5
62. Revelation 2:26-27
63. Psalm 2:7-9
64. I Corinthians 6:2-3
65. Revelation 19:11-15
66. Revelation 3:21

Epilogue

1. William J. Reynolds, *Companion to Baptist Hymnal* (Nashville, Tennessee: Broadman Press, 1976), 201.
2. George Duffield, Jr., "Stand Up, Stand Up for Jesus," in *Baptist Hymnal* (Nashville, Tennessee: Convention Press, 1975), 391.

Made in the USA
Coppell, TX
09 December 2021